I0760040

DIOGENES

DIOGENES

THE REBELLIOUS LIFE AND REVOLUTIONARY PHILOSOPHY OF THE ORIGINAL CYNIC

INGER N.I. KUIN

BASIC BOOKS
New York

Cover design by Ann Kirchner
Cover image © Scala/Art Resource, NY; Raphael Sanzio, Public Domain, via Wikimedia Commons
Cover copyright © 2025 by Hachette Book Group, Inc.

Basic Books
Hachette Book Group
1290 Avenue of the Americas, New York, NY 10104
www.basicbooks.com

Printed in the United States of America

First Edition: November 2025

Published by Basic Books, an imprint of Hachette Book Group, Inc. The Basic Books name and logo is a registered trademark of the Hachette Book Group.

Print book interior design by Bart Dawson.

Library of Congress Cataloging-in-Publication Data
Names: Kuin, Inger N. I., author.
Title: Diogenes : the rebellious life and revolutionary philosophy of the original cynic / Inger N.I. Kuin.
Description: First edition. | New York : Basic Books, 2025. | Includes bibliographical references and index.
Identifiers: LCCN 2025004812 | ISBN 9781541606470 (hardcover) | ISBN 9781541606487 (ebook)
Subjects: LCSH: Diogenes, -approximately 323 B.C. | Cynics (Greek philosophy)
Classification: LCC B305.D44 K85 2025 | DDC 183/.4—dc23/eng/20250613
LC record available at https://lccn.loc.gov/2025004812

ISBNs: 9781541606470 (hardcover), 9781541606487 (ebook)

LSC-C

Printing 1, 2025

CONTENTS

INTRODUCTION

SEEING THE WORLD DIFFERENTLY

Toward the end of the year 336 BCE, around the time when fall turns to winter, a young, newly crowned king traveled to Corinth. His father had been murdered at a wedding just weeks earlier, and the twenty-year-old had managed, with the help of a few powerful backers and some bloodshed, to claim the throne. The next task was to win favor with the Greek cities and to consolidate his late father's hard-won control of the region. During a council meeting, held at the nearby Isthmus of Corinth, Alexander III of Macedon managed to do just this: the so-called Corinthian League vowed their support for his campaign against Persia.[1] But there was one more thing on Alexander's mind. A philosopher by the name of Diogenes was staying in Corinth at that time too. Alexander had heard so much about him that he did not want to leave the city without having met the man.

The young king expected the philosopher would come to him. Everyone else who mattered had turned up to congratulate him on winning the backing of the Greek cities. But Diogenes did not come to Alexander. The philosopher forced the king to go to *him* instead. In order to meet Diogenes, Alexander had to ask the men in his retinue to take him to the outskirts of town, to a wooded area known as the Kraneion, where the famous thinker was living in a large clay pot laid on its side to make an improvised shelter. Let us go down with them and see how that meeting went.

When he sees Alexander and his men approach, Diogenes raises himself up on his elbow ever so slightly, to get a better view of what is happening. Once Alexander at last stands face-to-face with the philosopher, he asks Diogenes what he can do for him. Diogenes answers: "Just step aside, out of my sun." Alexander, stunned, does as he is told. Clearly, this great man has no use for him. On the way back to town, the king's men crack jokes about the strange philosopher. But not Alexander. He says (mostly to himself): "If I were not Alexander, I would be Diogenes."[2]

Diogenes' fearless and irreverent response to the most powerful man in the world as it was known to him encapsulates everything that he stood for: total independence, courage in the face of power, and joyful contentment with what nature bestows freely on us humans. Alexander's reaction is just as telling. A man used to being obeyed rather than obeying, he was completely taken by surprise. Yet instead of angrily telling his soldiers to arrest the insolent philosopher, the king obeyed him, and even wished to be him.

If the most powerful man in the world offered them the opportunity to make a wish, most people would either freeze, dumbstruck with fear, or seize the moment and ask for wealth, a job, a favor. Diogenes ignored both scripts. With complete disregard for Alexander's power, he answered him just as he would any other person. By refusing his offer, Diogenes refused to become indebted to the king. Diogenes did not accept Alexander's power and in that moment turned the tables on him.

But Diogenes' meeting with Alexander is important not only for what it teaches us about who he was and what he stood for. It is also a prime test case for how we go about telling Diogenes' story, and for understanding how difficult it is to do so. The encounter with Alexander is easily the most famous event from Diogenes' life. It has been told and retold, interpreted and reinterpreted, countless times. It was a popular topic in art in antiquity and has been ever since. But today most historians think the event never took place. I happen to think they are wrong.

SIDELINED

There are precious few things about Diogenes that scholars can agree on: he lived in the fourth century BCE, he spent most of his life as a wandering philosopher in Athens and Corinth after leaving his hometown on the coast of the Black Sea, he was outspoken and rebellious, and he inspired an equally outspoken and rebellious philosophical tradition. Venturing beyond these basics means entering the territory of debate. Of course, this problem is not unique to Diogenes: there are bound to be large holes in the historical record of anyone who has been dead for more than two millennia, no matter how famous they were in their own time. Unless new evidence comes to light, we will, for instance, never know the name of Diogenes' mother. The same happens to be true of Cleopatra.[3]

Trying to write Diogenes' life is made more difficult by the fact that no works by the philosopher himself have survived, and I argue in this book that he most likely did not publish anything during his lifetime. After he died, his followers kept his ideas alive, as well as they could, in quotations and anecdotes; even so, most of our information about Diogenes comes from authors who wrote centuries afterward, relying on what remained of those earlier oral and written traditions. Another, somewhat paradoxical problem when it comes to Diogenes is that many of the stories about his life are so good they are hard to believe. A meeting between the recalcitrant loner Diogenes and the young king Alexander III, who would soon become known as Alexander the Great? Yeah, sure.

The way scholars have approached Diogenes over the last century or so seems to have suffered from a kind of vicious cycle. In their eyes, the fact that no writings of his remain, let alone the kind of theoretical works expected of a philosopher, renders him unsuitable for serious scholarly attention. This in turn has made it easier to dismiss the traditions about Diogenes as unserious themselves, or as mere sensationalist stories with no basis in reality, and such dismissals further contribute to Diogenes' bad reputation as just a legendary madman, and so on and so forth. But what if the stories about Diogenes are shocking and seemingly far-fetched because this is precisely the effect that he set out to produce: to surprise people, in order to show them that it is possible to see the world differently?

For most of history philosophers and other people have admired Diogenes and his idiosyncrasies. He served as an inspiring model for what one can accomplish by thinking outside of the things everyone takes for granted. After his death toward the end of the fourth century BCE, reports about

Diogenes' life spread far and wide. They had a profound influence on the philosophical school known as Stoicism, and on the first Christians. All the way up to the end of the eighteenth century Diogenes' intellectual legacy was seen as an essential part of the philosophical canon. But this changed with the arrival of a new understanding of what does and does not get to be part of that canon.

In the early nineteenth century, the German philosopher Georg Wilhelm Friedrich Hegel formulated an influential new definition of the history of philosophy in a series of lectures. At his inaugural address as professor of philosophy at the University of Heidelberg in 1816 he said: "The bodies belonging to the minds who are the heroes of this history, and their temporal lives (the outward fates of the philosophers), have perished, but their works (the thought, the principle) did not follow them." For Hegel the only part that matters is the latter, the rational element, and ideally it is stripped of personality and individual character as much as possible. In his view philosophical material is valuable insofar as it belongs to "the general character of humans as humans" and is free from "peculiarity" (*Eigentümlichkeit*).[4] Hereafter, the history of philosophy increasingly became a history of ideas and theories, no longer of individual lives. Because there was no room for personalities or idiosyncrasies in the history of philosophy anymore, Diogenes was sidelined as a thinker.

Cutting Diogenes out of the history of philosophy creates several problems. Without him, it is difficult to explain why Stoic thinkers focused so much on personal ethics, or why a sober lifestyle was such a key virtue for them and for the early Christians—and these are just two of many developments for which Diogenes was either the source or a vital link between the earliest beginnings of Greek philosophy and its translation into the Roman era and beyond. But the bigger issue by far is this: by not taking Diogenes seriously as a philosopher, we are missing out. He was antiquity's most independent and original mind, and his vision of simplicity, autonomy, and living in accordance with nature has much to offer in our contemporary world.

INTO THE WOODS

To call it exile would be an exaggeration, but I did feel rather out of place. It was the middle of the summer, and I had just moved from Europe to a tiny college town in the woods in New England. I had landed there as a last-minute hire for a temporary job teaching in the classics department, starting in the summer term. People had recommended the college art gallery to me as something to do, so I went—and found myself face-to-face with Diogenes.

On the colorful painting I am looking at—eighteenth-century and French, so the label says—a bald, bearded man is sitting on the ground, his face shaded by trees hanging overhead. On the other side of the painting I see a group of men. Their faces catch the light, they are standing, and behind them the outline of a city is visible. The seated man gestures with his hand, palm turned downward, at the man who appears to be the leader of the group. Dazzling in shining armor and a bright red cape, that man is reaching out an open hand and seems to be offering something. But whatever it is, the guy in the shade is not having it.

Perhaps it had something to do with my own state of mind, but Diogenes' isolation and out-of-place-ness in the painting affected me. I had read about his meeting with Alexander many times and seen other visual depictions of it, yet this version of the scene truly brought home to me how extraordinary Diogenes' response was. He looks inferior to Alexander in all respects: he lacks an entourage, his clothes are dull, he is unkempt, and he is sitting on the ground while everyone else towers over him. And yet Diogenes seems perfectly content under these beautiful, shady trees. He does not look vulnerable or deprived in any way, even though he is a long way from home. The painter, Louis de Silvestre, has succeeded in illustrating why Diogenes did not need anything from Alexander, and why it was natural for him to rebuff the king. He shows that Diogenes did not fit in the world of cities and kings but had created his own world right outside. And from this place the philosopher could see more clearly than anyone the emptiness of Alexander's splendor.

Though Diogenes is less of a household name than, for instance, his contemporary Plato, he still has been written about plenty. But most if not all existing treatments fall into one of two traps. Many accounts present a sanitized version of Diogenes, in which much of what ancient authors tell us about him has been discarded as being either too scandalous or simply too good to be true. This procedure makes Diogenes into a skeletal, uninteresting figure, a mere conduit for a few seemingly unrelated philosophical notions that will be taken up in earnest only later by the Stoics. Alternatively, there are accounts that uncritically reproduce the ancient reports about Diogenes in sensationalist detail, without allowing for the possibility that his ideas and his life may have something of value to offer other than entertainment. In such narratives Diogenes is nothing but a cliché: a crazy provocateur who relieved himself in public and enjoyed shocking people with his antics. These two approaches, as different as they are, converge in selling Diogenes short as a thinker.

The story of Diogenes' life has something to teach us, and he intended it that way. With Diogenes, his thinking, lived experience, and corporeality were inseparable. He gave no lectures but lived out his ideal of radical autonomy in his large pot. If you wanted to learn from him, you had to join him and observe from up close, or ask a specific question. Because Diogenes himself intertwined his life and his ideas completely and on purpose, this book offers an integrated account of both. We will always be doing both history and philosophy, and we will continuously engage with him in two different ways: in the past tense, as a historical figure situated in a specific time and place, and in the present tense, as a philosopher who speaks and performs for us outside of time. We must do so even in cases when his ideas and experience overlapped in an unwanted, unintentional way: to understand Diogenes' unprecedented and unique philosophical critique of the institution of slavery, for instance, we have to also investigate how he was enslaved and sold, and lived in servitude in the house of a wealthy Corinthian family.

Reconstructing Diogenes' life and ideas is a difficult task because of the gaps in the historical record about him, and because over time both his admirers and detractors started making things up about him. Some of these fictions eventually got mixed in with true events in traditional narratives about his life, complicating matters even further. But we are not totally helpless. By tracing a given report about Diogenes as far back in time as we can, taking into account who transmitted it, when, and for what reason, we can make an informed decision whether or not to trust the reported event or quote. I have followed this method for everything that is included in my account of Diogenes and will explain my process in cases that are particularly vexed, like the meeting of Diogenes and Alexander. Sometimes I include fictitious stories about Diogenes—of course, clearly marking them as such—because they give us great insight into what he and his ideas meant to later generations. For the sake of readability this book contains endnotes rather than footnotes, and the notes are preceded by a brief explanation of how ancient and modern texts are cited in the notes. In the center a set of images is printed, including all images discussed in this book, like Silvestre's painting of the meeting of Diogenes and Alexander.

This book will start out with a historical sketch of Diogenes' life and the time he lived in. He was born in a prosperous, independent city-state located on the fault line between the Greek and Persian realms of power. By the time he died both realms had been brought under Macedonian control by Alexander's conquests. In the chapters that follow, we will explore the answers Diogenes' lived philosophy offers to five big questions: What can we know about the world? How should we treat our bodies? How can we stand up to rulers? How does one resist and survive slavery? How do we prepare for death? The book concludes by tracing the massive influence Diogenes' answers to these questions had, from the first generation of his followers all the way up to the twenty-first century. We will encounter Diogenes' ideas in early medieval Baghdad, at the time buzzing with the cross-pollination of Islamic and ancient Greek philosophy; in Parisian intellectual salons right around the time when the French Revolution was about to erupt; and in Friedrich Nietzsche's intensely original struggle for truth and meaning at the end of the nineteenth century, the beginning of the modern era. In dramatically different circumstances, Diogenes time and again provided the spark to let people think outside of the status quo and bring about change.

The aim of this book is to show how Diogenes became Diogenes, how his ideas have helped shape the world we live in, and what they can do for us today. Diogenes' philosophy teaches us to train our minds and bodies so that we can handle both hardship and pleasure. Because of the unpredictability of human existence, we should enjoy the present, yet be prepared for all circumstances. He modeled a truly independent life by needing nothing more than what he could easily provide for himself and by relying on his own reason alone to make sense of the world around him. The first recorded critic of slavery, Diogenes was able to think outside of his society's norms when no one else could. We set out to discover how he was able to do this, and to learn by his example how we, today, may start thinking beyond our own blind spots.

1

IN SEARCH OF A HUMAN BEING

Diogenes lived his philosophy, and to understand his ideas we must start by learning about his life. That this is not a straightforward matter has already been illustrated by the fact that the most famous event of his life, his meeting with Alexander, is strongly disputed, with most historians arguing that it never happened. This raises the question of how we know what we know about Diogenes in the first place. Where do the reports about him come from, how have they been passed down and preserved, and what kinds of information do we have? To answer these questions we will begin by tracing the earliest scattered references to Diogenes, starting with his lifetime, and consider how they relate to the much more abundant reports about him from the second and third centuries CE. We will then zoom in specifically on the chain of information that preserved Diogenes' encounter with Alexander for the historical record, before placing this particular event on the timeline of Diogenes' life.

Diogenes' philosophy consisted of intentionally spectacular deeds and equally memorable quips. The followers who attended him remembered these deeds and sayings and made every effort to pass them down, both orally and in written form. In Diogenes' lifetime and for many centuries afterward all sorts of information—reports about battles, family histories, love poetry, jokes, and so on and so forth—was shared and transmitted both ways: orally, through recitation, storytelling, and performance, as well as through writing and copying texts. Generations of scholars have taken it for granted that what little information we have about Diogenes is not to be trusted. But once we understand that Diogenes did and said surprising things on purpose, that these things would have been memorable precisely because they were surprising, and that both followers and foes passed them on through rich and diverse strategies of information transfer, it follows that we can know much more about Diogenes than modern historians have allowed for.[1]

As a non-writer, Diogenes is in good company. The Athenian philosopher Socrates, who was two generations older than Diogenes, famously did not produce any works either. But—and this is not true for Diogenes—we can read extensively about Socrates in surviving works by men who knew him: the historian Xenophon, the comedy writer Aristophanes, and Socrates' influential disciple Plato. As we read, however, we must always bear in mind that what Plato writes is not necessarily an accurate representation of Socrates' ideas: it is primarily a representation of Plato's thinking *about* Socrates. Still, the availability of several early and extensive accounts undeniably puts us on surer footing with Socrates than with Diogenes. Tracing and reconstructing his thinking is a difficult and sometimes frustrating task. In using reports about him we must always be mindful of what has been forgotten, exaggerated, or distorted. But abandoning this effort and dismissing *all* the ancient quotes and anecdotes as fictions is as good as writing Diogenes out of the history of philosophy, forgoing his still urgent exhortation to a good, self-directed life according to reason and with (not in spite of) our bodies.

SPARTAN CAFETERIAS

The earliest reference to Diogenes, as brief as it is, comes from the work of a contemporary. The multitalented philosopher Aristotle was born about twenty-five years after Diogenes. Aristotle does not exactly mention him by name, but the epithet he uses was so closely associated with Diogenes that we can assume it refers to him. In a discussion of metaphors in his *Rhetoric*, Aristotle says that the sculptor Cephisodotus calls triremes "decorated windmills" and that "the Dog" describes the taverns of Attica as "Spartan cafeterias."[2] Diogenes reportedly received the nickname "the Dog" from Plato, and it stuck. (We will return later to how this happened.) Attica is the peninsula where Athens is located, and Diogenes' quip was probably intended to make fun of the overly luxurious stylings of the Athenians and to praise the frugality of the Spartans, which aligned with his own austere way of life. Diogenes liked using humorous and confusing paradoxes, and the comment fits well into that pattern.

It is uncertain whether Aristotle and Diogenes knew each other personally, but they did move in similar circles. Aristotle was the teacher of young Alexander and a student of Plato, with whom Diogenes butted heads several times. Aristotle's successor as head of his philosophical school, Theophrastus, reportedly compiled a collection of anecdotes about Diogenes.[3] Unfortunately, it does not survive in its original form, but later authors frequently refer to it.

The second-oldest source about Diogenes is an anonymous work preserved on a papyrus that dates from the mid-third century BCE, less than seventy years after Diogenes' death. This means that the person who compiled the several anecdotes and conversations that make up the text could have received the information directly from someone who overlapped with Diogenes. Its most likely author, Metrocles, was a student of Diogenes' disciple Crates, so he was in a sense an intellectual "grandson" to the elusive philosopher.

All the anecdotes compiled in this text feature Diogenes outwitting the authorities. In one of them he is staying in an inn somewhere—the exact location is not mentioned—when guards of the governors ask him who he is and where he comes from. He says: "I am a Molossian mastiff." Here, as in subsequent sources, Diogenes embraces the nickname Plato gave him, identifying specifically with a breed of dog known for its ferocity and large size. Next, the guards ask him where he is going. He does not answer, and the guards hand him over to the governors. A hearing follows where the guards question him. Does he, as a stranger, despise the city and its laws so much that he does not even answer questions? Diogenes says that he answered the guards' first questions nicely, but by the last one he thought they had gone mad: "They asked me where I was going, seeing me sitting at the table!"[4]

Though their accusation that Diogenes despised the city and its laws is true, he tripped up his accusers with a savvy logical joke. Because Diogenes expressed much of his thought through witty quips, in tracing his ideas we also have to develop a sensibility for his style of humor, and for the social dynamics of joking. Just as during his meeting with Alexander, Diogenes was not at all impressed by the authorities and their threats of punishment. The witticism itself—at the moment the guards asked their question he was obviously going nowhere—fits well with one of Diogenes' core precepts: to live in the here and now. Because this text was written so soon after his lifetime, and most likely by someone close to Diogenes, we have good reasons to trust it. It also allows us to be a bit more confident about later accounts that paint a similar picture of Diogenes: a traveler and a stranger wherever he went, but never at a loss for words.

Unlike Plato and Aristotle, Diogenes did not himself found a philosophical school, but he had his followers, who came to be considered a distinct philosophical movement in their own right. They were called *kynikos* in Greek, derived from the Greek word for "dog" (*kyon*, genitive *kynos*); in Latin this was spelled *cynicus*, which in English became "Cynic." Teles of Megara lived in the mid-third century BCE, was a contemporary of Metrocles, and like him, followed the teachings of Diogenes. He also wrote several texts on Cynic philosophers. Excerpts of these have been preserved by the scholar Stobaeus, who produced a voluminous anthology of ancient Greek authors in the fifth century CE, with a special emphasis on philosophy. Teles devotes a handful of passages to Diogenes. In the longest of them, Diogenes meets with someone who complains that Athens has become an expensive city. They visit several shops together and ask the prices of perfume, meat, and a sheepskin. Each time Diogenes agrees with the complainer: the city is indeed expensive. Then they go to the stalls for lupini beans and dried figs, where the prices are much lower. Now Diogenes exclaims: "How cheap the city is!" He was trying to show that Athens was expensive for those who lived an expensive life but cheap for those who did not, Teles explains. The message: life is far easier if you practice living well on beans and figs, like Diogenes, than if you accustom yourself to luxuries.[5] This narrative, like the previous two, can be taken as fairly reliably grounded in fact, since Teles compiled it around the same time as when the papyrus was written.

In addition to Cynicism, two other major philosophical movements emerged in the third century BCE: Epicureanism, named after its founder, Epicurus, and Stoicism, named after the Stoa Poikile in Athens, where it was first taught. The differences between these movements and the influence of Diogenes on both of them will be of interest later on. For now, as we track the posthumous reports about Diogenes through the centuries, we turn to the Epicurean philosopher Philodemus, from Gadara, in modern-day Jordan. He lived at the beginning of the first century BCE and after Teles is the next author to discuss Diogenes, in his polemical treatise *On the Stoics*. Philodemus' works have been preserved only on charred papyrus scrolls found in a villa at Herculaneum, which together with Pompeii was buried under lava from the eruption of Mount Vesuvius in 79 CE. The text, consequently, is severely damaged and fragmentary.

As he discusses Diogenes' ideas on politics, Philodemus challenges the notion that Diogenes wrote nothing during his lifetime. He defends the view that Diogenes, just like Plato, wrote a political-philosophical work titled *Republic* (*Politeia* in Greek, which also means "constitution"). We can assume that the ideas Philodemus attributes to Diogenes' *Republic* derive from texts written by Diogenes' followers about his thinking, though the "summary" of Diogenes' *Republic* that Philodemus offers reads as rather polemic and extreme. Philodemus mentions the following views and proposals: weapons are useless, bones should serve as money instead of coins, there is nothing wrong with cannibalism, and there should be complete sexual freedom, including incest and sharing spouses. Some of these he also attributes to Zeno, disciple of Crates and the founder of Stoicism.[6] In his text he attempts to discredit the Stoics by linking them to Cynicism, and we might wonder if he sacrifices accuracy in the interest of scoring points against his intellectual opponents. Nonetheless, we will see that all of these proposals are ultimately rooted in Diogenes' thought. Philodemus seems to have chosen some genuine ideas of Diogenes—for instance, his rejection of the institution of marriage—and exaggerated them to create a scandalizing caricature.

The last of the early written sources about Diogenes is by the Roman orator and philosopher Cicero in the first century BCE. He is actually the one to give us the earliest preserved account of the meeting of Alexander and Diogenes. It is remarkably succinct: "Diogenes really answered Alexander in a rather brash manner when the latter asked him if he needed anything: 'Step aside, out of my sun.' He had clearly disturbed Diogenes' sunbathing."[7] Cicero places Diogenes' reply to Alexander in the context of exemplary asceticism: the sage needs no material goods to be happy, since only virtue matters. Cicero uses so few words to describe the event that his readers must already have been familiar with it from other sources that have since been lost.

From the first century CE onward many extensive texts on Diogenes have survived complete and intact. Some of these are explicitly fictional: they concern Diogenes only in the sense that he is a character in the work. Other texts are polemical, like Philodemus' work, which means that Diogenes' ideas may be presented tendentiously. Both types of texts are useful for understanding the influence of, and reactions to, Diogenes over the centuries, but only rarely can we use them as sources for statements and anecdotes that may actually derive from the historical Diogenes. If we do so, we should proceed with great caution.

In general, it is better to rely on other kinds of sources. Diogenes occasionally pops up in historical writing. These fortuitous glimpses of him are promising for reconstructing some parts of his life. An even more valuable resource is the so-called genre of doxography in this period: collections of philosophical views and statements of others. Diogenes features in the collections of several doxographical authors, but most importantly in the work of Diogenes Laertius. That the two men share a name is a coincidence, albeit a somewhat confusing one.

In his work *Lives of the Philosophers*, written in Greek in the third century CE, Diogenes Laertius describes more than eighty thinkers. These "lives" are not conventional biographies, but rather compilations of sayings and events in roughly chronological order. The biography of Diogenes is one of the longer lives in the collection. The author draws from the work of numerous predecessors, many of whom he mentions by name, going as far back as Theophrastus, Aristotle's successor and Diogenes' contemporary. In addition to relying on older sources, Diogenes Laertius selects and reports information largely without any apparent bias. Together with the earlier texts already mentioned, his biography is our best introduction to Diogenes' thought, even if he does partake of some sensationalism on occasion—in using his text, some caution is required too. An important virtue of his is the tendency to include alternative versions on genuine points of contention. For example, he gives a list of philosophical works and tragedies that Diogenes is said to have published but also writes that the philosopher never wrote anything at all according to two of his sources. Similarly, we find several conflicting accounts of Diogenes' death in Diogenes Laertius. And he writes about the time Diogenes got a visit from Alexander.

DID DIOGENES MEET ALEXANDER?

So, why are scholars so reluctant to believe Cicero, Diogenes Laertius, and others when they tell us of the meeting of Diogenes and Alexander? "It is hardly likely, for instance, that Diogenes would ever have met Alexander, or that the king would have been either interested in him or impressed by him." This is the translator and author Robin Hard, who in a recent publication uses the story of the meeting to support his assessment that many of the anecdotes about Diogenes are "surely fictional."[8] His reasoning shows how much the reputation of Diogenes as a crazy philosopher has shaped the interpretation of the material. But we can throw the question right back: Why would Alexander *not* have wanted to meet Diogenes? His own private teacher was the philosopher Aristotle, who, as we have seen, certainly knew of Diogenes, and perhaps even knew him directly. And we will see that there were still other connections between the young king and the old philosopher.

A more serious challenge to the historicity of the episode has to do with the chronology of the respective lives of the two men. At the end of the seventeenth century the Frenchman Pierre Bayle turned his back on the Catholic Church and his home country and traveled, via Switzerland, to the Netherlands. He settled in Rotterdam and in 1697 went on to publish his *Dictionnaire historique et critique*, a hefty encyclopedia of intellectuals of the past and their ideas. In this work Bayle subjects the received narratives about the likes of Diogenes to a critical analysis. Up to this point people had generally accepted the received narratives about such historical characters without asking many questions. By starting to do precisely this, Bayle was ahead of his time.

A large portion of Bayle's lemma about Diogenes deals with his relation with Alexander. He writes: "We cannot help but find greatness in the ways of Diogenes, if we imagine that they have some sense to them. Since Alexander, who certainly was able to judge such a thing well, found greatness in him, there must have been some."[9] Unlike Hard, Bayle assumes that the two men met *and* that Alexander was impressed by Diogenes. In his extensive footnotes, however, he demolishes some of the main source texts that up to that point had gone unchallenged.

The Roman philosopher Seneca, who at some point served as tutor and advisor to Emperor Nero, mentions Diogenes twice in his treatise *On Benefits*. In both passages he connects him to Alexander, who was "puffed up with pride beyond human measure" on the day he met Diogenes. The king was overcome by the philosopher because he was "neither able to give him anything, nor to take anything away from him."

Diogenes "stomped naked through the riches of the Macedonians and trampled the wealth of the king . . . who then ruled the whole world."[10] In this last part Seneca is speaking figuratively: Diogenes "trampled" Alexander's wealth by rejecting it. Bayle objects to Seneca's version of the episode, which he wrote around the middle of the first century CE, because of its problematic chronology. Diogenes and Alexander would have met before the Macedonian conquests in Asia, because afterward Alexander never set foot in Greece again. So at the time of his conversation with Diogenes, Alexander did not yet rule "the whole world," nor was he worshipped as a god ("pride beyond human measure"), not yet. Diogenes Laertius, writes Bayle, commits a similar error when he has Alexander introduce himself to Diogenes as "the great king." Alexander acquired that title only after his conquests.

For Bayle, doubts about the accuracy of the source texts for the interactions between Diogenes and Alexander could go hand in hand with full confidence regarding the historicity of the meeting itself. He even justified Diogenes' worth as a philosopher by means of Alexander's opinion, as in his eyes the Macedonian king was unassailable. But Bayle's misgivings about the source texts would take on a life of their own centuries later. At the start of the twentieth century the standard encyclopedia on classical antiquity, the German work *Paulys Realencyclopädie der Classischen Altertumswissenschaft*, references the "clumsy anachronism," as demonstrated by Bayle, of the story of the meeting of Alexander and Diogenes. It goes on to conclude: "It is probably best to leave open whether the encounter has any basis in history or not."[11] A few decades later an article that would influence scholars for decades to come claims that the narratives of the meeting "have been blown to pieces too often to notice," without citing Bayle or, in fact, anyone else.[12]

If Seneca and Diogenes Laertius were our only ancient sources for Diogenes' meeting with Alexander, with both of them dating it to a moment when the two men could not have been in the same place, it would be difficult to maintain its historicity. But this is not at all the case. In Cicero's version, which is about a century older than Seneca's, Alexander does not use any honorific titles during the meeting. Cicero goes on to narrate in the same passage how Diogenes "used to argue that while he had no needs, nothing would ever be enough for the king, in order to show how far superior he was to the king of Persia in life and fortune." Here Diogenes does describe Alexander as having defeated the Persians already, but this is at a later point in time, long after their encounter. In addition to Diogenes Laertius there are other Greek authors who report on their conversation, and it is in their works that we find clues as to who recorded the event in the first place.

Plutarch was a historian and philosopher who lived in the second half of the first century and the early part of the second century CE. He wrote a biography of Alexander, in Greek. A generation later another historian, named Arrian, did the same. Both authors describe the young king's meeting with Diogenes, placing it at Corinth, before his campaigns in Persia and beyond. Both authors also repeatedly reference a much earlier author by the name of Onesicritus. This Onesicritus was a follower of Diogenes, served in Alexander's army as chief helmsman, and wrote a work titled *On the Education of Alexander.* Several long fragments of this piece have been preserved, and these indicate that the work also covered Alexander's campaigns. It seems unavoidable that Onesicritus described the meeting between Alexander and Diogenes, and that Plutarch and Arrian based their accounts on his, even if this part of the work does not remain today.[13]

Alexander shared two connections with Diogenes—Aristotle and Onesicritus—and had an interest in philosophy. So he had a clear motive in wanting to meet him. He also had the opportunity: the two men were in the same place at the same time, since Diogenes had arrived in Corinth around the middle of the fourth century BCE and stayed there for a long time. Proof of the meeting was provided by Onesicritus himself in his account of Alexander's (young) life, and this is how a report of this remarkable event entered the historiographical tradition. Some scholars accept that Onesicritus indeed wrote about the meeting of Alexander and Diogenes, and that he was the source later authors used, but still consider "a literary origin . . . more plausible" because "the contrast between these two diametrically opposed, but paradoxically parallel personalities would have been so appealing to explore."[14] In other words, the story of their meeting is so good that Onesicritus must have made it up. This seems like an example where the shock value of Diogenes' way of life—did he really meet Alexander and tell him to get out of his sun?—works against him and prevents him from taking up his rightful place in history.

We have every reason to be apprehensive about what we can really know about someone who lived and died more than two millennia ago, but sometimes such skepticism goes too far. In reconstructing Diogenes' life we always have to ask *how* we know what we think we know, and whether the source (or string of sources) is good enough. In the case of the philosopher's meeting with the king we can answer this question affirmatively. So: yes, the two did meet. And, keeping this strategy close to hand, we are now ready to see how Diogenes became Diogenes.

ON THE BLACK SEA

For Diogenes, thinking and lived experience were inseparable. His way of life was his philosophy, and that is why this book must begin with an outline of his life. The following sketch is based on Diogenes Laertius' biography and is necessarily incomplete. The only remaining physical objects related (indirectly) to Diogenes are some coins bearing his father's name. Still, even if that was all we had, we would already know more about him than about the vast majority of people who were alive at the time. Across all the available types of ancient source material the sociocultural elite is much better represented than ordinary people. The wealthy could build temples and have their names inscribed on them; someone who ran a small workshop hung up a wooden sign. When it comes to durability the inscription in stone "wins" practically every time.

Diogenes was born in Sinope, a prosperous, independent city-state on the Black Sea that served as a hub for international trade. Today Sinope is called Sinop, and it is located in what we now know as northern Turkey. Diogenes Laertius offers us two clues about Diogenes' birthdate: he was ninety years old when he died, and he died in the same year as the Macedonian king Alexander. Since Alexander died in 323 BCE this gives us 413 BCE as the year of Diogenes' birth. The *Suda*, a voluminous encyclopedia in ancient Greek compiled in the tenth century CE, seems to differ on this point. It says Diogenes was born in 404 BCE, and it attributes various tragedies to him. (These are also mentioned by Diogenes Laertius, though he does not commit himself to Diogenes' authorship.) This poses a problem for the chronology of Diogenes' later life: it would mean that he could have overlapped only barely with some older philosophers in Athens whom he did meet, according to most sources. The *Suda* also calls Diogenes an Athenian, so we must conclude that the notice is about someone else and that *he* wrote those tragedies, not Diogenes of Sinope.[15] Going back to the age that Diogenes Laertius gives for him, we should note that the neat, round number ninety is somewhat suspect. We know from ages listed on tombstones that people commonly rounded these up or down in antiquity, simply because they did not know exactly how old they were.[16] It is therefore safest to say that Diogenes was born sometime between 413 and 408 BCE—in other words, around 410 BCE.

Diogenes' hometown, Sinope, was founded in the seventh century BCE. According to the historian Herodotus, its founders were Cimmerians, a nomadic people believed to have come from present-day Iran, though other historians credit people from Thessaly, in Greece, and assume that Sinope was only later taken over by Cimmerians and, still later, by settlers from Miletus. Archaeological remains indicate some presence of Milesians in Sinope as early as the seventh or sixth century BCE. Located in what is now western Turkey but was then known as Ionia, Miletus dated back at least to the Bronze Age, and Milesians spoke the Ionian dialect of ancient Greek that Herodotus also used. This became the common language in Sinope and was most likely either Diogenes' native language or one of his native languages. Sinope was part of the region of Paphlagonia, which was almost certainly under Persian rule in the fifth century BCE. It was also during this time that the

Persian king Darius, and his son Xerxes after him, tried and failed to add the cities of mainland Greece to their empire.

In the decades before the birth of Diogenes there were close contacts between Sinope and Athens. Pericles, the Athenian general immortalized by the historian Thucydides, sent ships and men to "help" the Sinopeans overthrow their ruler Timosileus in 436 BCE, but how welcome this intervention was we do not know. Afterward, six hundred Athenians remained in Sinope and settled in the homes of the expelled supporters of the old government.[17] In early September 400 BCE, when Diogenes would have been about ten years old, a motley army of around ten thousand mercenaries under the command of an Athenian general named Xenophon passed through Sinope. The troops were on their way back from their attempt to help the brother of the Persian king overthrow his sibling and take the throne for himself. The pretender to the throne had been killed in his first major battle, and now the mercenaries faced the difficult task of getting themselves safely back to the Ionian coast after their failed mission. We have a detailed account of the march because the general Xenophon was also a historian and recorded their experiences in the famous work *Anabasis* (literally "march upcountry"), sometimes also called *March of the Ten-Thousand*. Xenophon's report on his encounter with ambassadors from Sinope gives us a brief glimpse of what life was like there during Diogenes' youth.

Xenophon's men are met by the ambassadors when they are encamped at the nearby town of Cotyora, which was one of the three colonies of Sinope. Their spokesman is named Hecatonymus, and he implores the soldiers to stop pillaging the town. In his speech he appeals to their shared Greekness: because of their Milesian roots the Sinopeans are Greeks like

Xenophon himself, and the soldiers should treat them and the Cotyorites well. But if they will not—Hecatonymus immediately launches into a threat—the Sinopeans will call in the Paphlagonians and make an alliance with them against Xenophon's army. Xenophon responds that he does not care one bit whether or not the cities and communities they pass through can claim Greek origins. Whoever welcomes him and his soldiers peacefully will be treated in kind, *and* vice versa. This is just as true for the "barbarians" (*barbaroi*) they meet with, he says, applying the term Greeks used to lump all non-Greeks together.

Given that Xenophon's men had already begun pillaging the land of the Cotyorites before meeting with the ambassadors, it is clear that he did not always live up to this stated ideal of reciprocity. And it turns out that the "Greekness" of the Sinopeans was rather superficial: something that could be invoked when it seemed opportune to do so but that was just as easily put aside when circumstances changed. In the end both sides decided to proceed on friendly terms and, in this instance, further violence was averted.[18]

The meeting between the Sinopeans and Xenophon's mercenaries tells us something about Sinope's prominence in the region, but also something about the messiness of geopolitics and ethnic identity at the time. Sinopeans saw themselves both as Milesian Greeks and as Paphlagonian "barbarians," placing emphasis on one or the other of these depending on the context and occasion. Xenophon the Athenian was unequivocally Greek but fought for a Persian would-be usurper together with an army of men who hailed from all over the ancient Mediterranean. By choosing allies on an ad hoc basis, Sinope managed to hold on to its independence in the following decades, but around the year 370 BCE the Persian general Datames took control of the city after several sieges. This remained the status quo until the start of the campaigns of Alexander.[19]

In a relatively recent biography, Diogenes has been called "purely Greek" with respect to his "language and heritage," because he came "from the same Milesian stock from which philosophers like Thales, Anaximander, and Anaximenes did," referencing three famous thinkers from the city of Miletus.[20] But being a philosopher did not necessarily make Diogenes Milesian or Greek, let alone "purely" so. To call Diogenes "Greek" is an oversimplification that fails to do justice to his background and experiences. Although he spent much of his life in prominent Greek cities like Athens and Corinth, he always remained an outsider there, without civic rights in those places. As Xenophon's account shows so clearly, Diogenes' birthplace was in the middle of the "barbarian" territory of the Paphlagonians, on the fault line between the Greek and Persian spheres of influence, and we can only guess at the precise origins and ethnicity of Diogenes' family. Moreover, as this book will document, Diogenes was influenced by philosophical traditions flowing into Sinope from several directions, west and east.

Diogenes' father was named Hicesias, and his mother's name, as we already said, is lost to us. She is not mentioned at all in Diogenes Laertius' biography, though there is one statement attributed to Diogenes in which his mother appears that has been handed down in a Byzantine collection of quotations. Upon finding out that someone had written something negative about her, Diogenes said that one tear from his mother could erase all allegations. The precise meaning is hard to grasp out of context, but it suggests—if indeed he said this—that he felt the need to defend his mother and was unimpressed by the allegations against her.

Hicesias was a banker and in that capacity responsible for the coinage in Sinope. Given the likelihood that Diogenes received some form of education as a young man, it seems that he came from a fairly well-to-do family. The name Diogenes means "son of Zeus" in Greek: *dio-* is the genitive of the name Zeus and *-genes* is derived from the verb meaning "to be born," *gignomai.* "Son of Zeus" seems like an impressive name, but it was quite common, and in the reported sayings Diogenes never discusses it. Laertius' biography does quote a short poem by one Cercidas, who explains the etymology of the name and writes that Diogenes was rightly called "son of Zeus and heavenly dog" because of his fortitude. The poet wrote this in the third century BCE. The title "heavenly dog" for Diogenes stuck and would still be in use in Cynic literature of the first centuries CE.[21]

COUNTERFEITER OR REVOLUTIONARY?

Of Diogenes' youth we know little. The major events of his time in Sinope are his possible involvement in "defacing the currency" and, shortly thereafter, his banishment from the city. In Greek his father's job is called *trapezites*, which basically means "someone with a table." Originally the main task of *trapezitai* was to exchange money and test the authenticity of coins. In the course of the fourth century BCE they also began to take on the management of accounts and lines of credit. *Trapezitai* usually did their work outdoors, setting up their tables in the busy marketplace. It makes sense that Hicesias would have been commissioned to oversee the mint in Sinope because of his expertise as a banker.

Diogenes Laertius gives two alternative scenarios for exactly what happened in Sinope: either Hicesias tampered with the coinage and both he and his son Diogenes were exiled from the city as a consequence, or Diogenes was responsible for the disruption and this led to exile for both father and son. When we think of counterfeiting in a modern context, we generally think of the production of false money. But the Greek term consistently used for what occurred at Sinope under Hicesias' watch has a broader meaning: *paracharasso* can refer both to minting false coins with a fake stamp and to damaging coins already in circulation as an act of vandalism or to cause unrest.

Compared to other types of sources, coins from the ancient Mediterranean have survived in great numbers and relatively well preserved. No fewer than nine coins minted in Sinope in the early fourth century BCE with the name Hicesias on them have been found. It was common at the time for the mint master to put his name in the legend, which is the text on the coin. From roughly the same period we have dozens of coins that imitate Sinopean money but seem to have been minted elsewhere because they contain Aramaic instead of Greek letters, or Greek letters with many errors. Most of them were rendered unusable with a chisel shortly after they were minted.[22] These finds make the story of Hicesias' involvement in a disruption of the currency plausible, but the exact circumstances remain a matter of speculation. Perhaps the goal was to drive up the value of the coins minted in Sinope to make a profit. There may also have been a political reason to destroy coins coming from elsewhere, possibly against a larger background of unrest leading up to the Persian takeover by Datames. It was, in any case, common for a son to have the same profession as his father, so Hicesias and Diogenes may well have acted together, and faced exile together.

Later generations looked to the affair of the coinage as an explanation for Diogenes' exile and his departure from Sinope. But from early on the episode was also assigned metaphorical significance, perhaps first by Diogenes himself. Diogenes Laertius connects the story of the defaced coins with a later visit by Diogenes to one of the oracles of the god Apollo. Again, he gives two scenarios. In the first, Diogenes was pressured by the men working at the mint to deface the currency and turned to the oracle for advice. There he was told that it was permissible to disrupt "the public *nomisma*." *Nomisma* can mean "coin" as well as "institution" or "accepted custom" in a broader sense. (The word derives from *nomos*, which can mean "law" as well as "custom.") In this scenario, Diogenes' offense stems from a mistake: he thought the oracle gave him permission to disturb the coinage, when actually he was supposed to go after the institutions and customs. Because of his mistake, Diogenes is banished, or else flees out of fear. In the second version, Diogenes is responsible, but his father winds up in prison because he entrusted the minting to Diogenes. After his father dies Diogenes goes to the oracle to ask how he can become famous. The oracle's answer is the same: disrupt the accepted customs.

Both scenarios connect the oracle to the exile and the (metaphorical) disruption of the *nomisma* and thereby turn Diogenes into a man with a divine mission. The question remains whether it all really happened that way. The episode closely resembles an event from the life story of another famous philosopher, so it may be a borrowing that was incorporated into

Diogenes' biography erroneously: Socrates, in the defense speech recorded by Plato known as *Apology*, also claims that he performed his philosophical interrogations because of an oracle from Apollo. The god said that no one was wiser than Socrates, who "knows that he knows nothing," so Socrates tried to show that others also "know nothing" to prove the oracle right.[23] Another issue is Diogenes' often disparaging attitude toward religion. Would he really have let Apollo dictate his actions? But perhaps he had an ambivalent relationship to the divine. In any case, with or without encouragement from the oracle, Diogenes managed to reemploy the potentially negative reputation of "counterfeiter" he carried with him to Athens as a pithy metaphor for his philosophical rallying cry of subverting societal norms.

IN EXILE

After leaving Sinope, Diogenes struck out for Athens, a trip that would have taken about ten or eleven days by sailboat, which was the fastest way to go. Athens was the intellectual center of the Greek-speaking world at the time, and the city presented itself as a refuge for those who had been forced to leave their homeland. But this did not mean that newcomers had the same rights as (male, free-born) Athenians. They were not allowed to vote in the public assembly, nor to own land.

Exile was a lifelong punishment, unless the banishment was officially revoked, but it was one that Diogenes embraced. Diogenes proclaimed that he became a philosopher thanks to his exile, hinting at the many philosophers before him who also left their native land, forced or not, and praising Athens for offering him such a stimulating environment. In another quote reported by Diogenes Laertius, Diogenes taunted the Sinopeans: sure, they condemned him to exile, but he condemned *them* to stay home. With this playful inversion the philosopher probably meant to say that although Sinope was an important city, it could not match Athens' intellectual climate.

Upon his arrival in Athens Diogenes contacted someone who was supposed to have a small house for him, but the man did not immediately come through. Diogenes did not want to wait and moved into a *pithos* instead: a large earthenware pot normally used for storing wine. (Some accounts erroneously refer to this as a barrel or a bathtub.) Placed on its side, a *pithos* forms a small, humble cave. In the many, many depictions of Diogenes and his pot—from the first century BCE to the present—he sits up front in the opening, framed perfectly by the rim. Diogenes hardly could have foreseen how clever his selection of a pot would be as iconography, but ever since then, the *pithos* has embodied the distinctive paradox of lonely seclusion in the middle of the marketplace.

According to Diogenes Laertius, Diogenes' *pithos* stood in the Metroön, a temple complex for the goddess Meter (the Mother) bordering the marketplace in Athens. This information is problematic, because this complex was not built until two centuries after Diogenes' lifetime. Perhaps at some point in the oral tradition "on the site where the Metroön now stands" was shortened to "in the Metroön"? Or Diogenes may have lived in the ruins of an older temple to the Mother that was destroyed during the Persian Wars in the fifth century BCE. Either way, the marketplace was the beating heart of the city, the center of commercial activity, and a great place to meet a lot of people. Here Diogenes could exhibit his life of seclusion and self-sufficiency to as many passersby as possible.

Living in a *pithos* was also a way of signaling austerity and humility. A short reference in the comedies of Aristophanes renders it plausible that poor Athenians indeed used large pots as dwellings. One of the characters in *Knights* describes how people lived in "pots, nooks, and sheds" during the Peloponnesian War, fought by Athens and Sparta (and their respective allies) at the end of the fifth century BCE.[24] So Diogenes was probably one of many who had made a makeshift shelter for himself in the city in this way. But his *pithos* would become the most famous one by far.

In Athens, Diogenes became a follower of Antisthenes, who had been one of Socrates' disciples. Like Diogenes, Antisthenes led an unconventional and sober life. Already in antiquity some pointed to him as the actual founder of Cynic philosophy. Because of the undogmatic nature of Cynic thought, it is better to see Antisthenes as an inspiring example to Diogenes than as his teacher. Antisthenes died around 365 BCE, so if they met Diogenes must have arrived in Athens at least before then. It was also in Athens that Diogenes clashed with most of the philosophers of his own generation, Plato foremost among them.

Diogenes did have followers during his lifetime, but, as mentioned, he did not establish a formal school. He must have undertaken some travels (Diogenes Laertius places him in Olympia and Megara, among other places) but otherwise spent his time on the streets of Athens. It was expected of philosophers that they would spend time in public spaces, since intellectual life took place in the marketplace, on the steps of temples, and in open-air sports facilities, the famous *gymnasia*. A major difference between Diogenes and his peers, however, was that his peers went home at the end of the day. Diogenes slept in his *pithos* and lived off alms and dinner invitations.

In Athens Diogenes also acquired his nickname. According to Diogenes Laertius, Plato at one point insulted him by calling him a dog. The specific reason remains unmentioned, but it must have occurred in the context of their larger rivalry. Diogenes took it in stride and quickly adopted the name, reminding others of it constantly, as we already saw in the papyrus text. In the biography, he explains his moniker as follows: "I wag my tail when someone gives me something, I bark when someone gives me nothing, and when someone is a bad person I bite!" In Greek, just as in English, "to bite" (*dakno*) can have a metaphorical meaning, and Diogenes uses it here to refer to his verbal aggressiveness.

Dogs have been loyal friends to humans for millennia, and yet "dog" is an insult in many cultures. Freud explained this apparent contradiction as a consequence of repressed sexuality.[25] Dogs defecate and masturbate shamelessly in public. According to his analysis, in this way they remind us humans of our own barely contained impulses. "Dog" became an insult for those who did not conform to the generally accepted standard of civilization. Diogenes thought it nonsense that we eat in the company of others while we hide anxiously to fulfill other bodily needs. And he was not afraid of acting on that conviction.

TO CORINTH

At some point after moving from Sinope to Athens, Diogenes was traveling to Aegina, an island strategically located between Athens and the Peloponnese. Citing two different sources, Diogenes Laertius describes how on this trip he was ambushed and captured by pirates, who took him to Crete.

There Diogenes was offered for sale as a slave. He was reportedly bought by a wealthy Corinthian merchant named Xeniades. We will go into the details of this episode and Diogenes' ideas about slavery later, but for now it suffices to note that the story of his abduction and sale at the slave market is plausible enough. During the fourth century BCE, and for a long time afterward, the Mediterranean was plagued by pirates. One of their pursuits was human trafficking. Those who ventured on a sea voyage ran a real risk of ending up as merchandise in a slave market.

Diogenes must have arrived in Corinth, possibly enslaved by Xeniades, at some point in the 340s BCE, and wound up living there for many years. According to Diogenes Laertius, he stayed in the household into old age and served as a teacher for Xeniades' sons. This would not have been unusual: raising and teaching children was often left to enslaved workers. Diogenes Laertius nowhere mentions release. In the Greek world, an owner could free an enslaved person in various ways and for various reasons, but it was not common. There are several anecdotes suggesting that after a while Diogenes stopped living in Xeniades' household, including the one about his meeting with King Alexander. In most versions the encounter takes place in the Kraneion in Corinth, where Diogenes is said to have lived in a *pithos* again. Alternatively, Xeniades may have given him a lot of freedom of movement without formally releasing him. According to the biography, he said of Diogenes: "A good deity [*agathos daimon*] has entered my house."

Several different stories circulated about Diogenes' death, at about ninety years old. He is said to have died either by holding his breath, from a cholera-like disease after eating a piece of raw octopus, or from a dog bite after one of his dogs attacked him while he was feeding them octopus. As is often the case in Diogenes Laertius, there is a connection between the cause of death listed and the philosophy of the biography's subject. In the second scenario, Diogenes behaves like a dog by eating raw food; in the third, the Dog is killed by his own dogs. The first scenario clearly taps into Diogenes' radical autonomy and self-control: he took the end of his life into his own hands by voluntarily renouncing even the most basic necessity of life, oxygen. In the account of this scenario Diogenes' friends found him in the Kraneion in Corinth, wrapped in his cape. When he did not wake up, his friends attributed his death to suicide and started spreading the story of him holding his breath. In fact, committing suicide in this way is physiologically impossible. A more plausible explanation would be that Diogenes went into cardiac arrest in his sleep.

For Diogenes to have lived to around ninety is impressive, especially considering the average life expectancy at the time of around forty. If he really lived that long, he would have been an unlikely outlier, though that is not impossible. In antiquity several philosophers were said to have grown very old, and a long life was considered proof of the strength of one's philosophy. There is a chance that his followers exaggerated Diogenes' longevity for this reason. All in all, we cannot be sure exactly how old he was when he died. Diogenes was buried at Corinth next to the gate to the isthmus that connected the Peloponnese to mainland Greece. On his tomb stood a column topped with a marble statue of a dog. In the second century CE the writer Pausanias recounts seeing the tomb in that location, though he gives no further details.[26] The Sinopeans reportedly set up several bronze statues of Diogenes with inscriptions thanking him for demonstrating the virtue of a self-sufficient way of life.

Of those bronze statues no remains have been recovered, but today his birthplace does honor its most famous son with a white stone monument, standing nearly eighteen feet tall.

The monument was designed by the Turkish sculptor Turan Baş and installed in 2006. It depicts Diogenes twice: standing on top of a barrel and on the front of the same barrel, sitting in a round window. The Diogenes on top of the barrel is accompanied by a seated dog and is holding a lantern. The Diogenes on the front of the barrel is reading a piece of papyrus, and a nameplate above his head bears his name in Latin capitals. Both Diogeneses are bald, bearded, and dressed in a loose-fitting cape. The Diogenes standing on top of the barrel is remarkably muscular for a middle-aged beggar. It is clear that the monument took inspiration from earlier Diogenes iconography. Many paintings from the early modern and modern periods show Diogenes living in a barrel instead of a pot, and with a similar glass lantern in his hand. In antiquity, however, portable oil lamps were terra-cotta (like a Roman one on which Diogenes himself is depicted) or, occasionally, bronze. The way Diogenes is framed by a window on the front of the barrel evokes works of art that depict him sitting in the round opening of his *pithos*.

At the base of the barrel stands a plaque in the form of an open book. In Turkish, its inscription reads: "Stand out of my sun, that is the only thing you can do for me" (*Gölge etme, başka ihsan istemem*). This version of Diogenes' famous answer to Alexander is still used as an expression in Turkey today. It pretty much means "Leave me alone!" and is typically used to rebuff someone who offers unsolicited help. In collective memory the phrase—found in song lyrics, as the title of a self-help book, and in political speeches—is still known to derive from

Diogenes. In 2017 there was an attempt to have the monument removed on account of it being an effort to pin "Greek philosophy and Greek ideology" on Sinop. The campaign seems to have been motivated by a mix of nationalist sentiment that saw Diogenes as not being Turkish enough and religious conservatism uncomfortable with Diogenes' radical views on the family and sexuality.[27] Pride in the homegrown but world-famous philosopher who stood up to Alexander of Macedon prevailed, however, and at the time of this writing Diogenes still stands on his barrel.

Equipped with a sense of what there is to know about Diogenes' life, and how we know these things, we are now able to grasp what he himself viewed as his most important accomplishment: to redefine the nature of philosophical inquiry. Plato was becoming well known for his attempts to answer conclusively the question "What is a human?" In response Diogenes reached, among other things, for an oil lamp and set out on his own search in broad daylight. It was a philosophical rebuttal by means of an absurdist performance, with a serious message behind it. For Diogenes, Plato's search for sophisticated definitions and theoretical abstractions to capture the world was the opposite of what philosophy should be about. What mattered to him was the ethical problem: How can we be good humans? Judging by their behavior, Diogenes felt, so few people know the answer to the latter question that they are very hard to find, even with a lamp in broad daylight.

2

WHAT IT MEANS TO KNOW SOMETHING

DIOGENES IS SITTING in his jar in the marketplace in Athens. He is minding his own business, much like when Alexander came to see him in Corinth. A man is walking toward him. We do not know his name, but he is clearly very excited. He has a question for Diogenes that he thinks is going to stump the great thinker. He has learned about this particular philosophical problem only recently himself, and he is eager to put it to the famous philosopher. He hopes it will leave him speechless. "Diogenes, did you know that movement does not *exist*?" Diogenes gets up and walks around the questioner, one lap. Then he sits down again.

Although in this moment Diogenes did not say anything, he was not quite speechless either. He simply did not need any words. The brief anecdote comes from Laertius' biography, which does not record how the questioner reacted when Diogenes moved around him in a circle, but it seems safe to assume that he was disappointed. People were probably present to witness the exchange in the crowded marketplace. Laughter rose up, and he felt publicly shamed and ridiculed.

Diogenes developed his way of doing philosophy in confrontation with his contemporaries, undermining their ideas and methods through humor. These confrontations were sometimes with other philosophers, sometimes with unnamed individuals. Even in the case of the latter we can often trace the underlying question to a philosophical problem that was well known at the time. This is certainly true of the man who asked the question about movement, which goes back to the ideas of the philosopher Zeno of Elea. Zeno lived in the southern, Greek-speaking part of Italy in the fifth century BCE, so Diogenes would not have been able to meet him. The man who asked the question might have read about Zeno's ideas or learned them from other philosophers. There is some evidence that Zeno visited Athens and read from his works to live audiences there.[1]

One of the problems Zeno dealt with was the principle that any distance in physical space is divisible into an infinite number of smaller distances. According to Zeno, this infinity theoretically makes movement from one place to another impossible. He illustrated this idea using the paradox of Achilles (the hero from the Homeric epic) and the tortoise. His example became famous in antiquity: a fifth-century BCE drinking cup found in Falerii in Etruria, Italy, shows Achilles just as he has overtaken the tortoise—a joke or a counterargument in cup form, since this is the very thing Zeno insisted would never happen. In the original thought experiment the tortoise always gets a head start of about thirty feet, and the race starts over each time Achilles reaches the tortoise's starting point. Since the tortoise will always cover some distance, no matter how small, while Achilles rushes to the tortoise's starting point, the hero will never actually catch up with the tortoise even if he gets incredibly close. Diogenes did not find Zeno's speculation about the meaning of categories like space and time worthwhile: if he could successfully set his own body in motion, that was all he needed to know.

Intuitively it seems as obvious that Achilles would overtake the tortoise as it is that Diogenes *could* move, but to prove mathematically that this is so is actually quite difficult; it is necessary to show that an infinite series (the ever-shortening but accumulating distances that the tortoise travels while Achilles reaches the tortoise's starting point) can converge to a finite number (a distance Achilles can complete). It would take until the nineteenth century for mathematicians to be able to capture this phenomenon in an effective formula.[2] Zeno wrote thousands more paradoxes like the one about Achilles and the tortoise. He seems to have focused on how the natural world can be captured through quantitative conceptions and mathematical notions. With his response to the man who asked him about Zeno's ideas, Diogenes signaled his outright refusal to engage in this type of inquiry. But most early Greek philosophers were like Zeno. They were engaged first of all in natural philosophy: the quest to understand the nature and structure of the cosmos.

In antiquity Thales was often identified as the first Greek philosopher. He lived in Miletus at the beginning of the sixth century BCE and thought that the cosmos is composed entirely of water. He considered water to be a divine soul that permeates everything: humans, animals, and matter. The most famous story people told about Thales was that he once fell into a well because he was not looking in front of him but gazing at the stars in the sky. One time Diogenes said that he wondered why scientists stare at the sun and moon but overlook the things right in front of them. This was a clear stab at Thales, given how well known the story about his tumble into the well was.[3] The message: Diogenes is a very different kind of philosopher.

Diogenes' strong rejection of earlier thinkers like Zeno and Thales hinged on a profound disagreement about the central problem of epistemology, or the theory of knowledge: To what extent is the universe knowable? And, by extension: What should philosophy be about, and what is it capable of? Diogenes thought philosophy should focus on human existence. Claims that go beyond our immediate experience in the physical world are, in his view, by definition unprovable and therefore a waste of time.

When Socrates appeared on the scene in the fifth century BCE, initially he was also drawn to natural philosophy in the style of Thales and other predecessors. But, as Plato vividly describes in his dialogue *Phaedo*, Socrates became disillusioned and frustrated with this pursuit. He was looking for the cause of being as such and found their strictly materialist answers unsatisfying. The overall image we get of Socrates, from Plato and other authors, is that he then went on to make philosophy more everyday by dealing with questions like how people should live together, what happiness is, and how to define justice. Socrates' most important and still famous imperatives were to strive to know oneself and to avoid acting unjustly at all costs. But although his objectives were worldly, he did turn to theoretical abstractions—for instance, to define what "the good" and "the just" are, at least in Plato's account of his life and thinking.[4] The generation of philosophers after Socrates, Plato himself and also Aristotle, viewed philosophy's task as all-encompassing. To be a philosopher meant studying everything—the cosmos, nature, arts, and politics—in order to formulate a blueprint for the good life of men in the city.

Someone once said to Diogenes that they were not fit for philosophy, Diogenes Laertius reports. Given how demanding philosophy was as it was understood by Diogenes' contemporaries, this would be a pretty understandable concern. The man received the following reply: "Then why do you live, if you do not think it important to live well?" At first glance Diogenes' answer to the man's concern does not seem revolutionary, since Plato, Aristotle, and others certainly also thought it was important to live well. But once we understand that for Diogenes that is *all* that philosophy is, to live well, its radical implications become clear. To do philosophy means using human reason, available to us all, to live one's life in accordance with nature. It is unnecessary to go beyond the everyday, the here and now. One does not need to understand the origins of the cosmos to live a good life. Everybody can do it, and everybody *should* do it.

With his narrower understanding of what philosophy should be about, Diogenes was out of step with his contemporaries, but he greatly influenced thinkers after him: in the following centuries, philosophy would increasingly look inward. In the Hellenistic period and even more so under the Roman Empire the main question philosophers pursued was how to live your life well as an individual. This also meant that philosophy was no longer just for members of the elite (the future leaders of the state) but was for everyone.

EMBODIED PHILOSOPHY

Diogenes did philosophy with his body in two ways. How he inhabited his body in his everyday life was an essential component of his philosophy. As we will see, he trained and hardened his body to be prepared for anything yet still allowed it many pleasures. But he also used his body to make specific arguments by performing them.

Diogenes walked through the streets in broad daylight with a lamp, in search of a (good) man. He ridiculed Zeno's paradox, which was meant to show that movement is impossible, by moving his body. And in response to someone using a syllogism to argue that he had horns—once again we get no name—Diogenes grabbed the man's head and said, "Well, I do not see any." This anecdote too points to a philosopher who was well known in antiquity: Eubulides of Miletus. He was a contemporary of Diogenes, and even wrote about him, so it is possible that they actually interacted directly. Alternatively, it may have been one of his students, or someone who merely had heard about the syllogism, who raised it with Diogenes. Eubulides was interested in logic. One of the paradoxes that has survived under his name begins with the proposition "That which you have not lost, you still have." The syllogism continues, "Horns you have not lost, therefore you have horns." The argument rests on the false premise that the person being addressed had horns to begin with.[5] But Diogenes did not see fit to enter a debate of that sort. Invariably he refused to answer philosophical questions on someone else's terms. With his performative, bodily responses, Diogenes disrupted the prevailing discursive parameters for philosophical thought: he does not need to "win" the game; he shows that it is not even worth playing.

Someone could not stop talking about celestial bodies. Diogenes silenced him with a playful question: "Say, how long ago did you arrive from heaven?" In other words, we do better to keep quiet about the things we cannot see up close. Diogenes' strong philosophical commitment to the here and now occasionally poured over into a broader anti-intellectualism and a rejection of the arts. Two times (that we know of, at least) he went to an orator's lecture and disrupted it by ostentatiously eating something, as if to say: You cannot satisfy your hunger with fancy words, so what is the point? On another occasion he attacked orators as a group for hypocrisy: they have much to say about justice but do not live by their words. He called the plays performed in honor of the god Dionysus during his festival "spectacles for morons." Music, geometry, astronomy, and "such things" are useless and unnecessary, he said, sweeping the entire traditional curriculum off the table with one pithy remark.

At the same time, Diogenes peppered his words—at least as they are reported by Diogenes Laertius—with quotations from poetry, just like other philosophers before him. When he said that in his own way Plato also went around begging, just like him, he quoted a verse that occurs twice in the *Odyssey*: "He does it with his head down, so that others will not notice." In the original context this is about Odysseus' son having conversations he does not want to be overheard.[6] The verse makes Plato seem sneaky and secretive. Diogenes' anti-intellectualism clearly did not prevent him from quoting famous literature. The Homeric epic was by far his favorite literary source, but not the only one. He occasionally drew on the tragedian Euripides too. This is an indication of the extent to which poetry, especially the *Iliad* and *Odyssey*, was part of the everyday cultural vocabulary in all walks of life. Still, it also shows that Diogenes was a bit of a hypocrite. He mocks the orators for their fine words, but language is a major weapon for him as well: he will not pass up the opportunity to be clever and employ an appropriate line of poetry when it suits his message.

ABOUT THE GODS

Diogenes lived in a profoundly religious society where festivals and rituals to worship the gods set the pace for everyday life and the cityscape was littered with statues of gods, temples, and sanctuaries. This would have been true as much of Sinope as of Athens and Corinth. Given that the existence and nature of divine beings is a subject that generally (depending on one's outlook) eludes direct human observation, Diogenes preferred to apply his time and efforts to other things. He did, however, see fit to criticize those who claimed to have reliable knowledge of the gods, or behaved as if they did. He found religious institutions particularly irksome. On the matter of the gods Diogenes, as far as we can tell, resigned himself to a disinterested agnosticism.

Whenever he spotted a soothsayer, dream interpreter, or anyone who listened to one of them, man seemed to him the dumbest of all creatures, said Diogenes. The notion that the gods communicate with humans through dreams and through other signs and omens was mainstream in ancient religions, but he found it utterly ridiculous. When a woman prostrated herself on the ground to the gods in an unflattering pose, he walked up behind her and said, "Are you not afraid that if a god comes and stands behind you, he will see how you are lying here, since everything is filled with gods, right?" With some cheekiness Diogenes pointed out how strange it was that the woman was addressing the gods as if they were facing her, when of course they could be anywhere. By standing behind her Diogenes played the role of a god, as it were, and reinforced his point: if he could startle her like that, a god could do it all the more. This is not to say that Diogenes himself believed that gods could be anywhere. He poked fun at other people's assumptions, while maintaining his own agnostic attitude.

Another element in religious practice that Diogenes disliked was that in his view people depend on the gods instead of taking responsibility for themselves. And they do so in counterproductive ways. They may ask the gods for good health by means of a festive ritual and simultaneously stuff themselves with food. They may pray to the gods for things that are bad for them, or they ask for one thing when they should be asking for something else. When Diogenes, for instance, saw a couple making a sacrifice to the gods because they wanted a son, he asked them: "Should you not rather ask for a child who will grow up well?" To someone undergoing a ritual sprinkling—it was custom to have the moral stain incurred by committing a crime (*miasma* in Greek) ritually washed away to enable you to rejoin the community purified in the eyes of the gods—he said, "You can no more erase your misconduct with sprinklings than you can erase your spelling mistakes." Diogenes did not believe in these kinds of rituals: even something as trivial as a language error cannot truly be undone, let alone a greater offense. To erase a spelling mistake on a piece of papyrus, the writing surface of choice at the time, you could try to wash out the ink with water, but unless you were a highly skilled professional scribe, you were bound to make a mess.[7]

Diogenes' rejection of authority caused him, as we would expect, to be unsympathetic to the religious institutions of his day. Theft from a temple complex was generally considered one of the worst possible offenses, but Diogenes was very lighthearted about it. He reasoned that if everything belongs to the gods—as a religious person would say—you cannot steal from them. When he saw a man being led away by two temple officials for stealing a bowl from the treasurers of the shrine, he said, "The big thieves lead away the little thief." In other words, not the small-time temple robber but those who claimed to guard the treasures of the gods were the real criminals. They cheated people out of money in the name of religion and, Diogenes thought, most likely skimmed something off the top for themselves.

During his lifetime Diogenes was already known for his unconventional attitude toward the gods. A pharmacist named Lysias asked him bluntly if he believed in the existence of the gods. Diogenes replied, "How could I not believe in them, when I see how they hate you?" With this classic witticism—we find a variation on it in a comedy by Aristophanes from 424 BCE—Diogenes wanted to mock the questioner.[8] To say that someone was hated by the gods could mean that they were very unfortunate, but it could also mean that they were very ugly or morally depraved (or both). Diogenes certainly was using the phrase in the latter sense here. At the same time he skillfully avoided giving a real answer to the serious question that Lysias asked him.

Not so long before, in 399 BCE, Socrates had been sentenced to death partly because of his views on the gods, so it is possible that Diogenes' evasive response was motivated by fear. But it seems more likely that he acted on principle. Within the parameters of Diogenes' theory of knowledge, Lysias' question is unanswerable—that the gods do not exist is just as impossible to prove as the opposite. Diogenes' agnosticism places the gods at a distance and leads him to a non-teleological worldview: unlike many of his contemporaries, he did not believe in a higher purpose or a providential plan for mankind designed by the gods. Instead, he devoted himself to a philosophy that prepares humans "for all possible circumstances."

LEARNING FROM ANTISTHENES

Diogenes' philosophy was different in scope, purpose, and methodology from what other philosophers were doing at the time, and from what had come before. He did not lecture students or debate opponents but expressed his position with a pithy answer or some other act. Diogenes' thought was a lived philosophy, without an underlying theory or system, and it was averse to authority. This raises the question of how one can learn it, and even whether it can be taught at all. According to tradition, Diogenes did have a "teacher"—or at least an inspiring model. He became a follower of Antisthenes after arriving in Athens as an exile. Antisthenes was born there and had been a prominent student of Socrates. He did not have Athenian citizenship because his mother was from Thrace, where she grew up in slavery. When someone brought up that he did not have two freeborn parents, he replied, "Nor are both my parents wrestlers, and yet I am a wrestler." He clearly had some kinship with Diogenes.

Though we should take "wrestler" primarily in a metaphorical sense in Antisthenes' quip, meaning someone who is eager to fight people with his words, he did spend his days in a gymnasium in a wooded area called Kynosarges just outside Athens. The name translates roughly to "white dog," and already in antiquity that fact was used as an alternative explanation for why Diogenes and his later followers were called dogs. But Antisthenes himself is never described that way. Asked why he had so few disciples, Antisthenes said, according to Diogenes Laertius, "Because I chase them away with my silver staff." To the follow-up question of why he scolded his pupils so viciously, he answered, "Doctors do the same thing to the sick." The silver of Antisthenes' staff symbolizes the philosophical wealth he has to offer. But the road to this wealth is rough: just as the sick person must sometimes undergo a painful surgery to get better, the aspiring philosopher must be able to endure hardships.

The only follower of Antisthenes mentioned by name in the sources is Diogenes. At first Antisthenes sent him away, according to Diogenes Laertius, because he did not want any disciples, but Diogenes did not accept this. When Antisthenes then proceeded to threaten a beating, Diogenes said, "Hit me. As long as I think you have something to say you will not find a staff hard enough to keep me away from you." Diogenes, paradoxically, showed himself disobedient yet simultaneously as faithful as a dog. He was the only one who had fully recognized Antisthenes' wisdom and wanted to learn from him at any cost. He gladly would take the blows if that was the price he had to pay for his training. In doing so, he anticipated the contempt for physical suffering and discomfort that would later come to characterize his lived philosophy.

Xenophon, the historian and general we encountered before, includes Antisthenes as one of the interlocutors in his dialogue *Symposium*. Just as with Plato's dialogues, we should not take this work as a faithful account of a conversation that actually took place, but we can assume that Xenophon would have wanted to represent Antisthenes in a way that would have been recognizable to those who still remembered him. In the piece someone asks Antisthenes why he is proud of his wealth when he hardly has any possessions. He replies that people who have only the bare minimum and want nothing more are best off. And people who aim for "frugality" (*euteleia*) are more righteous than those who make possessions their goal. As an example of the latter, Antisthenes brings up rulers who engage in the slave trade just for profit and order mass murders. The "wealth" of a frugal life, Antisthenes adds, makes people generous and freethinking, as was true of Socrates, who shared his wisdom with him.[9]

Aside from their first meeting, Diogenes Laertius describes only one other moment between Antisthenes and Diogenes that we could label as educational. When Diogenes asked him for a coat, Antisthenes instructed him to fold his cape in half. In the anecdote, which Laertius reports in his biography of Antisthenes, we hear nothing about Diogenes' reaction, but the biography about him states that Diogenes had a double-folded cape that he also used as a blanket to sleep under, suggesting that he did follow Antisthenes' frugal advice.

The fact that this is all that has been transmitted about Antisthenes and Diogenes underscores how difficult it is to imagine the two as a teacher-pupil pair. But the similarity between them with respect to their austere habits is undeniable, and it is likely that Diogenes was indebted to Antisthenes for this, even if he took these practices much further. Antisthenes still had a small house, while Diogenes preferred his pot. Unlike Diogenes, Antisthenes showed an interest in rhetoric: he took lessons from the famous orator and sophist Gorgias and wrote speeches, a few of which have survived.[10] Some of Diogenes' core values, such as his rejection of social norms, the importance of physical training, and his shamelessness, are completely absent from Antisthenes' thought. For these elements we will do better to look at influences from outside Athens.

PHILOSOPHY IN SCYTHIA AND INDIA

Diogenes' followers retroactively adopted a Scythian prince named Anacharsis as a proto-Cynic. Anacharsis lived in the sixth century BCE, some 150 years before Diogenes was born. Scythia is located on the northern coast of the Black Sea and the Caspian Sea, in present-day Ukraine and southern Russia. Its people were made famous by the historian Herodotus, who praises them for their nomadic existence. The Scythians always take their homes with them. This makes them intractable and therefore, in a sense, unbeatable. Herodotus singles out Anacharsis for praise as a wise man. He describes how the prince visited all the Greek cities. On his return to Scythia Anacharsis reports that all the Greeks except the Spartans are constantly preoccupied with wisdom, but that the Spartans are actually the most prudent. He implied that the other Greeks lose themselves in intellectual, abstract speculation, while the Spartans get closer to attaining true wisdom precisely by ignoring all this.

In antiquity Anacharsis was considered one of the so-called Seven Sages, together with the lawgiver Solon and the philosophers Thales and Pythagoras. He came to symbolize the outsider who observes the customs of the Greeks with a critical, often astonished eye. We can no longer establish with certainty how much of what Herodotus and later authors tell us stems from the life of the real Anacharsis—some scholars believe that he never existed at all—but it most likely corresponds to what people told each other about him, inside and outside Scythia.

At the time it was a popular cliché that the Spartans, maintaining a strict regime of military exercise, lived "in their bodies," while the Athenians lived "in their heads," carrying on endless philosophical and legal debates. What seems to have been true is that Spartan freeborn men, would-be soldiers, spent large amounts of time on their fitness. Like Anacharsis, Diogenes praised the Spartans, in line with his anti-intellectual attitude and interest in physical training. Both men opted for a nomadic, homeless existence. Both spent time in Athens as foreigners, and both were critical of Athenian customs and laws after experiencing them up close. The crux of Anacharsis' worldview, as described by Herodotus, is that customs are not universal but culturally determined, and that therefore no one set of norms is superior, not even those of the Athenians. Tragically, Anacharsis was murdered soon after his return to Scythia, according to Herodotus. In his telling the king murdered Anacharsis because he practiced a religious rite in the Greek way upon his return, but this may be an overinterpretation on the part of the historian, who paints the Scythians as resistant to all things foreign.[11]

From the third century BCE onward, after both Anacharsis and Diogenes were dead, Cynics adopted the former into their ranks. Given the similarities between the two men, it is easy to understand why. But in one important respect Diogenes went further than Anacharsis. By questioning the usefulness of social norms as such, he pushed the Scythian's cultural relativism to a new level. Is it possible that Diogenes was actually influenced by the stories about Anacharsis, and that Anacharsis' ideas about norms and nomadism were a stepping stone for him? We cannot know for sure whether or not Diogenes knew about him. Still, Sinope's location on the southern coast of the Black Sea, just across the water from Scythia, increases the likelihood that a young Diogenes had heard stories about Anacharsis' travels and ideas from people who were from there, or from merchants returning from Scythia.

After considering the possible effects of ideas that traveled from the north, it is necessary to look at what was happening, philosophically speaking, to the east of Sinope. Before and during Diogenes' lifetime the epic *Mahabharata* circulated orally in ancient India, which included modern-day Pakistan. It would be written down in Sanskrit later. The *Mahabharata* and also early Buddhist texts feature people who pursue an ascetic lifestyle by imitating animals. Some imitate cows by eating whatever they come across and sleeping wherever they happen to be. Others follow the example of dogs, walking on all fours and picking up food from the floor with their mouths. In ancient India there were also people among the followers of the Hindu god Shiva who displayed exhibitionist and animalistic behavior as part of their asceticism. They were known as the Pasupatas. According to Indian sources from the period, such activities were aimed at provoking insults and disgracing oneself.

The question of influence from India on ancient Greek philosophy has long been a vexed one within ancient studies. Pythagoras' ideas about the reincarnation of the soul from the sixth century BCE (later used by Plato) have, for instance, often been connected to Buddhist notions, but specific evidence for such early contact has never been found.[12] For the fourth century BCE, however, things are a bit different. As with the Scythian Anacharsis, it is possible that thanks to Sinope's location on the trade routes to Persia and India, Diogenes already knew about these particular forms of Indian asceticism before he came into contact with the philosophers in Athens. Both imitating animal behavior and seeking out humiliation would become part of Diogenes' daily life and, thereby, part of his philosophy. He wanted to show that he was above social norms and therefore simply could not be humiliated. In Buddhist and Hindu practice this behavior probably aimed at displaying endurance and overcoming one's own pride by taking insults. Unlike Diogenes' choice to be "a dog" for life, the Indian forms of asceticism through provoking humiliation are temporary: you commit yourself to it for a certain period of time and afterward, enlightened, you either return to ordinary life or move on to the next stage of asceticism.[13]

During Diogenes' later life the cultural exchange between the Greek-speaking world and India increased enormously because of Alexander's campaigns. From this period on we also find in Greek sources descriptions of Indian asceticism that, again, resemble Diogenes' way of life significantly. The historian Onesicritus, who was also the first to record the meeting of Alexander and Diogenes, reports traveling to Taxila, not far from present-day Islamabad in Pakistan, as Alexander's representative. There he meets with men he calls "gymnosophists," or "naked wise men." He describes how they stand, sit, or lie around naked all day in the blazing sun in various positions—probably yoga poses—and live off what is offered to them on the street. One of the men tells Onesicritus that "the best teaching" (that is to say, their own) removes both suffering and pleasure, that suffering and toil are not the same thing, and that toil makes the mind stronger.

We cannot determine for sure which specific group Onesicritus met, but his portrait generally fits well with what in Sanskrit is called a *sadhu:* an ascetic beggar who may adhere to Buddhism, Hinduism, or Jainism. This way of life still exists today. It dates back to at least the fourth century BCE, when Onesicritus wrote, but is probably even older. We can easily imagine that in Sinope Diogenes had already heard stories about *sadhus* before Alexander's conquests and was impressed by those accounts. Although Diogenes' asceticism is unique in several respects, the outward similarities with the practitioners in ancient India seem too great to be purely coincidental.

DIOGENES VERSUS PLATO

Even if Diogenes was already aware of the possibility of animalistic asceticism before he came to Athens, it was there that he was first called a dog by Plato. Now, Plato was in many ways exactly what Diogenes was not: Athenian, a citizen, wealthy, and established. He had been born in the city in 424 or 423 BCE to parents who both could claim famous statesmen as their ancestors. His father's family reportedly even traced its lineage back to the god Poseidon.[14] By the time the two men met in Athens—probably after 360 BCE but before Plato's death in 348 or 347 BCE—they were both older men: Diogenes in his fifties, Plato in his mid-sixties. But they were spending their middle age very differently. Plato had started a philosophical school with its own building, known as the Academy, two decades earlier. The Academy, where he also lived, was located in the peaceful, green suburbs. He had plenty of students in Athens, typically upper-class young men, and in 366 and 361 BCE he traveled to Syracuse, in Sicily, to interest and instruct two consecutive rulers (Dionysius I and II, respectively) in philosophy, at the invitation of their close relative Dion. He had written and published several philosophical works already.

Diogenes, as we know, was homeless. He slept in his large jar in the marketplace in the center of town. He refused to lecture, let alone take students in any formal capacity. Anyone who wanted to ask him something could do so. All they had to do was show up. He had no books to his name. One might wonder how they ever met. But they did.

Plato is Diogenes' most frequently recurring interlocutor in the biography by far. They met in the street as well as at dinner parties at people's homes, and on at least two occasions Diogenes made the trek out to the Academy. Even Plato had to go to the *agora* sometimes, and Diogenes did get invited to parties, presumably because of his sharp wit. Although there were now established schools, philosophical conversations and confrontations still took place in more informal settings too. In Diogenes Laertius' descriptions of them, the clashes between Plato and Diogenes at first look like petty, very personal brawls, but there is usually a lot more going on.

For Diogenes, confrontations with Plato were opportunities to raise his profile: Plato was the well-known authority figure, Diogenes was the rebel. And it is precisely their conflict that allows us to see the contours of Diogenes' lived philosophy of shamelessness and austerity most clearly. He disagreed with Plato on the purpose and methods of philosophy, the existence of the gods and the afterlife, the importance of the laws and the city, how to treat rulers—in short, on pretty much everything. But they were also connected in one very important respect: they shared in carrying on the legacy of Socrates. Plato had been Socrates' student when the Athenian jurors sentenced him to death, and he remained deeply affected by this loss for the rest of his life. Diogenes came to Athens only after Socrates' trial and execution, but he was a follower of another of Socrates' students, Antisthenes.

When Plato gave Diogenes the nickname "the Dog," Diogenes appropriated it immediately and used it with pride. But Plato called him something else too. When someone asked him what sort of a man he thought Diogenes was, he answered: "A raving Socrates." With this insult Plato tried to dismiss his adversary as a lunatic. But at the same time he drew attention to Diogenes' philosophical affinity with his own teacher. Diogenes was indeed a raving, out-of-control Socrates to the extent that he went even further in choosing poverty, devotion to philosophy, and independence from the city (*polis*). In the eyes of his followers this made him, not Plato, the true heir to the heroized martyr Socrates.

For his part Diogenes called Plato's lectures a waste of time. While he certainly wanted to needle Plato with this remark, Diogenes believed that lectures were useless in general. Through his insult he was broadcasting how far removed that mode of instruction was from how he practiced philosophy, even if he probably thought Plato's lectures were particularly useless on account of their content.

The direct exchange between the two men that seems the most childish is about arrogance. We see Diogenes in Plato's living quarters at the Academy, trampling on his carpet. Diogenes says, "I trample on Plato's conceitedness." Plato replies: "Yes you do, with your own conceitedness." Plato's point is that Diogenes needs an audience for his action, which exposes him to the charge of being vain and conceited himself. The carpet stands for what Diogenes thought of as Plato's appetite for luxury and feeling important. Earlier, Antisthenes too had attacked Plato for his arrogance. But in Plato's case this was not only a personality trait; it was also connected to his philosophy. Antisthenes and Diogenes were concerned with the everyday, things that are tangible and humble. In their view, Plato's interest in the transcendental, in the divine—in what goes beyond human experience—and his rejection of bodily, earthly experience were further expressions of his arrogance.

Probably the most famous component of Plato's philosophy was, and is, his theory of forms (sometimes also called theory of ideas): the thesis that what we see around us are mere reflections of higher, abstract forms, which are divine. A beautiful man, for example, ultimately derives his appearance from the immortal and immutable concept of beauty. Humans can approach these "ideas" only via an infinitely long and difficult path of philosophical study; meanwhile, thanks to the sight of beautiful people, we catch indirect glimpses of beauty as such, and the same is true of other forms and their earthly reflections.

One of the lengthier confrontations between Diogenes and Plato was about the theory of forms. It is not clear where their conversation took place; it could have been at the Academy or at a social event at someone else's home. Diogenes Laertius reports:

> While Plato talked about his ideas and talked about table-ness and cup-ness, Diogenes said, "Plato, I see a table and a cup, but table-ness and cup-ness I do not see at all." He said, "That is to be expected, you have the eyes with which a table and a cup can be viewed, but you do not have the mind to contemplate table-ness and cup-ness."

This account of Plato's theory of forms may sound like a bit of a caricature, but it does accurately reflect his own writing. The tenth book of his dialogue *Republic* discusses how furniture makers produce tables and couches as reflections of the corresponding forms "table" and "couch."[15] Plato's response was no doubt intended as an insult, but Diogenes probably would not have taken it that way. Sense perception was all that mattered to him. People in their right mind do not bother with metaphysical abstractions—after all, you can eat from a table, but not from table-ness.

Diogenes' search for a man with an oil lamp in broad daylight likewise was a critical response to Plato's philosophy, and a reaction to an earlier incident. Diogenes had heard that Plato was being admired for defining man as "a biped without feathers." He plucked a rooster and brought it to Plato's Academy, presenting the animal triumphantly: "This here is Plato's man!" Plato then, according to Diogenes Laertius, decided to amend his definition, adding "with broad nails." In Plato's dialogue *Statesman* we do encounter "a biped without feathers" as the definition of man, but the addition that Diogenes' action forced on Plato is absent from the surviving works.[16]

In the plucked rooster scene the respective approaches of Plato and Diogenes collide head-on. Plato's definition "a biped without feathers" was the outcome of rigorous philosophical research, in which a given hypothesis is tested and refined through questioning, also called dialectics. Diogenes grabbed an actual biped without feathers so that everyone could see for themselves that the definition Plato's method had produced did not hold up in practice. He refused to engage in a philosophical debate with Plato, for to do so would legitimize the latter's approach. The plucked rooster was a rejection of philosophical dialectics as such. The theatricality of the action purposely ridiculed Plato's method, which, in Diogenes' view, was as absurd as looking at a plucked rooster, or the sight of someone walking down the street in broad daylight with a burning oil lamp.

The rest of the known, direct confrontations between Diogenes and Plato dealt with questions of austerity and power. Diogenes linked the grandeur and ambition of Plato's all-encompassing philosophical project, sometimes implicitly, to gluttony and a desire for luxury living. When they ran into each other on the street, Diogenes offered to share his dried figs with him. Plato ate them all, much to Diogenes' indignation. But the lack of moderation also went in the other direction: when Diogenes asked Plato for a few figs, he sent a whole jar of them. Diogenes then said, "If someone asks you how much is two plus two, do you say twenty? That is what it looks like, since you neither give what is requested, nor answer what you have been asked." Diogenes Laertius explains that Diogenes was making fun of Plato's long-windedness, but he also seems to be hinting at the grandiose scale of Plato's philosophical project.

Finally, Diogenes used accusations of gluttony to criticize Plato's relationship to rulers. Plato twice traveled to Syracuse to reside as a philosopher at the royal court there. We know that Diogenes, who categorically rejected Alexander's overtures, never would have accepted such a position, and he used every opportunity to chastise Plato for having done so. When he saw Plato eating only olives at a fancy banquet, he said, "As a wise man, you sailed to Sicily for these kinds of dishes. Why do you not enjoy them now?" Plato replied that he ate only olives in Sicily too, prompting Diogenes to ask why he had gone there in the first place, since olives also grew in Attica. In this conversation the food must be a metaphor for the payments Plato had or had not received in Sicily, which was a hotly debated question already in antiquity. Diogenes' use of Homer to paint Plato as someone who was a beggar but tried to hide it must have been a reference to Plato's relations with the Syracusans as well. In another confrontation about the same issue Plato said to Diogenes, "If you had served Dionysius [of Syracuse], you would not be washing lettuces now." Diogenes replied, "If you had washed lettuces, you would not have served Dionysius." The message is abundantly clear: to preserve his freedom, Diogenes will happily eat lettuce for the rest of his life. It is unforgivable to him that Plato made a different choice.[17]

The conflict between Plato and Diogenes was about the purpose of philosophy, but also about the role of the philosopher in society. Plato worked from within, educating the Athenian elite, and even foreign rulers. Diogenes felt it was necessary to be an outsider, in order to stay self-sufficient and independent, and to maintain enough distance to be able to see all the ways in which society's customs and mores fall short. This allowed Diogenes, but not Plato, to understand, for instance, the fundamental injustice of the institution of slavery, as we will see. For Plato, ultimately, the universe is well run; it is a good place, under the auspices of a good, providential divine, as long as we manage to transcend through philosophy the earthly plane of our lowly bodies, of mere appearances. Diogenes is in and of this world, and in his body, which he sees as nature's gift. Life is unpredictable, but by using our reason, we can prepare ourselves for anything, come what may. This, says Diogenes, is what philosophy is.

DIOGENES AS A TEACHER?

We have seen that Antisthenes' mentorship of Diogenes was highly unusual: he was reluctant to take him on, and downright hostile toward him. Diogenes, as mentioned, did not have any students in the conventional sense either, but we know that he did have followers during his lifetime—they were the first ones to pass on his ideas and sayings, starting the centuries-long chain of transmission. How Diogenes treated these followers is a lesson in lived philosophy and iconoclasm in itself.

Diogenes Laertius writes that there was a man (his name is not mentioned) who was eager to study philosophy with Diogenes. The philosopher gave the man a fish and ordered him to walk behind him, holding the fish. The man got embarrassed, threw the fish down, and ran away. When they met again later, Diogenes laughed and said, "A fish killed our friendship." The anecdote presents a distorted mirror image of the story of the first meeting of Diogenes and Antisthenes. Diogenes was not deterred even by beatings from Antisthenes, but this would-be student thought he was too good to carry a fish for Diogenes, which already rendered him completely unfit for the Cynic life. The fish was a test of the man's loyalty and his mentality. He failed on both counts.

But there were other followers who were successful. A man named Xeniades put Diogenes in charge of the education of his sons while Diogenes was enslaved by him. Diogenes taught the boys to live on bread and water, to go around barefoot wearing only a cape, and to disregard their appearance. The historian Onesicritus, writes Diogenes Laertius, first sent one of his sons to Diogenes to learn from him, then the other one, and finally apprenticed himself to him—so strong was the "enchantment" of Diogenes' words. Among his pupils Diogenes Laertius also lists the Athenian statesman and general Phocion; the philosopher Stilpo of Megara, who in turn would become the teacher of the founder of the Stoic school, Zeno of Citium; and "many more distinguished men." He conspicuously omits one man: Diogenes' most famous and important follower, Crates. His biographies of both Antisthenes and Crates, however, make it abundantly clear that Crates was a disciple of Diogenes, and sources earlier than Diogenes Laertius report this too. Crates probably lived from about 365 to 285 BCE, so he may well have spent some time with a rather old Diogenes in Athens. Like Stilpo, he functioned as a link between Cynic and Stoic philosophy by taking Zeno under his wing.

Crates was originally from Thebes and came from a wealthy family. Diogenes convinced him to renounce his possessions. Quite unlike Diogenes, Crates went door-to-door in Athens asking people what he could do for them, and he was welcomed everywhere. He did gymnastic exercises in the middle of the city and emulated Diogenes' austerity: he drank only water and said he called "disgrace and poverty" his homeland and Diogenes his "fellow countryman." Crates had a reputation for being very unattractive and seeking out humiliation. He ridiculed Nicodromus, a musician, and received some bruises in return. Next, he tied a writing tablet around his forehead that read, "Made by Nicodromus." The message of this surreal joke—the wording imitates the way craftsmen signed their work in antiquity—is that those who follow the Cynic way of life are invulnerable. If you never feel humiliated, you cannot be humiliated. Crates deviated from the Cynic lifestyle in one important respect: he married Hipparchia, another follower of Diogenes, and even had a child with her. Most Cynics felt, like Diogenes, that family life was at odds with their ideal of total self-sufficiency.

Although conversations and lectures were still the primary vehicles for philosophical instruction in the age of Diogenes, many philosophers did write down their ideas at some point, just as Plato did, so that they could circulate among a wider audience. It was also common for students to take notes during lectures, and these notes could be copied and sold. As discussed, there is conflicting information about what Diogenes left in writing: Diogenes Laertius provides a list of works attributed to him but immediately adds that according to multiple sources Diogenes wrote nothing and that his works are also attributed to other people. No substantial fragments survive of any of the works on this list, let alone complete versions.

Diogenes' recorded sayings suggest that he had little interest in being a writer. He joked about how tiring it was to read long texts, and when a certain Hegesias asked Diogenes for his writings, he replied, "What an idiot you are, Hegesias! When it comes to figs you would not choose painted ones, but only the real thing. Still, you are ignoring the real instruction and rushing to the written version instead." Those wanting to follow Diogenes' example have to change their own lives and, as with eating figs, you do that with your body. You cannot accomplish the exercise of body and mind he orders us to undertake just by spending time with a book any more than you can learn to swim by reading about it. All things considered, it seems unlikely that Diogenes published any writings during his lifetime or that he left behind a body of work upon his death.[18]

The Diogenes tradition shows how, in line with his criticism of Plato for long-windedness, he was even concise when speaking. His answers and comments were always pointed, often expressed in a punch line, sometimes just with a wordless motion. By making himself available and visible in public spaces, Diogenes was a teacher to many more people than the individuals labeled as his followers. Anyone who talked with him in the street, listened to him speak to someone else, or even just saw how he lived could learn from him, if they wanted to.

Diogenes once described himself as a choir conductor who sets the tone just a little too high so that the others will hit the right pitch: the choir members cannot reach the note the conductor sings and will inevitably sing a little lower. Though he thinks his followers and everyone else with an interest in his philosophy should actively and earnestly attempt to follow the example of his way of life, Diogenes is realistic enough to recognize that very few will fully achieve this goal.

So what was so difficult about following Diogenes' example? In many ways it seems easy enough. He distanced himself from the natural philosophers who came before him, and from Plato and other contemporaries by refusing to engage in their way—dialectics, paradoxes, categories—of doing philosophy. He turned the focus away from contemplating the cosmos and onto lived experience, making philosophy accessible to everyone. For his would-be followers there were no books to read, no lectures to attend, and no complex, abstract theories to learn. Philosophy is just something you have to do. But that also means you have to *do* it. To be a follower of Diogenes means you have to change your life. The first step, to which we will turn in the next chapter, is to radically rethink your relationship to your body. Diogenes' approach to human pleasures, needs, and desires was entirely new and would redirect the course of philosophy for centuries to come.

3

ON HAVING A BODY

It looks like a dinner party: a group of men and women, including one child, sits at a long table. They are wearing nice clothes and seem to be engaging in polite conversation. Or are they? As it turns out, the topic of conversation is digestion. And if you look closely, you see that all the guests are sitting on toilet bowls. They are defecating, their underwear dangling around their knees. Then someone gets up from the table and leaves the room. The scene cuts to a shot of the guest locking himself in a closet to wolf down some food before returning to his toilet bowl.

This unforgettable scene is part of the 1974 surrealist comedy *Le Fantôme de la liberté*, by the Spanish-born Mexican filmmaker Luis Buñuel. It forces viewers to ask themselves why in human communities it is acceptable and even desirable to eat together, yet we prefer to seek, as far as possible, total isolation for the end of the digestive process. The scene derives much of its power from the actors' convincing rendering of a state of utter boredom: a bourgeois toilet party turns out to be just as lame as a bourgeois dinner party. The underlying idea seems to be that the cultural norms about which acts are acceptable in the company of others and which ones are not are so unimportant that they could be reversed entirely without causing significant changes to how we live.

Eating, digesting, and evacuating one's bowels are among the most essential things we do with our bodies in order to sustain them. How, what, and where to eat and how and where to relieve oneself were among the many norms Diogenes challenged. His relation to his body was made up of complex contradictions. He prided himself on his hardiness and austere habits and on his control of his body. He needed no fancy food, no house, not even a soup bowl. He slept in his cape, harmed by neither cold nor heat, because he had trained his body to withstand both. And yet he did not hesitate to masturbate or relieve himself in public—in other words, to let himself go completely. Diogenes turned both punishing his body and giving in to his bodily needs into a public performance. His self-denial and his choosing and preaching poverty would prove enormously influential in later periods, especially within Christianity. But giving in to sexual urges became unthinkable even when done secretly.

If we take the inversion of norms as our starting point, as Buñuel does, we could simply say that Diogenes turned several norms upside down at once. In Athens and Corinth in the fourth century BCE the norm was to pursue at least some degree of comfort and financial security. Diogenes did neither. There was also an expectation for everyone to relieve themselves in private—the ancient public toilets that have been excavated date to the Roman period, a few centuries after Diogenes lived, and they were mainly used by poor people. Masturbation also was not considered an activity that should be enjoyed in public. Outdoing even Buñuel, Diogenes took a step beyond the imaginative medium of art and did all these things in real life.

These acts were as shocking to Diogenes' contemporaries as they now seem to us when we read about them. So why did he do these things, with what purpose? How could he treat his body in such contradictory ways? How did people respond? And did he expect his followers to imitate these behaviors? We begin this chapter by jumping ahead in time a bit, to two admirers of Diogenes living in the first and fourth centuries CE. Their reactions to this aspect of the Dog's life show us how lasting an impression his behavior made, and how strongly it motivated people to be fearless in their own lives.[1]

CLEANING AUGIAS' STABLE

The traveling orator and philosopher Dio Chrysostom identified strongly with Diogenes both because of his austere lifestyle and because Dio too was an exile. In 83 or 84 CE, Dio was banished by Emperor Domitian from his hometown, Prusa (modern-day Bursa in Turkey, located just across the Sea of Marmara from Istanbul), and from Italy. The reason was his close association with a cousin of the emperor who had fallen out of favor and was executed. Dio's exile lasted until 96 CE, when Domitian was assassinated.[2] In one of his speeches, Dio talks about Diogenes' time in Corinth. He depicts him giving a lecture on suffering and pleasure to an audience gathered for the Isthmian Games, the local version of the Olympic Games. Although Dio Chrysostom was writing before Diogenes Laertius, we cannot understand the words he attributes to Diogenes as authentic. Unlike the short sayings in Laertius, this is a long speech, and it is highly unlikely that it would have been transmitted intact orally. Also, what we know about Diogenes from other sources suggests that he was averse to giving long speeches in the first place. Dio's account of Diogenes is best understood as a kind of fan fiction, and it is of interest to us as a response to, and interpretation of, his thinking. Just as with fan fiction, the ideas at the heart of it do truly belong to Diogenes. And Diogenes Laertius reports that Diogenes did attend the games on several occasions.

In Dio's narrative, Diogenes begins by telling the crowd that it is many times more difficult and laudable to suffer hunger, cold, or even torture than it is to compete in sports. In Laertius' biography Diogenes disparages athletes and spectators several times, and along similar lines. Dio's Diogenes goes on to praise the divine hero Heracles, because he completed his famous labors, ordered by King Eurystheus, without complaining. Heracles easily withstood extreme cold and heat while dressed in nothing more than his worn-out lion skin. He also, very humbly, cleaned up the gigantic pile of manure in Augias' stable. Diogenes claims that Heracles completed this task as well because he wanted to show that he was not only doing glamorous works. He believed, says Diogenes, that above all else humans should vanquish their desire for glory. This is where Dio lets Diogenes' speech end, but his narrative continues. He describes how Diogenes crouched down and did "something shameful" (*adoxon*, literally "without repute"). Dio adds: "I suppose Diogenes was thinking of Heracles' act when he did this." He also reports that the people in the crowd were shocked and called Diogenes crazy. In the last words of the piece Dio mocks their outrage and calls them frogs.[3]

Due to the many different layers in Dio's speech and his euphemistic language, the episode is a bit difficult to follow. Nonetheless, Dio clearly suggests that Diogenes concluded his speech by relieving himself in public, in a sort of reverse imitation of Heracles' shoveling in Augias' stable. In both cases, the excrement represents the heroic willingness to do what is *adoxon*.

The connection between Heracles and Cynicism was not invented by Dio. Diogenes Laertius writes in the biography that Diogenes himself thought of Heracles as a model. The philosopher used the Greek word *ponos* for the trials that he deliberately subjected his body to. This word was traditionally used for Heracles' labors because it means "hard labor," but it also could mean "suffering" or "trouble." Later followers of Diogenes adopted Heracles, just like they did with the Scythian prince Anacharsis, as a Cynic philosopher *avant la lettre* because of his hardships, and because he too was a wanderer for much of his life.

In Dio's interpretation, Diogenes relieved himself in public to show that, like Heracles, he did not strive for glory and did not care about public opinion at all. What other people would shy away from out of shame, Diogenes embraced. But the speech is also about Dio himself: like Heracles and Diogenes, he will not be put down by criticism or challenges. The emperor may have exiled him, but this is an *adoxon* that Dio can use to show his strength. The implicit, subversive takeaway of all of this is that Emperor Domitian is no different from the cruel king Eurystheus and the Sinopeans who exiled Diogenes: in each instance the underdogs beat those in power, who sought to humiliate and silence them, by refusing to be ashamed.

We encounter the same image of a crouching Diogenes about three centuries later in a speech by a philosophically inclined Roman emperor named Julian. He is often called "the Apostate" because he turned his back on the newly institutionalized Christian religion and promoted the restoration of the traditional Greco-Roman cults. Like Dio, Julian was not, strictly speaking, a Cynic philosopher, but he was no less a great admirer of Diogenes. His speech mounts an attack on Cynic philosophers of his own day, who, in his view, disgrace their founder by behaving shamefully out of opportunism and fail to commit to the Cynic way of life in earnest. Julian then moves to defend Diogenes' shameful acts. Many people, he says, hide in the dark to do nature's business, while they do the worst things in the middle of the marketplace: embezzle money, accuse others falsely, initiate unjust prosecutions, and the like. When Diogenes was in the marketplace and relieved himself or farted, his aim was to attack people's vanity. After all, the crimes others engage in openly are far worse than what Diogenes did there. When it comes down to it, nothing was wrong with Diogenes' actions, which were in accordance with nature, Julian concludes. The criminal misconduct other people engage in in the marketplace is, in sharp contrast, entirely unnatural.[4]

Dio and Julian offer slightly different interpretations of Diogenes' propensity for doing his business out in the open. Dio focuses on his shamelessness and the rejection of norms: Diogenes denies himself not only bodily comforts but also the comfort of having a good reputation, as do Heracles and Dio himself. The contradiction in Diogenes' behavior, the tension between self-control (for instance, withstanding cold) and letting oneself go (pooping in public), is resolved, because Dio shifts attention away from the bodily aspect onto the psychological. He is interested in the mental fortitude required to live without heat *and* without honor. Julian's interpretation is more moralizing. He argues that Diogenes does something that seems bad but is actually harmless in order to show the actions of others as truly bad. As a yardstick for measuring which actions are good and which are bad, he applies the criterion of whether or not something is "in accordance with nature."

But the responses of these two admirers also have a lot in common. Both acknowledge that most people were shocked by this aspect of Diogenes' behavior and reacted negatively to it. Both go against common opinion to defend his acts against this criticism and give philosophical meaning to it. Remarkably, neither Julian nor Dio attempts to deny that Diogenes ever did these things. Finally, nothing suggests that they felt any pressure to enact similar behaviors in their own lives. Rather, they present themselves as drawing the correct lesson—as they see it—from Diogenes' act, and living by it as it applies to their own situations. Dio embraces the "shame" of his exile with gusto; Julian fearlessly exposes the moral faults of his contemporaries.

Diogenes Laertius' biography retells one anecdote that deals explicitly with Diogenes' toilet habits. The story places him at a dinner party at someone's home. The other guests, Laertius tells us, kept throwing bones at Diogenes, "as you would to a dog." On his way out he repaid them in kind: he urinated on them, "like a dog." Laertius, as is customary in his work, offers no interpretation beyond foregrounding the connection between Diogenes' behavior and his nickname. The anecdote itself seems to confirm Dio's reading. The other guests tried to shame Diogenes for being called "the Dog." Instead of resisting or fleeing the situation, he embraced it fully and showed the bone-throwers how utterly their attempt had failed by choosing to become even more like a dog. But we also catch a glimpse of Julian's way of thinking. Diogenes' performance of dog-ness points to Julian's distinction between what is "natural" and what is not. Dogs (and other animals) cannot but live "in accordance with nature." The fact that Diogenes did so too is another reason the nickname suits him so well.

Diogenes Laertius does not say in so many words that Diogenes also defecated in public—there is one passage where he may be implying it, as we will see—but it seems extremely likely that he did. Perhaps Laertius held back in this regard, out of propriety and respect for the philosopher, or for his own readers. It would befit Diogenes as the Dog to have done so, and his ardent admirers Dio and Julian do not attempt to deny it. In light of his thought and lifestyle more broadly, his reason for publicly relieving himself was to showcase that he was above shame and did not need the approval of others in any way. From Diogenes' point of view, it is silly to be ashamed of our bodily functions in the first place: few things are more natural than having to poop, and living in accordance with nature should be our only rule.

Diogenes' attitude toward his body went much further than Buñuel's relativism: not only are cultural norms interchangeable, but we would actually be better off without them. Going to the bathroom in public was Diogenes' way of showing that this is so. Those wanting to imitate Diogenes' lifestyle, as the examples of Dio and Julian show, need not do exactly the same thing. What matters is to be fearless and to be above shame and cultural norms. Everyone can do this in their own way.

CONTROLLING SEXUAL DESIRE

Diogenes did everything in public, both "the things of Demeter and those of Aphrodite," writes Diogenes Laertius. What does this mean? Demeter was, among other things, the goddess of grain and the harvest. So the "things of Demeter" refers, in the first instance, to food. There are other anecdotes in the biography to the same effect. When people commented on the fact that Diogenes ate in the marketplace, his response was: "It was in the marketplace that I got hungry." He gave a more elaborate explanation in another anecdote, which sounds like a philosophical syllogism:

> If it is not strange to eat breakfast, it is not strange to eat breakfast in the marketplace.
> It is not strange to eat breakfast, so it is not strange to eat breakfast in the marketplace.

Here Diogenes gave us a parody of a syllogism, by means of wordplay. The Greek word that I have translated as "strange" is *atopos*, which literally means "out of place" (*topos* means "place," as in "topography"). If having breakfast as such is *not* out of place in the world, if it is, in other words, in its place here, it cannot be that one specific place, like the marketplace, is exempt from this principle.

Arguing over what is out of place and in its place brings us back once again to the scene from Buñuel. In Diogenes' time social dining indoors was a normal and desirable pastime, but eating in the street was seen as uncivilized. Up until relatively recently, the latter was true of the United States as well. For Diogenes to have flouted this social expectation is hardly surprising, given the scenes described in the previous section. (And it seems plausible enough that when Laertius speaks of "the things of Demeter" he may also be referring euphemistically to what happens to our food after we have digested it.) But his reasoning for doing so is interesting. Diogenes' disregard for what is and is not allowed in certain places points ahead to his fundamental rejection of community norms. Such norms in particular determine how things are done in a specific location—that is, in the *polis*. As we will see in the next chapter, Diogenes did not see himself as a citizen of Athens, Corinth, or anywhere else, but as a citizen of the universe. This is why he is subject only to the laws of nature.

The "things of Aphrodite" can refer to sex in general, but in the case of Diogenes it refers specifically to masturbation. Laertius writes that Diogenes, when he was occupied with his "manual labor," used to say: "If only it were as easy to get rid of hunger, just by rubbing your belly." Here he equates masturbating with satisfying hunger for food, the difference being, according to Diogenes, that it is far easier to fulfill sexual desire than it is to satisfy one's hunger. And this is something we should be glad about, Diogenes wants to say, instead of anxiously hiding it. For him, doing it in public is also a way to promote the virtues of masturbation as such. This sets it apart somewhat from his public eating and toileting, where the primary point is to move a normal, regular activity to an irregular context.

It will, again, be instructive to look at a later response to Diogenes' enthusiasm for masturbation. The writer and physician Galen lived in the second century CE. He systematized Hippocratic medicine, and in some parts of the world his ideas influenced medical training into the twentieth century. The doctor took an interest in Diogenes precisely because of his treatment of his body. Galen praises his approach to sex and connects it to his principle of "living in accordance with nature":

> We all agree that Diogenes the Cynic was the strongest man in the whole world with respect to any activity that requires self-control and fortitude. But even he engaged in sex, wanting to relieve himself from the painful pressure of withheld semen, *not* because the pleasure connected with ejaculation is itself a good thing. Once, when he had hired a prostitute and she was late, he had already grabbed his penis before she even arrived, they say, and relieved himself from the semen by rubbing. When she appeared afterward, he sent her away saying his hand had already sung the wedding song. It is abundantly clear that wise men do not pursue intercourse on account of pleasure, they just want to heal the painful pressure, as if this occurs without pleasure. I believe that other animals seek out sexual intercourse in a similar way, not because they have become convinced that pleasure is something good, but because they have found that withheld semen hurts—so, just as they naturally defecate and urinate.[5]

Galen's interpretation comes across as a little forced, because he is so adamant that Diogenes, as a wise person, was impervious to pleasure (*hedone*). He is trying, in his own way, to resolve the apparent contradiction between Diogenes' extraordinary capacity for self-restraint and his unbridled self-gratification. Galen's reasoning is that as long as the latter is not about pleasure at all but has a purely medical reason, it is compatible with Diogenes' otherwise austere lifestyle.

Modern medicine agrees with Galen that ejaculation is healthy, but precisely because it produces pleasure by releasing certain hormones in the brain. Failure to ejaculate in itself is, on the contrary, not harmful to the body. Galen presents ejaculation as medically necessary, an assertion that chimes with Diogenes' own comparison of the (male) orgasm to the food necessary to quell hunger. By introducing the question of how and why animals have sex, Galen tries to push his point even further: sex is equivalent to emptying your bladder, as long as you are not doing it for pleasure, following the example of animals *and* Diogenes.

But this clinical interpretation misses a key dimension of Diogenes' attitude toward sex. Galen seems to think that Diogenes preferred masturbation as a less pleasurable yet effective alternative to having sex with a mate. For Diogenes, however, couple sex was distasteful, whether with men or with women, paid or unpaid, marital or not—in the biography Diogenes scoffs at all of it. His disdain for people who seek out prostitutes casts doubt on Galen's narrative, which may have served merely as a frame for introducing the topic of masturbation.[6] Diogenes actively discouraged marriage and thought children were bothersome. This element of his thinking is actually at odds with his intention to live in accordance with nature: although almost all animal species masturbate and seek out same-sex unions—which does undermine Galen's assumption that animals are not motivated by sexual pleasure—they also actively pursue intercourse with members of the opposite sex, and they do, of course, procreate. The real reason Diogenes advocated for masturbation over sexual intercourse was that it allows for self-sufficiency and avoids the stresses that threaten those who go in search of a partner.

In Laertius' biography, Diogenes addresses the topic of love (*eros*) on two occasions. He says: "People in love are unhappy for fun / their pleasure [*hedone*]." He also says: "*Eros* is being busy for people who have leisure." Both quips revolve around the idea that people who fall in love cause themselves unnecessary suffering. In the first phrase the word for pleasure (*hedone*) is used ambiguously: Diogenes simultaneously says that lovers are unhappy "for fun," that is, they do so voluntarily, and that they do so "with pleasure as their goal." The second phrase plays with the Greek word for leisure (*schole*): people in love give up their leisure and cause themselves unnecessary "busyness" (*ascholia*, literally "a lack of leisure"). The point of his wordplay is that, according to Diogenes, those who fall in love make themselves dependent on someone else, which can lead to all sorts of trouble: disappointment, obsession, jealousy, and sadness. But there is no need for any of this, because pleasuring yourself carries no such risks.

Another premise of Galen's interpretation is that Diogenes' philosophy preached the avoidance of pleasure. This is not true either. Diogenes teaches that we must be on our guard against developing a need for forms of pleasure that are difficult to obtain, because both failure to obtain them and, if we are successful, even the trouble of obtaining them disturb our peace of mind. Diogenes chose to masturbate *not* to avoid the pain caused, supposedly, by holding back semen. As we will see in the next section, bodily suffering was not something he was afraid of. His true motivation was that one can get attached to the pleasure of pleasuring oneself risk-free. Unlike someone else's sexual favors, masturbation is always at our disposal, without going through any trouble or risking disappointment. He did not care one bit about the social norms telling men and women to get married and have sex in order to procreate. While in Diogenes' view there are strong reasons to avoid other forms of sexuality, there is no reason not to masturbate, nor is there anything shameful about it. He did it in public to underscore this philosophical lesson.

A MODEL OF SUFFERING

When Socrates was on trial in 399 BCE he gave an account of his life and his choices. According to Plato, this is when he said that he was poor because he had been too busy questioning his fellow Athenians to engage in politics or deal with his household finances. In ancient philosophy this would go on to become somewhat of a cliché: the true intellectual has no time to concern himself with money and things like that. Poverty—or what passes for it in a given context—could function as a badge of intellectual superiority.

As far as poverty was concerned, Socrates' students Plato and Aristotle did not quite follow in their teacher's footsteps. In their respective worldviews it would be reprehensible to pursue a large amount of wealth over all else, but taking care of one's family property—including real estate, enslaved workers, livestock, and valuables—is an important task for the wise man. Diogenes, with Antisthenes as intermediary, was the true heir to Socrates in spurning property.

Diogenes Laertius writes in his biography of Antisthenes that he acquired his toughness and insensitivity to bodily suffering from Socrates, who reportedly always walked barefoot. When Diogenes arrived in Athens, he joined Antisthenes immediately and copied his austere lifestyle. Initially the biography presents this as a practical choice rather than a principled one. Diogenes came to the city as an exile, having left his home and possessions in Sinope, and simply had to start over from scratch. But it becomes clear pretty quickly in Diogenes Laertius' narrative that Diogenes had no intention of trying to rebuild his life by amassing new belongings—that is, in the conventional way.

The philosopher Theophrastus—Aristotle's successor and a younger contemporary of Diogenes—also wrote down a collection of anecdotes about him and sayings by him. It is now lost, but Laertius cites one of these anecdotes, about a mouse. Theophrastus describes how Diogenes observed a mouse at some length and learned from the animal how to adapt himself to his circumstances. The mouse runs around without looking for a bed to sleep in or any fear of the dark. The mouse does not desire the fancy things that seem enjoyable to humans. Thanks to the mouse, writes Theophrastus, Diogenes "discovered the resource [*poros*] of circumstances." The Greek word *poros* literally means "path" but often was used metaphorically to refer to a contrivance, as in "finding a way through." So what Diogenes learned from the mouse was to view difficult circumstances not as an obstacle or a hardship but instead as a resource and a "path" in themselves.

From then on, Diogenes decided that he could use his cape, folded in half, as a blanket. He carried his food and utensils in a pouch, and he engaged in his main pursuits—sleeping, eating, and carrying on philosophical conversations—wherever he happened to be. Eventually he realized he needed even less. When Diogenes saw a boy drinking water from his hands, he threw away his water cup and exclaimed: "A child has defeated me in austerity!" (The seventeenth-century Italian painter Girolamo Forabosco chose this very moment as the subject for his painting of Diogenes.) In another anecdote, it is said, he saw a boy using a piece of bread to receive his portion of lentils, because he had broken his bowl. Diogenes decided he did not need a soup bowl either and got rid of it. These two anecdotes are so similar that they may well be variants of the same story. They show, in any case, that what began as a practical necessity seemingly turned into a contest: Diogenes wanted to make sure that he was living his life in the simplest, most austere way possible.

For all intents and purposes, Diogenes chose to live like a homeless person. He begged in order to survive. He slept on the streets, either in his big clay pot or under his folded cape. He lived on water and simple food. Like Socrates, he walked the street barefoot. And all of this was still not enough suffering: to test himself he rolled his naked body in hot sand in summer and embraced snow-covered stone statues in winter. In pursuit of freedom and independence, Diogenes chose to live a life that most people try to avoid. His first step was to determine what is natural to a human being.

LIVING IN ACCORDANCE WITH NATURE

The fact that Diogenes looked to a mouse for inspiration about how to live brings us back to his intent to live in accordance with nature. This was partly why he did not wear shoes and willfully exposed his body to the elements. Following the example of animals means dispensing with clothing, housing, and cooked food. Later followers of Diogenes ate only raw food, refusing to use fire at all. The biography tells us that Diogenes himself tried this too but got a stomachache from it. Also, one of the possible causes of death Laertius reports for him is food poisoning from eating raw octopus. Living in accordance with nature is more complicated than it may seem at first. Diogenes might have wanted to live like an animal, without the laws of the city, without culture, and without (basic) technology, but in many ways humans are not equipped to do so. Animals can eat raw meat; humans, for the most part, will get indigestion. The mouse has its fur to sleep in; Diogenes still needs his cape. Humans have evolved to be sufficiently different from animals that our bodies cannot handle living *exactly* like them.

Diogenes' adversary Plato was also thinking about humans and animals: what they share and what divides them. His dialogue *Protagoras* contains the myth of the divine brothers Epimetheus and Prometheus, which offers an explanation for the inferiority of human bodies to animal bodies: mistakes were made during creation. The story tells us how Epimetheus, whose name means "afterthought," was a bit too generous while he was handing out useful physical attributes, like furry skin. As a result, these useful ones had run out by the time humans got their turn to receive their attributes. Prometheus ("forethought") had to fix his brother's mistake. He did this by giving humans fire, as well as the necessary skills to live together well in the *polis*.[7]

The *Protagoras* myth illustrates how central living-in-the-*polis* was to human nature in the eyes of Diogenes' contemporaries. Plato's student Aristotle famously described man as "an animal of the *polis*" (*zoion politikon*).[8] Diogenes' rejection of the *polis* and his intent to emulate the way animals live are obviously intertwined, so much so that it seems like a zero-sum game: either you embrace living in the *polis* or you join the animals in the wilderness. But faced with these two opposing alternatives, Diogenes actually searched for a small opening, for some in-between.

In Diogenes' view humans are like other animals—much more so than most people think—but not identical to them. At several points in the biography he talks about the importance of reason (*logos*), both as a general organizing principle and as a guide for humans. He says, according to Laertius, that he rallies courage against misfortune, nature against the law, and reason against emotion. Life is worth living only when one lives in harmony with reason. The Greek word *logos* also means "speech" in addition to "reason." Both speech and reason, according to Aristotle, are unique to humans among animals. Although Diogenes admires how animals live and thinks humans can learn from them, he agrees with Aristotle on this fundamental point. He, too, believes that human nature is characterized by *logos*: it is precisely through the use of reason that humans have to strive for a better understanding of their own nature, and live accordingly. If they do so, they will find that in some respects their nature is quite close to that of animals. When it comes to nice foods and housing, for example, or social norms like relieving oneself in private, humans are actually like animals in that they do not need these things. But, Diogenes thinks, humans also will find that procreation and couple sex are necessary features only of animal nature, not of human nature, and that we are better off staying away. Reason leads humans to such insights, but not animals.

Of the two fundamental distinctions his contemporaries drew between humans and animals, Diogenes accepted one but not the other. He saw *logos* as a necessary and exclusive feature of human nature, but not life in a *polis* and everything that entails. In reality Diogenes' retreat into the wilderness was far from perfect. He lived alongside and even from the community, in the urban wild instead of the wild wild. Louis de Silvestre's painting of the meeting of Alexander and Diogenes, as already mentioned, shows precisely this tension: in the scene Diogenes' jar sits exactly on the border between the city of Corinth and the forest. Behind him we see trees; behind Alexander, city buildings. As a beggar, Diogenes lived on the fringes of society, but he was not a bit less proud or outspoken because of it, to Alexander and other passersby. He was not at all ashamed or meek as he asked people for money: "If you have already given to someone, give to me too. If you have not, you might as well start with me." He also said: "All things belong to the gods. The wise are friends of the gods. Friends have things in common, so all things belong to the wise." Here we see Diogenes defend his begging with an appeal to traditional religiosity in the form of another parodic philosophical syllogism. And it shows that he ultimately thought of himself not as a beggar dependent on the city dwellers of Corinth or Athens but as a member of a universal community of men and gods (if the latter do indeed exist).

FREE FROM DESIRE

Understanding human nature truly and choosing to live by it is crucial for Diogenes, but in many ways this is just the first step. Learning how to respond to our bodily wants on a day-to-day basis is equally important, and a far from straightforward process.

Diogenes' adamant rejection of comfort and his interest in making his body suffer seem to support Galen's view that he avoided pleasure. His chosen path looks like an extreme version of how Socrates neglected his private interests: poverty and harsh circumstances build toward a disregard for the needs of the body. The ultimate purpose would be to achieve a higher, enlightened state of consciousness and insight. If we attribute such a motivation and way of thinking to Diogenes, his lived philosophy would closely approximate religious asceticism, like that of the so-called gymnosophists in ancient India (see Chapters 2 and 4). These naked monks stand completely still for hours in the burning sun, lie down on hot stones, and live on what little food they are given as alms. The objective of their suffering is to prepare the soul to commune with the divine, freed from sensitivity to pleasure and pain.

One major obstacle to interpreting Diogenes' treatment of his body in this vein is, as already discussed in this chapter, his enthusiasm for masturbation. But his attitude toward food is also less than straightforward, and often at odds with a categorical rejection of pleasure. Once, Laertius' biography tells us, Diogenes found a pastry among his olives, and he threw it away while mumbling an appropriate quote from a tragedy by the fifth-century BCE playwright Euripides: "Stranger, be gone from the king's path!"[9] The pastry is a luxury item entirely out of place among the modest olives and unsuited to Diogenes as a "king" of austerity. But on a different occasion, when someone asked him whether wise men eat pastries, he said that they eat all sorts of sweets, just like other people. About wine, Diogenes said that he liked best the ones he did not have to pay for. When someone criticized him for drinking at a tavern, his witty answer was that he also went to the barbershop to get his hair cut. In other words, drinking is simply what you do when you are at a bar. These exchanges show that Diogenes was not trying to avoid all sensory pleasures, unlike people committed to religious asceticism. Should we just chalk up his varying choices and behaviors to inconsistency or hypocrisy on his part and consider Diogenes a failed part-time ascetic? Although initially it seems reasonable enough to draw such a conclusion, doing so would be to miss the point of the nuanced understanding Diogenes had both of his body and of his mental well-being.

A far greater threat than pleasure, Diogenes said, is desire (*epithymia*): it is the constant and often fruitless pursuit of pleasure that ruins people because it makes them unfree. To avoid falling victim to this dynamic, people must, through exercise, habituate their bodies to scarcity and discomfort. Diogenes rolled his body in hot sand and hugged snowy statues to prepare himself for extreme heat and cold. But he did not make a habit of exposing himself to extreme circumstances, since for him bodily suffering was a means to an end, not a way of life in itself. For the same reason, we must teach ourselves to be satisfied with lentils and olives, even as there is also nothing wrong with accepting wine or pastries from time to time, as long as we do not get used to fancier fare or, worse, become dependent on it. We must keep ourselves safe from desiring pleasure, but not from pleasure as such.

Diogenes says in the biography that nothing in life turns out well without "training" (*askesis*). From this Greek word the modern term "asceticism" is derived, but the two are not completely identical. His *askesis* is mostly like exercise, a preparation of body and mind for all circumstances. With this, he says, we can conquer everything. Without it we accomplish nothing. Living a life of happiness is possible for those who, instead of choosing useless suffering, choose things that are in accordance with nature. Diogenes explains that people are unhappy because they make the wrong choices out of thoughtlessness. Nature has made a relatively easy existence available to them, but they hide this from themselves by "desiring honey cakes, perfume, and the like." In contrast, ignoring pleasure, once you have practiced doing so, "brings more pleasure than pleasure itself." This puzzling, seemingly circular reasoning is, in fact, a powerful redefinition of what pleasure is. When we only consider the bodily aspect in thinking about pleasure, we overlook the fact that many things that are typically seen as sources of pleasure (like honey cakes and perfume) require money and effort, contribute to worry and stress, and, ultimately, leave people in an unpleasant state of dependence. Diogenes added a psychological element to what constitutes pleasure: people who accustom themselves to being satisfied with water and olives can take good care of themselves relatively stress-free under all kinds of circumstances. Such freedom is more pleasurable than the smell of perfume or the taste of honey cake.

Living well, for Diogenes, is something we do with our bodies and our minds. Nature has given us bodies that are wonderfully strong if we train them through suffering. With trained bodies we can withstand most anything and live well on minimal resources, enjoying simple foods, the warmth of the sun, and other "safe" (that is, easily sustainable) pleasures. Such an existence is preferable by far to a life of luxury, because that life burdens our minds with constant desire for pleasure and constant worry about how to keep up such a high standard of living. And, most importantly, a life of luxury does not prepare us for adverse circumstances. A change of fortune will easily ruin the untrained, but not those trained through *askesis*.

There is, sadly, no record of Plato and Diogenes ever debating what it means to live in a human body. If they ever did talk about this to each other, it certainly would have been interesting. As discussed in the previous chapter, the two men disagreed on pretty much everything, and this topic is no exception. To return briefly to the myth of Prometheus and Epimetheus from Plato's *Protagoras*, one of the remarkable things about that narrative is how it emphasizes the shortcomings of the human body. Because we had been shortchanged and lacked adequate protection, Prometheus had to come to our rescue by giving us technology and cities. But it would be a simplification to say that Plato sees no beauty or usefulness in the human body or that he does not see the value of physical exercise. On the contrary, taking care of the body is pretty important in his philosophical outlook. The reason is that the body is the vessel and instrument of the soul. Yet precisely this point, that the body is nothing more than an instrument, is where Plato and Diogenes diverge.

Plato's Socrates describes the body as a prison or a tomb on no fewer than four occasions in the dialogues. This is because our bodies are part of the world of mere appearances, which is devoid of truth and real beauty. For Plato the ultimate purpose of philosophy is to leave our bodies behind and to commune with the divine good as souls. The metaphor of the body as a prison Plato likely found in earlier texts, such as works belonging to the Orphic or Pythagorean tradition. Central to this shared strand of ancient Greek thought, which was diverse and complex in its own right, was some notion of a soul that survives, cycles through different bodies (human and animal), and ultimately is rewarded with a disembodied, purely spiritual immortality on the divine plane. That is to say, in the end the soul is *freed* from the body. Plato teaches how to prepare for and approximate this process through philosophy while still in this world. Treating the body well as an inferior instrument for the superior soul is a vital part of this, but the body can never become an end in itself.

One of the passages where Plato's Socrates describes the body as a prison is in the dialogue *Phaedo*, which dramatizes the last days of Socrates' life. He says:

> Lovers of learning recognize that philosophy takes up their soul, which is entirely bound up in the body and fastened to it, forced to examine reality through it, as if through prison bars, instead of by itself on its own, and is wallowing in total ignorance; and that philosophy has discerned that the dangerous thing about the prison is that it comes from desire, as if the prisoner himself was the main accomplice in his being locked up.[10]

Interestingly, Plato, just like Diogenes, is worried about desire: this is what forces people to seek and satisfy bodily pleasures and prevents them from understanding that they should attend to their souls first and foremost. Plato's solution is that we tame our desire and make the appetites, the lower part of the soul, subject to the higher, rational part of the soul and, ultimately, that we free ourselves from our bodies entirely.

In Laertius' biography, Diogenes concludes his discussion of pleasure with a claim that he lives "the same life" as the hero Heracles, "who chose freedom above all else." While for Plato the ideal is to live free from the body, Diogenes wants us to live free with our bodies. For him the mind is not superior to the body. Both are worthy, both are capable of improvement, and both can give us true pleasure, as we savor our psychological freedom from desire alongside the (occasional) pastry or glass of wine. Diogenes' *askesis* is focused on the here and now, on the well-being of the bodies equipped with reason that humans are born with and that will die with them. The training to reach such well-being, to live more in keeping with human nature, is something everyone can do. It means not depending on precious or precarious forms of pleasure, because those who do will sooner or later face unnecessary physical and psychological suffering—they are too "soft" for the unpredictability of life in this world. Philosophy, says Diogenes, must prepare people for all circumstances. The example of animals shows us that social norms are unnecessary and limit us in our freedom and independence. Striving for a more "natural" relation to our bodies and rejecting social norms are two sides of the same coin: both are strategies for achieving self-reliance. And that is what, in Diogenes' view, freedom is.

ASKESIS AFTER DIOGENES

No part of Diogenes' thinking has been more influential than his redefinition of pleasure and his version of *askesis*. In the late fourth century BCE a man named Epicurus, who was originally from the island of Samos, founded a philosophical community in Athens. He acquired many followers who kept his creed, known as Epicureanism, alive into late antiquity. During the Enlightenment his ideas were popular among intellectuals in Europe, inspiring something of an Epicurean revival. Epicurus was a prolific writer, but his works were almost completely lost. In his case too Diogenes Laertius is an important resource: he has included three long letters by Epicurus and a summary of his philosophy, the forty so-called *Principal Doctrines* (*Kyriai Doxai*). Of these, about one-third are about pleasure and desire.

For Epicurus, the most important goal in life is pleasure. By this he does not mean expensive wine or nice food but the absence of physical and mental pain. Sensual pleasure in itself is not harmful, but obtaining it often causes discomfort that outweighs the pleasure. Only the desire for basic necessities is natural, according to Epicurus. All other desires are unnatural and must be unlearned. What we know about Epicurean attitudes toward love and sex we know mainly from Lucretius, a follower and philosopher in his own right who lived in Rome in the first century BCE. In his monumental poem in epic hexameter on Epicurean philosophy, titled *On the Nature of Things*, he describes being in love as a terrifying, insane mania that only gets worse as you feed it. The safest solution, writes Lucretius, is to seek out some prostitute and allow yourself to be "cured," while staying away from your beloved completely. If you want to start a family, Lucretius recommends marrying a woman who is not very pretty and gradually building a good relationship with her. Anything to stay out of the savage clutches of passion.[11]

Around the same time that Epicurus started gathering students and meeting them in his famous garden, Zeno of Citium, himself a pupil of Diogenes' follower Crates, started to teach philosophy in the Stoa Poikile in Athens. The philosophical school that would grow out of his group of philosophers came to be known as Stoicism, after the brightly painted covered porch where they met. After Zeno's lifetime the school was led by Cleanthes and Chrysippus, respectively, and it would go on to become hugely influential in Rome, even more so than Epicureanism. The Stoics adopt Diogenes' notion of *askesis*, but they give it even more of a psychological focus. The mind must be trained to choose and pursue only those things that are "in accordance with nature" and ignore everything else. To good Stoics it does not matter, strictly speaking, whether or not they obtain what they pursue, as long as they have made the right choices.

Just like Diogenes, Stoics are concerned with the dangers of desire, but unlike him (and Epicurus) they privilege mental over physical well-being. Also, even though they adopted the phrase "living in accordance with nature" from Diogenes, they mean something else by it. For the Stoics what suits someone and is, therefore, in accordance with their individual nature is whatever divine providence has assigned to this person. As a result, options that would not at all seem "natural" to Diogenes and the Epicureans, like choosing to participate in political life, can be "natural" to the Stoics if this is something that was fated for you.[12] Nevertheless, the idea that your task is to find out, through philosophy and reason, what is in accordance with your nature was formulated by Diogenes and taken over by the Stoics. Also, the central Stoic notion that it is possible to train yourself through *askesis* to live without luxury goods and to be happy under all sorts of different circumstances comes straight from Diogenes' playbook.

Rejecting wealth and comfort, living the life of a wanderer, and disregarding existing social norms—these were all choices

Diogenes made, but they are also rather reminiscent of that other troublemaker from antiquity: Jesus of Nazareth. His austere lifestyle and the ascetic practices of Christian monks in subsequent centuries are quite similar to the Cynics' way of life and were in some cases influenced by it. We will properly consider the topic of Diogenes' influence on Christianity in Chapter 7, but for now we will conclude the theme of living with a body by a brief comparison with the ideas of one of Jesus' followers, the apostle Paul. He lived in an intellectual climate shaped by Hellenistic philosophy—a term commonly used to group together Stoicism, Epicureanism, and Cynicism—and we find many traces of this in his writings.

Paul writes about the topic of sexual desire in his first letter to the Corinthians. He writes that for people like himself, the best choice is to remain unmarried. One must try to live without distractions and worries as much as possible (since the world is about to end), and this is more attainable without a husband or wife. Unmarried people can devote themselves completely to God and for this reason are happier. If this path is not possible for you, writes Paul, you must get married, and both husband and wife must fulfill marital duties to the other. Extramarital sex must be avoided at all costs. Fornication is the only sin, according to Paul, that affects the body itself, and our body is the temple of the Holy Spirit, part of the body of Christ himself. That extramarital sex is fornication is crystal clear in Paul's first letter to the Corinthians, but he does not say anything about masturbation specifically, although for centuries this Bible passage, and a few others, would be interpreted as prohibiting it.[13] Paul's apprehension about the intensity of sexual desire is palpable in his words, and in this respect he is of one mind with Diogenes. The two men also agree on the fact that marriage occupies people excessively—but this is where the similarities end. Paul's abstinence, unlike Diogenes' training, was aimed at devoting body and mind completely to God. Diogenes' body belonged to him and to no one else.

What Diogenes was after in relation to his body was freedom: freedom from desire, and freedom from social and cultural norms. He achieved both through his *askesis*, his redefinition of pleasure, and his shamelessness. A persistent tension in Diogenes' life was his position in the *polis*. In stark opposition to his contemporaries, he rejected the notion that humans need to participate in a community to live full and happy lives. But he still wanted to share his ideas and therefore needed a city like Athens or Corinth for the marketplace that would provide him an audience.

How was Diogenes able to live out his ideal of self-reliance in the middle of the city? And how did he maintain his radical freedom in relation to power and authority while living through the major political turmoil of the fourth century BCE? In the next chapter we will see Diogenes shake the ideological fundaments that prop up rulership with his words, and even more so with his way of being in the world. As we have already seen, Diogenes was famous in antiquity in the first place for standing up to King Alexander, and it was as a man who spoke truth to power that he would inspire people to do the same all the way into the twenty-first century.

4

SPEAKING TRUTH TO POWER

For those living in Athens and Corinth, the fourth century BCE was an eventful time. In 404 BCE the Peloponnesian War between the two large Greek power blocs had ended in a decisive victory for Persian-backed Sparta over Athens and its allies. Still, new conflicts between city-states kept erupting, and new efforts at cooperation failed time and again. Meanwhile, the Macedonians in the north were becoming more and more powerful under the leadership of the ambitious Philip II, Alexander's father. The Athenians debated each other fiercely in the assembly: Should they seek an alliance with Philip, or should they defend their independence at all costs? Before they managed to reach a consensus Philip beat the Athenians decisively at the Battle of Chaeronea in 338 BCE. The Macedonians were now in charge.

Over the course of a decade, during the 340s, Athens' most famous orators tried to rally their city to one or the other side of the cause. Demosthenes gave no fewer than four orations against an alliance with Macedon, which together would come to be known as the *Philippics*. Isocrates spoke in favor of Philip and campaigned for a united Greek attack on Persia, led by the king. From time to time these ongoing efforts were punctured by armed hostilities with Philip, culminating in his invasion of central Greece in 339 BCE and the defeat of Athens together with Thebes at Chaeronea in Boeotia. Diogenes spent part of this decade in Athens and another part in Corinth. At the time of the decisive battle he would have been living in Corinth, just across the water (now called the Corinthian Gulf) from Chaeronea. But these battles and debates surface so infrequently in what we can read about Diogenes, you would hardly know he lived through such a pivotal time in history for the region.[1]

One rather obvious reason that Diogenes would not be participating in the debate carried on by Demosthenes and Isocrates is that he was not allowed to. He was a foreigner and would not have had civic rights in Athens or Corinth. In most Greek cities foreigners were given citizenship only under very rare circumstances, so with his forced departure from Sinope Diogenes had effectively turned his back on political life. But he also steered clear of it on principle. As a self-sufficient lone wolf, he had no use for the *polis* except as a place to share his philosophy with others. He refused to conform to the existing norms and laws, which he viewed as arbitrary infringements on his independence.

Still, there is one surviving anecdote about Diogenes in which the battlefield of history does push directly into the philosopher's world, even though it only serves to underscore his aloofness from such events. Lucian, a satirical author from Samosata (today in Turkey, near the Syrian border) who lived and wrote in the second century CE, tells the story at some length:

> People were saying that Philip was already on his way. All the Corinthians were hard at work: someone was preparing weapons, someone else was bringing up rocks, yet another was fortifying the city wall, someone was shoring up a battlement, and yet another was busy doing all sorts of different useful things. Diogenes stood by and watched. Since he had nothing to do—no one had any use for him—he fastened his cape zealously and began to roll the pot that was his home up and down the Kraneion. One of his followers asked him: "Why are you doing that?" Diogenes said: "I am rolling my pot up and down so that I am not the only person doing nothing in the midst of all these people who are so busy."[2]

It seems unlikely that Diogenes would actually worry about looking idle or lazy. His answer to his follower was entirely tongue-in-cheek. Rolling his pot up and down the Kraneion was a kind of commentary on what was going on around him: the efforts of the Corinthians were just as useless as what he was doing. Philip did not advance on Corinth until after the Battle of Chaeronea. He had already won, and there was nothing the Corinthians could do about it. So it made no real difference whether you were desperately trying to defend the city or calmly rolling a pot up and down the street. Lucian certainly interpreted Diogenes' action in this way. He brings it up in a work that mocks ambitious historians of his own day as useless. In his view there was no longer any point to writing history, since under the autocratic rule of the Roman emperors it was impossible to do so impartially and independently.

We cannot be sure whether or not Diogenes actually rolled his pot while Philip marched.[3] Either way, it stands as a strong image for his rejection of patriotism, of saber-rattling, of politics, and of any kind of heroism. Even if Corinth had been salvageable, Diogenes likely would not have seen the use of resisting Philip militarily. Whether Corinth was independent or under Macedonian rule would not have mattered much to him. He considered himself a citizen of no city or empire. At most he was a member of the community of all living things.

But his indifference to politics did not make Diogenes indifferent to power and authority. On the contrary, it was through his confrontation with Philip's son Alexander that he expressed his defiant stance toward power in the first place. We begin this chapter by returning to this clash and another one very much like it. Diogenes' ability to maintain his independence from rulers is the starting point for understanding how he viewed his role in society, and in the world. His resistance, in turn, had a massive impact on his followers. It served as an inspiring model, but it also forced them to make difficult choices about how they themselves should navigate this explosive political moment.

LIKE FATHER, LIKE SON

Before Diogenes met Alexander, he actually met his father. Shortly after when Diogenes would have been rolling his pot, Philip's army paused during their approach to Corinth.

According to Laertius, Diogenes then wandered into the camp. Somebody noticed the disheveled old man, who must have looked decidedly out of place, and he was apprehended. Diogenes was immediately brought before Philip on suspicion of being a spy for the Corinthians. When questioned, he said: "I have come to spy on your insatiable greed." Philip was impressed with the response, writes Laertius, and let Diogenes go.

Just as in the anecdote about Diogenes rolling his pot, others assumed that he was contributing to the war effort, while in reality he was doing anything but. There is also a clear similarity with the meeting with Alexander: Diogenes was completely fearless. Though this time in a much more threatening situation, since he was in custody and suspected of spying for the enemy, he still did not hesitate to say something provocative to Philip. The combination of his boldness and the surprise effect of his answer caused the king to be impressed rather than angry. Much the same scenario played out when Diogenes stood up to Alexander.

The similarities between Diogenes' respective meetings with father and son raise the suspicion that perhaps the anecdote of the exchange with Philip is a made-up variation on the narrative about the meeting with Alexander. But there are good reasons to accept it as true. Laertius cites as his source Dionysius the Stoic, a student of Zeno's who was born around the end of Diogenes' life. He could have heard about the meeting from any number of people who spent significant time with Diogenes, and he wrote on Cynic philosophical themes like *askesis* and pleasure. The historian-philosopher Plutarch also reports on the meeting with only slight variations.[4]

So what was the point of Diogenes' answer to Philip, other than provocation? When he met Alexander, Diogenes told the young king to get out of his light so that he could continue to enjoy the sun. This response communicated a refusal to accept anything from Alexander, so as not to be in his debt and, thereby, in his power. For exactly this reason, Diogenes attacked Plato for his stays at the royal court in Syracuse, because in his view Plato had given up his independence, even if only temporarily, in exchange for comfort and luxury. His own response to Alexander was also a statement about what is worthwhile in life: not riches, influence, or status but the simple pleasure of enjoying the warmth of the sun. The first three are pleasures not in accordance with nature, while the last, of course, is. Diogenes' response to Philip was just as meaningful. The older king and his retinue assumed that Diogenes wanted something from them, in this case strategic information. In fact, the philosopher had something to give to Philip: a pointed reminder that greed and desire know no bounds and that pursuing them in wartime ultimately does at least as much harm to the plunderers as it does to the plundered.

As it turns out, Diogenes' dual pursuits of freedom from desire and freedom from power are closely connected. In the same way as he made himself impervious to desire, by training his body and mind to enjoy the pleasure of living only with basic necessities, he also protected himself against the power of rulers. Because he did not want or need anything from the Macedonian kings, they could not give him anything, and he eluded their grasp—unlike so many others. Callisthenes, a great-nephew of Aristotle, was a historian who, like Onesicritus, accompanied the young king on his campaigns east. Laertius writes that someone kept talking to Diogenes about how fortunate Callisthenes was, because he got to live a life of luxury in Alexander's retinue. Diogenes' answer: "No, he is unfortunate, because he eats breakfast and dinner only when it suits Alexander."

The other component of Diogenes' attitude toward rulers, as already mentioned, is his fearless irreverence. This is well illustrated by a second conversation reported by Laertius between Alexander and Diogenes. Laertius does not give us any indication as to how this meeting relates to the other one. We can imagine Alexander going back to Diogenes the day after, or—which would run counter to how Plutarch reports the meeting—it could be the king's response to the philosopher's request that he get out of his sun. The exchange goes as follows:

> Alexander: "Are you not afraid of me?"
> Diogenes: "Why? Are you something good or something bad?"
> Alexander: "Something good."
> Diogenes: "Well, who would fear something good?"

In this conversation Diogenes skillfully turns Alexander's own question back on him. The king *assumes* that the philosopher will be afraid of him. Since people generally only fear what is bad, this must mean that deep down Alexander understands that his power as king is based on the fear and dependence of his subjects. In other words, he is something bad, no matter what his answer. Diogenes' final rhetorical question is entirely sarcastic.[5]

But Diogenes is not most people, and he is not afraid of Alexander. Why? There is nothing Alexander can do to him or take away from him that would make Diogenes suffer. He will not accept favors or riches in the first place, so withholding those does not affect him. But Diogenes is not afraid of physical pain or suffering either, nor does he fear death. His answer to Alexander is meant to show both that the power of the ruler is based on fear and that it is possible to undermine this power by getting rid of one's fear, by being like Diogenes.

Another anecdote, albeit much harder to accept as historically grounded, features Diogenes in dialogue with a different ruler. A "tyrant" (*tyrannos*) asked the philosopher what kind of bronze would be best to use for a statue of himself. Ancient Greek has two different words for autocrats: a "bad" ruler who is perceived as abusing his power or as having come by it illegitimately is typically called *tyrannos*, while someone who is viewed as a "good" ruler is called *basileus*, often translated as "king." Why any ruler would ask Diogenes a question about bronze is difficult to imagine, but Diogenes reportedly answered: "The kind of bronze from which Harmodius and Aristogiton were cast." At the time this joke would have been easily understood: in antiquity these two men were known as the "tyrant-killers," and at Athens they were honored with two statues in the *agora*. In the sixth century BCE Harmodius and Aristogiton had murdered the brother of the ruler of Athens, Hippias, an event that was seen by the Athenians as the beginning of the end of his reign and a catalyst for the birth of Athenian democracy.[6]

Diogenes' joke referencing the tyrant-killers may have been added to the tradition by his followers during or after his lifetime. Either way, it confirms his reputation as someone with a strong dislike for autocrats. Diogenes would not bow to anyone, but especially not to those who expected him to. He was able to live by this until his last day. But both during and after his lifetime, autocratic rule was decidedly on the rise in the region. The victory of Philip at Chaeronea effectively meant the end of democracy and independence for the Greek cities: after about 170 years of Macedonian rule, the Romans would take over. This means that in the centuries to come Diogenes' followers would always have to figure out a way to live out their Cynic views within autocratic systems. To understand how this could be done, we might look to the example of Onesicritus, Diogenes' follower who served in Alexander's army and wrote down the first report of their meeting.

A PHILOSOPHER AT THE HELM

Onesicritus was likely born a little before 380 BCE on the island Astypalea in the southeastern Aegean Sea and may have moved to the island Aegina at some point in his life. As mentioned, he became interested in Diogenes' philosophy through his sons, whom he sent to Athens to study with him, and eventually followed them there to learn from the Dog himself. This period of study must have taken place just before Diogenes ended up in Corinth, so around the middle of the 340s BCE. At some time before 330 BCE he joined Alexander's eastward expedition. He steered the king's own ship down the Indus River and was chief helmsman of the fleet for the journey from the Indus to the Persian Gulf. Onesicritus' *On the Education of Alexander* covered Alexander's early life, but also the expedition, in which he himself had been a key participant.[7]

Onesicritus' three very different roles already raised questions in antiquity, with his portrayal of Alexander being criticized as too favorable. Lucian, in his satire on writing history, writes that even Alexander himself thought that Onesicritus had gone too far. The king reportedly said to his helmsman that he wanted to return after his death in order to hear how people really felt about him, since now everyone just praised him in hopes of favors.[8] It is difficult to see how a follower of Diogenes, the man famous for standing up to Alexander, could choose to participate in the king's military campaign and even write an excessively flattering biography of the same man Diogenes mocked.

In the surviving fragments of his *On the Education of Alexander* Onesicritus mentions Diogenes only once, but in a highly relevant passage. In this section of the work he describes his visit to the people he calls "naked sophists" or "gymnosophists" at Taxila, in ancient India. Alexander has heard that the men are famous for their strength and endurance but refuse to visit other people. Whoever wants to meet them will have to go to Taxila. He sends Onesicritus to investigate. The first "gymnosophist" Onesicritus talks to on his mission is named Calanus. He ridicules Onesicritus' nice clothes and says he can teach him only if he takes off his clothes and lies next to him on a hot stone. Onesicritus hesitates, and immediately another "gymnosophist," named Mandanis, intervenes.

Mandanis strikes a milder tone. He begins by praising Alexander for his wisdom: "He is the only philosopher in arms I have seen. This is the very best thing: that those who are wise and have power convince others who are willing to also have self-restraint, and that they force the ones who are unwilling to do so." This idealized portrait of Alexander as a philosophizing ruler would have much influence on later authors. Mandanis goes on to tell Onesicritus that their philosophy removes both suffering and pleasure from the soul, that suffering and toil are not the same thing, and that toil makes the mind stronger. A mind strengthened by such training is equipped to prevent conflict and to give good advice. In this way he himself, Mandanis says, has counseled his king, Taxiles, to work together with Alexander.

At the end of their conversation Mandanis asks Onesicritus whether among the Greeks there are any thinkers with such ideas. Onesicritus answers that Pythagoras, Socrates, and Diogenes espouse something similar and that he himself listens to Diogenes. But Mandanis is not convinced: these Greeks may have some clue, but they still go wrong because they put "the law above nature." Otherwise they too, like him and his fellow wise men, would walk around naked without any shame and live simply because, he says, "the best house needs the least furniture." In a quasi flash forward Onesicritus adds that Calanus will later join Alexander's retinue and will end his life "in the traditional way," that is, through self-immolation.

In this account Onesicritus seemingly attempts to reconcile the tension between his own relation to power and his philosophical outlook. Just like Diogenes, the "gymnosophists" initially refuse to play by Alexander's rules by staying in Taxila instead of going to him. Calanus and Mandanis, respectively, represent more extreme and more conciliatory versions of their philosophy—which shows obvious kinship with Cynic philosophy—and the latter clearly wins out. In Mandanis' words we can read a justification of Onescritus' relation to the philosophically inclined Alexander, since it is similar to Mandanis' relation to Taxiles.

But Mandanis' reaction to what Onesicritus says about Pythagoras, Socrates, and Diogenes is rather confusing. Does his critique stem from the fact that their teachings do not seem to have any effect on how the Greeks live, or does he think that these philosophers are not outspoken enough? Diogenes did place nature above the law, walk around naked from time to time, and lead a very simple and sober life. The discrepancy between Mandanis' response, as quoted by Onesicritus, and what we know to be true about Diogenes could be a strategic ploy on the author's part, who himself preferred to wear clothes and was less radical than his teacher. Having the "exotic" foreigner Mandanis say that by his standards Diogenes' philosophy did not go far enough might have been Onesicritus' way to reassure his Greek-speaking audience about Diogenes and make them more sympathetic to him.[9]

As is becoming clear, Onesicritus' own background and ideas colored his reporting. Mandanis' praise for Alexander may well have been exaggerated, and this would be an example of the flattering nature of his work. Because there are other sources attesting to ascetic monks living in this way in ancient India at the time, we do not need to doubt that Onesicritus had an opportunity to meet these men, and did so. That Alexander sent Onesicritus to study their ways stands as further testimony to his interest in philosophy, and Onesicritus' self-identification as a follower of Diogenes in his own work aligns with Diogenes Laertius' account of him.

Onescritus' report of his meeting with Calanus, Mandanis, and the others shows that he was aware of the complexity of his own position, and the episode illustrates vividly how hard it is to follow Diogenes' example in the real world. Calanus' ribbing of him might as well have been Diogenes speaking: What are you doing here in your shiny uniform, Onesicritus, doing Alexander's bidding? Have I not shown you a different way? Have I not shown you how to stand up to him? At the same time there are also several things in this episode pleading for Onesicritus, and for the sincerity of his devotion to Diogenes' way of life. The task he fulfills for the king is to study Indian ascetic philosophers, rather than, say, go on a pillaging raid to obtain as much valuable booty as possible. He has managed to insert a philosophy lesson about living in accordance with nature, shamelessness, and asceticism in the middle of a biography of the king. Onesicritus, ultimately, still gets Diogenes' message across. Perhaps we can see this as his act of resistance, his small way of speaking truth to power. Unlike Diogenes, Onesicritus did not categorically choose self-sufficiency and rebelliousness over everything else. But he did choose to promote Diogenes' philosophy in his biography of Alexander, showing that it is possible to engage in a Cynic act even when one is not living a fully Cynic life.

ALEXANDER BECOMES DIOGENES

The preservation of some of Onesicritus' own writing allows us a glimpse into what it might be like to be a Cynic and a royal subject. But what about being a Cynic and a ruler? This very question captivated Plutarch of Chaeronea, who in addition to his historical biographies wrote many philosophical essays. In these he regularly returns to the meeting of Alexander and Diogenes. He was not, like Onesicritus, writing as someone who knew both men up close, but studied them many centuries after the fact, by which time the Romans were in charge of the Greek-speaking world. Nonetheless, Plutarch still struggled as intensely with the same issue—how to reconcile what Diogenes stood for with power and rule—but he pursued this tension from the perspective of the king.

In Plutarch's account of the meeting in his *Life of Alexander* and also in Laertius, the king reacted to Diogenes' irreverence toward him by saying: "If I were not Alexander, I would be Diogenes." In his essay *On the Fortune or Virtue of Alexander* Plutarch writes that afterward the king reminisced often about his meeting with the philosopher and was in the habit of repeating this phrase to himself, almost like a mantra. Why did he do this? And what did he mean by it? What he did *not* mean by this, Plutarch writes, is that Alexander would be Diogenes if he were just a poor man. That would be kind of a silly and opportunistic thing to say. Rather, Alexander means that he cannot be Diogenes, because he must rule. He fulfills his role not because he is hungry for power or because he loves wealth, but purely from a sense of duty.

Plutarch proceeds, in the same essay, to put a lengthy statement in Alexander's mouth, almost like a daydream, in which he asks Diogenes for forgiveness for not choosing the path of philosophy: because he has to be Alexander, he has to extend the Macedonian Empire all the way to the edges of the known world and bring "Greek justice and peace" to all peoples. Alexander would expand the empire that he inherited from his father, as Plutarch well knows, by so much that when he died it stretched from modern-day Albania in the west all the way up to and including modern-day Pakistan in the east. The members of the Macedonian court had prided themselves on having Greek roots since the early fourth century BCE, and some living in the Greek cities indeed saw them as fellow Greeks. But others continued to see them as hostile foreigners. In Plutarch's time the Greeks, now living under Rome, retroactively adopted Alexander as being fully one of their own.

Plutarch lets the daydream conclude with the notion that, thanks to Alexander, remote peoples will know Diogenes because Alexander will "disrupt the institutions / coinage [*nomisma*] and transform all that is barbarian by means of the Greek form of government [*politeia*]." Plutarch continues the thread of the symbolic interpretation of Diogenes' involvement in messing with the coinage at Sinope. With his comparison he draws a direct line from Diogenes' role as a contrarian who wants to overthrow all norms and institutions to the changes brought to India and Persia by Alexander's conquests. Plutarch seems to suggest that Alexander's meeting with Diogenes had major consequences for Alexander and for the world. But Diogenes' rejection of any form of *politeia*, Greek or otherwise, has vanished into the background.[10]

In his essay *To an Uneducated Ruler* Plutarch goes even further still in likening Alexander to Diogenes. In the piece he depicts kingship as a sea voyage in bad weather:

> By philosophizing Alexander managed to become Diogenes in his outlook but to stay Alexander in his allotted fate and actually to become Diogenes even more because he was Alexander: his important destiny involved a lot of wind and being tossed around and he needed a lot of ballast and a great helmsman.[11]

Just like his source, Onesicritus, Plutarch is deeply invested in reconciling philosophy with power. The contradiction between Diogenes' anti-political and anti-authoritarian bent and Alexander's position is explained away. Alexander became a better king because he let Diogenes convert him to philosophy. He needed Diogenes' good influence all the more because of his position, and for the same reason this "ballast" had an outsized effect, impacting millions of people. Diogenes functions metaphorically as Alexander's helmsman, the job that his follower

Onesicritus had in actuality. According to Plutarch, Diogenes' rejection of the king laid the groundwork for Alexander's successes. If true, this would, from Diogenes' own point of view, have been a dubious, even horrifying achievement.

On the basis of the sources available to us we cannot know in what ways Alexander was affected by his meeting with Diogenes, beyond the fact that the philosopher made an impression on him. Plutarch's speculations fall squarely in the realm of philosophical fan fiction. He wants to demonstrate that Alexander was a good follower of Diogenes, just like Onesicritus, because he contributed to disseminating his ideas. Plutarch was an ardent admirer of Alexander, like many Greek intellectuals living under Rome. His starting point is the profound contradiction between Diogenes' rejection of political power and Alexander's admiration of the philosopher. The exercise that Plutarch engages in is worthwhile, but in a paradoxical way. It simultaneously highlights what benefits a ruler might derive from Cynic philosophy—staying calm in difficult circumstances, a willingness to bring change to institutions—and how impossible it would be to be a Cynic ruler in reality. Plutarch fails to convince us that Diogenes would *not* be rolling over in his grave at the thought that he inspired Alexander's imperialism. The only way for Alexander to actually listen to Diogenes would have been for him not to be Alexander in the first place.

LIVING WITHOUT A POLIS

Diogenes' aversion to autocrats is the most well-known and most influential aspect of his relation to power. But his resistance to political authority went much further still. And while it may be tempting to think of Diogenes as a democrat, Laertius' biography tells a different story.

As mentioned, Diogenes was not able to participate in the assemblies of Athens or Corinth in the first place because he was a foreigner. The takeover by the Macedonians in 338 BCE meant that the political institutions of the Greek cities became much less powerful, but they did continue to function and remained active in the areas in which they did still have a say. Diogenes viewed these institutions as playgrounds for vain busybodies, manipulated by the two archetypes of ancient democracy: the populist flatterer who incites and inflames the masses and the opportunistic snitch who prosecutes political enemies for his own gain. To him, playing this game is not much better than entering the service of a king.

Diogenes' rejection of the existing laws and customs (described in Greek by one and the same word, *nomoi*) is so fundamental that it does not matter to him whether they were mandated by an autocrat or by a democratic legislature. Either way, the agreed-upon norms are arbitrary, not universal, in his view. They make people interdependent in an undesirable way, and enforcing them requires some degree of authoritarian use of power. For this there is no room in Diogenes' egalitarian worldview. He used an ironic syllogism, reported by Laertius, to express his disdain for *nomoi* and the processes that produce them. It contains so much wordplay that it is hard to translate, but it is helpful to know that the adjective *asteios* (derived from *astu*, another Greek word for "city," virtually synonymous with *polis*) means both "of the city" and "sophisticated." Diogenes used to say:

> Without the nomoi, it is impossible to play the citizen
> *[politeuesthai];*
> Without the polis there is no use for city-stuff
> *[asteion];*
> The polis is city-stuff *[asteion];*
> Without the polis there is no use for nomoi;
> Therefore the nomoi are city-stuff *[asteion].*

The syllogism is logically flawed, but this is Diogenes' intention. He is having fun with the form and mocking this kind of philosophical methodology. Nonetheless, the underlying message shines through loud and clear: *nomoi* are useful only for those people who, frivolously, want to play the citizen in the *polis.*

The accomplished Cynic needs neither *polis* nor *politeia* to meet their needs, while participating in it would involve an unacceptable restriction of freedom. Laertius writes that Diogenes "truly disturbed the *nomisma*" because he ascribed value not to "the things in accordance with the *nomoi*" but only to "the things in accordance with nature." As discussed, the latter entails using one's own reason to find out what human nature is—namely, much closer to animal nature than most people think—and live by it. Nobody needs any *nomoi* for this.

Diogenes clearly rejected the *polis* as he knew it. But he did have ideas about how his followers should live. If like-minded people lived together without *nomoi* on the basis of equality to implement his ideas, their community would be unlike any existing ancient societies, not least because they would not be waging any wars.

A CYNIC'S PARADISE?

In antiquity the Epicurean philosopher Philodemus from Gadara thought that Diogenes wrote a political-philosophical work titled *Republic* (*Politeia*), just like Plato did, and he summarizes it in his anti-Stoic polemic *On the Stoics*. While Diogenes did not write this piece, Philodemus' description of its contents likely derived from texts written by Diogenes' followers, texts that, in turn, were inspired by Diogenes' ideas about how to live. Philodemus ascribes three proposals to Diogenes. The first is, simply put, pacifism. According to Philodemus, Diogenes rejected war and thought weapons were useless. This position fits well both with the anecdote about Diogenes rolling his jar up and down the Kraneion in Corinth and, in a larger sense, with his aversion to exertions of power. So if we imagine a community of his followers, it would not have an army and would not use physical violence to defend itself.

The second proposal mentioned by Philodemus is that small bones be used as coinage. Getting rid of gold and silver coins is in line with Diogenes' rejection of wealth, and it recalls the story of him disrupting the *nomisma*. Turning to bones as an alternative seems somewhat morbid, but it may be connected to Diogenes' interest in the animal world, and to his nickname "the Dog" in particular—dogs do like getting a bone, after all. Also, the Greek word used for "bones" in the passage is *astragaloi*, which often refers specifically to the knucklebones that people used for dice games. If Diogenes indeed said in so many words that *astragaloi* should be used as coins, this would be a way to emphasize that life is just as unpredictable as gambling with dice: wealth and riches are nothing more than chips in the casino. It is hard to decide whether Diogenes literally meant that if his followers were to form a community, they should use knucklebones as coins. Possibly we should understand this idea not as a policy proposal but rather as a thought experiment, meant to show the insignificance of the gold and silver coins that most everyone else pursued so ardently.

The third and last proposal that Philodemus cites as coming from Diogenes' *Republic* is to remove the taboo on cannibalism. Laertius also writes that according to Diogenes there is nothing wrong with eating human flesh, because the customs of other peoples show that cannibalism is not considered a crime everywhere. And in the biography Diogenes says that all matter is suffused with all things: there are tiny bits of meat in bread, tiny bits of bread in vegetables, and so on. On the face of it, this sounds like an inscrutable, odd comment. It could, however, be a first glimpse of the philosophical materialism that Epicurus and his followers would go on to develop: the notion that humans, animals, plants, and the earth are all, ultimately, composed of the same kinds of particles. If this is so, there is no real difference, Diogenes would argue, between eating bread, rabbit, and human flesh. We have no evidence to suggest that Diogenes or his followers actually practiced cannibalism. If anything, their diet appears to have been largely vegetarian, because of their austere lifestyle. Diogenes argued that eating human flesh is not an evil mainly to show that the taboo on cannibalism is an arbitrary rather than universal or natural rule and to remind people that we are actually much more similar than we think to the other animals we eat without any scruples.

Following his discussion of these three "proposals" from Diogenes' (presumed) *Republic*, Philodemus switches to a general discussion of the lifestyle of Diogenes and his followers. Most of what he mentions is familiar: coarse language, wearing a cape and folding it up to sleep under it, disregard for the *polis* and its *nomoi*. But Philodemus gets riled up the most about their loose sexual morality. He writes that among Cynics anything is permitted, including incest and sharing spouses. Laertius tells us that Diogenes indeed deemed marriage unnecessary as a ritual and institution: the only union that matters is whether a man and a woman want to be together with mutual consent. Any children should be raised communally, instead of by their parents. In short, Diogenes wants to get rid of the traditional family just as much as he wants to get rid of the *polis*. Some of these ideas are surprisingly close to aspects of the ideal city sketched in Plato's *Republic*. There too, traditional family structures are abandoned. But, in sharp contrast to Diogenes' outlook, they are replaced with a state-run system for raising and educating children, as well as a eugenic program for reproduction, both organized by the *polis*.[12] For Diogenes to reject marriage and the family in favor of letting people choose sexual partners at will—including incest, for maximum provocation, though it is also possible that Philodemus added this element to discredit the Cynics—aligns well with his overall efforts of fighting against the accepted *nomoi* and getting people to understand that everything could be different, that nothing about society and its customs is actually necessary. Still, Diogenes felt that remaining childless and abstaining from sexual relations with others altogether was actually the most suitable choice for his followers.[13]

It is difficult to picture a "free state" for Cynics organized around these principles, and nothing like it ever materialized—outside of the literary fantasy of Lucian, that is, who brought the spirits of the Cynic philosophers together in the underworld. What Philodemus and Laertius have preserved of Diogenes' political thought is sparse and was never intended as a blueprint for an actual community. A more fundamental problem is that Diogenes' radical independence and self-sufficiency are ill-suited for defining new ways of communal living, let alone putting them into practice. But if we take the term "community" more broadly to also include collaborations fueled by ideas, there does emerge after Diogenes' death something like a community of Cynics. His thinking was preserved by informal networks of traveling and corresponding followers, who shared their stories about Diogenes with each other and passed on his quotes to younger generations.

The notion that it is possible to feel kinship with others who do not live in the same region or country as yourself brings us to a final aspect of Diogenes' attitude toward power and politics: his invention of the basic principle of cosmopolitanism. His rejection of the *polis*, of autocratic rule, and of empire is ultimately grounded in his conviction that the only meaningful unit to be a part of is that which is shared by all living creatures but controlled by no one—the world. That this view still differs from modern cosmopolitanism in important respects has often been overlooked.

THE FIRST COSMOPOLITAN

"The cosmopolitan political tradition in Western thought begins with the Greek Cynic Diogenes." This claim is printed on the jacket of a book titled *The Cosmopolitan Tradition: A Noble but Flawed Ideal*, which was published in 2019 by the American philosopher Martha Nussbaum. She is certainly not the first (and probably will not be the last) to claim Diogenes as the founder of modern cosmopolitanism, the idea that all humans are equal members of a world community and should be treated as such. Two sayings in Laertius' biography are typically used to bolster this claim. The first one is Diogenes' response to the question of where he is from, posed to him by an anonymous interlocutor. Diogenes answered: "I am a *kosmopolites*." The Greek word *kosmos* can mean, among other things, "world" or "universe" and is here combined with *polites*, the Greek word for citizen, derived from the word for city, *polis*. This is the first time this word occurs in any ancient Greek text, and it is possible that Diogenes invented the neologism himself. In the other relevant passage Laertius writes that Diogenes mocked "high birth, reputation, and all those sorts of things" as "showy ornaments [*prokosmemata*] covering up vice" and said that "the only true *politeia*" is "the one in the *kosmos*." In this saying we see yet another example of Diogenes' love of wordplay: the word meaning "showy ornaments" is derived from *kosmos*, which in addition to "world" and "universe" also means "adornment" (hence also English "cosmetics").

Martha Nussbaum writes that Diogenes refused to define himself through his lineage, city, social class, or gender. He chose to define himself, instead, in terms of a characteristic that he shared with all human beings and called himself not simply a "dweller in the world" but a "citizen of the world." In this way he introduced "the possibility of a politics . . . that focuses on the humanity we share" rather than what divides us. Nussbaum connects Diogenes' sayings about cosmopolitanism to his request that Alexander get out of his sun. She interprets the meeting as an "image of the dignity of humanity, which can shine forth in its nakedness unless shadowed by the false claims of rank and kingship, a dignity that needs only the removal of that shadow to be vigorous and free." According to Nussbaum, Diogenes' dignity is connected via a straight line to the modern human rights movement.[14] But she also criticizes him.

The most significant shortcoming of the cosmopolitan tradition, according to Nussbaum, is that it does not pay enough attention to the basic material needs that have to be met for people to be able to express their inborn human dignity. This problem, she argues, started with Diogenes. She writes: "Why didn't he say to Alexander, 'I want you to give all your subjects a decent minimum living standard, including adequate nutrition and basic health care'?" Answering her own question, Nussbaum goes on to write that Diogenes was unable to say this, because by doing so he would have acknowledged that Alexander had power over him. Any request to correct social relations because they are harmful implies that the person asking has been harmed themselves and is therefore vulnerable. This is what Diogenes emphatically did not want. Human dignity is complete in and of itself, no matter what circumstances one is in. The only way Cynics can prove that this is so is by showing that they need none of the things a king can give them, writes Nussbaum. Diogenes "appears to think that he can say give me respect only if he totally refuses to lay claim to food and shelter." In Nussbaum's view, this was a mistake that would go on to have major consequences in the cosmopolitan tradition, such as its disregard for people's basic needs.[15]

Other thinkers have connected Diogenes' supposed cosmopolitanism with Alexander's expansionism, taking an approach rather akin to Plutarch's interpretation of their meeting. Alexander's attempt to found a world empire, some twentieth-century historians believe, was aimed at removing the differences between peoples and having all of humankind live together harmoniously under his rule. In other words, Alexander's conquests were intended to realize Diogenes' cosmopolitan ideal. As we said before, we cannot tell from the sources available to us what motivated Alexander. We certainly cannot exclude the possibility that he was driven simply by a lust for power. (His large empire, incidentally, would disintegrate almost immediately after he died.) We do know that Diogenes would have had no sympathy for Alexander's warmongering and ambition. In the end, living as equals with everything and everyone in the cosmos without regard for borders or differences is really not the same thing as conquering everything and everyone in the cosmos without regard for borders or differences.[16]

Would Diogenes have recognized himself in the image that Nussbaum paints of him, as the founder of the notion of universal human dignity? This question is difficult to answer. It is, for starters, surprising how easily she portrays Diogenes as Greek and as part of "Western thought." As discussed, Diogenes' hometown, Sinope, was as Persian and Paphlagonian as it was Greek, and he always remained a foreigner in the Greek cities where he lived. This very circumstance may have contributed to his feeling like a *kosmopolites* and not like a *polites* of a specific place. It is possible to counter Nussbaum's view with a minimalist interpretation of Diogenes' claim that he is a *kosmopolites:* He did not see himself as a member of a universal human community. He just wanted to signal that he was a citizen of no Greek *polis*, or any other community, and brought up the *kosmos* merely to strengthen his point. But this seems a bit too narrow. Against the background of Diogenes' incessant resistance against divvying people up by ancestry, social status, or wealth, it is justified at least to ascribe to him the notion of universal human equality, which was radical enough at the time. His critical views on slavery also support this.

When Nussbaum credits Diogenes with believing in the "dignity of humanity" that "shines forth . . . vigorous and free," however, she probably goes too far. Her premise that every human is "a precious being" is not something Diogenes would readily assent to. His defense of cannibalism, even if only in theory, is dramatically at odds with such an outlook. Because humankind exists, Diogenes is invested in showing all humans the road to a better life through philosophy, but he is not attached to the human species in the same way as Nussbaum is. An anonymous Cynic author, writing around the first century CE, has laid out the problem clearly in a letter in character. He impersonates Diogenes in what purports to be a response to the Stoic Zeno of Citium. Zeno, supposedly, was worried that if people stop having children, influenced by Diogenes' ideas, humans will go extinct. "Diogenes" writes that this would be as bad as flies or wasps going extinct—in other words, not bad at all.[17]

TOGETHER FOREVER

According to the tradition, Diogenes and Alexander died on the same day, June 10, 323 BCE. Initially this seems like too much of a coincidence to be anything other than a symbol of how strongly the two men were connected in the collective cultural memory, but we cannot exclude the possibility entirely. After all, John Adams and Thomas Jefferson—rivals, friends, former presidents both—also died on the same day, on the fiftieth anniversary of the signing of the Declaration of Independence no less, July 4, 1826.[18] In any case, Diogenes and Alexander continued to be thought of as a pair in the following centuries. Their meeting was the perfect scene for thinking through the philosophical problem of how the philosopher should relate to power. One medium for doing this was iconography.

A marble relief dated to the first century BCE, so around the same time as Cicero described the meeting in his *Tusculan Disputations*, shows the two men. It was found at Monte Testaccio in Rome, which is essentially an ancient garbage heap. To the left Diogenes sits in the opening of his pot, with his arms crossed. Alexander is standing to the right, stretching his arms toward the philosopher. Their body language depicts the core contradiction of their meeting: Diogenes' lower status is clear from his seated position, while Alexander towers over him, and yet Alexander is the one who is being rejected. A drawing made of the relief shortly after it was found in the eighteenth century shows how drastically it has been restored. Diogenes' head was missing, and originally the only thing left of Alexander's body was one hand. The identification of the headless man as Diogenes is supported by the dog sitting on top of the jar, the jar itself, and the pouch—all his characteristic accoutrements. That he was indeed accompanied by Alexander on the relief also seems inevitable. The fact that Cicero needed so few words to describe the meeting indicates that at the time it was the most famous story being told about Diogenes.

Dio Chrysostom from Prusa, as mentioned, was an orator and philosopher in the late first and early second centuries CE. In one of his lectures he takes the meeting of Diogenes and

Alexander and expands it into a long dialogue: fiction, inspired by true events. In the conversation Diogenes is the dominant interlocutor. He takes the lead early on and has the last word in the end. Dio has Alexander ask how he can be a good king. Diogenes answers that he has to start by working on his self-knowledge and self-restraint. These things are much more important than riches or military success. To reinforce his lesson Dio's Diogenes closes with a colorful description of the three ways in which a lack of self-restraint typically manifests itself: desire for material gain, excessive ambition, and lust for bodily pleasures (food and sex). The message to Alexander—and perhaps also to Trajan, who was emperor when Dio wrote the speech—is that those who lack self-restraint definitely cannot rule others. Much of what Dio's Diogenes says goes back to the central Cynic values of austerity and practical and psychological self-sufficiency. But there is one thing that Diogenes, strikingly, does not say: that being king, ruling over others, is reprehensible as such. In this way Dio's interpretation of the meeting is similar to the attempts of Onesicritus and Plutarch to show that Alexander's interest in Diogenes benefited his kingship.[19]

In Lucian's interpretation of the relation between the king and the philosopher, they are stuck with each other even in death. In one of his *Dialogues of the Dead* Diogenes teases Alexander by saying that he is surprised to run into him. Alexander is an immortal god, is he not? What is he doing in the underworld? Lucian's Diogenes character is alluding to the fact that Alexander was venerated as a god already during his lifetime, and to the rumors that his real father was the Egyptian god Ammon. Alexander counters by saying that his body will be taken to Egypt and that he will join the Egyptian gods when he gets there. Diogenes laughs at him and begins listing all the things that Alexander is missing out on now that he is dead: his elephants, his purple robe, his many subjects, his servants, and all of his gold. This brings Alexander to tears, and Diogenes seizes the moment to inquire whether Aristotle perhaps forgot to teach him about the fickleness of the goddess of fortune, Tyche. Alexander erupts in a fit of rage: Aristotle is nothing but a lying flatterer who convinced him that wealth and beauty are part of "the good." Diogenes, who decides to show some compassion after all, tells Alexander to drink a lot of water from the river of forgetfulness, the Lethe. He also points him toward an escape route—Alexander is being pursued by hordes of people he abused during his rule and who are now set on revenge.[20]

Lucian's version of the meeting mirrors their encounter while they were still alive. Now, in the underworld, it becomes clear how much Alexander depended on all the things he offered to Diogenes in vain. Lucian also has Alexander blame Aristotle for his predicament: his philosophical training caused him to become attached to power, status, and wealth. While his contemporaries tried to reconcile the tension between Diogenes' anti-politics and Alexander's kingship, Lucian leaves it fully intact and puts the brightest possible spotlight on it. If Alexander had really listened to Diogenes while he was alive, he would have known that power corrupts the ruler as much as the ruled and would have abandoned his kingdom.

In all ancient societies, the institution of slavery was part of everyday life, and in many places it was a significant part of the economy. The ancient Greek cities were no exception, and this is why we will turn to this subject in the next chapter. We have seen how Diogenes responded to one type of domination, that of kings and governments over their subjects: he rejected and undermined it. When we look at what he had to say about the realities and ideology of enslavement, we find that Diogenes was equally outspoken and critical. This may seem unsurprising in the context of his other views, but he was in fact the *only* unambiguous critic of slavery in the ancient Mediterranean we know of, and would remain so for a few centuries. He was also one of the few philosophers to be enslaved for an extended period of time. Knowing how Diogenes ended up enslaved, and how he bore this burden, is vital to understanding his unique stance on slavery, which was rooted in his own experience.

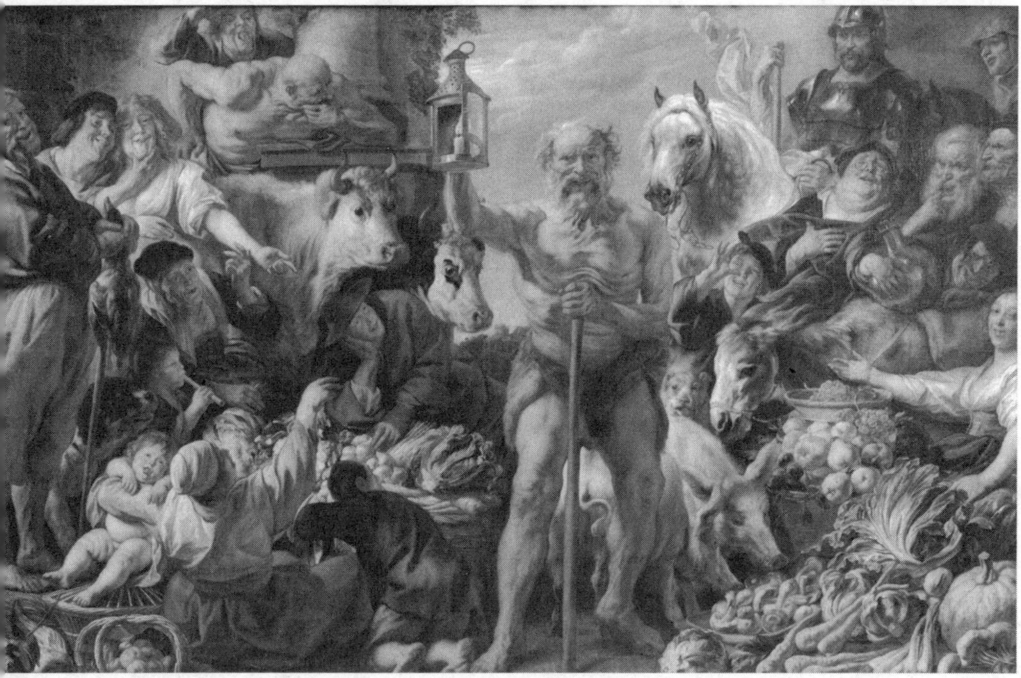

)iogenes in search of an honest human being (1642) by the Antwerp-based painter Jacob Jordaens. Gemäl-legalerie Dresden. Wikimedia Commons

\lexander and Diogenes (ca. 1750), oil paint on canvas, by the French portrait painter Louis de Silvestre. Hood Museum of Art, Dartmouth College, Hanover, New Hampshire. Purchased with support from the Mrs. Harvey P. Hood W'18 Fund; P.933.6

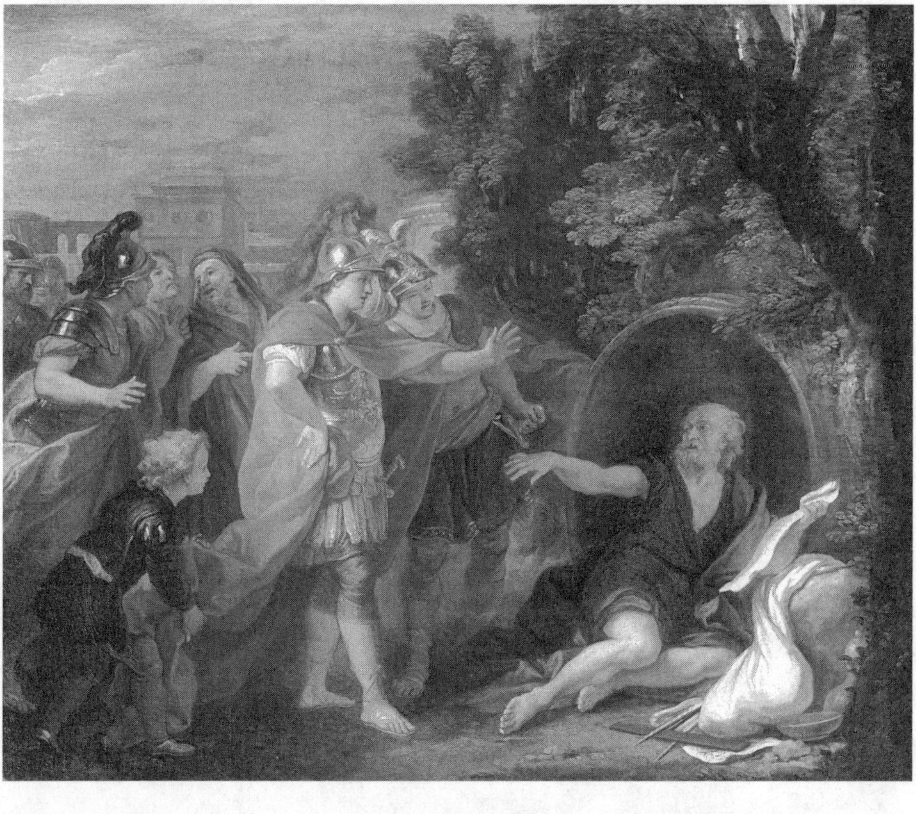

Alexander and Diogenes on a heav ily restored marble relief (first cen tury BCE) found in Rome o Monte Testaccio in the eighteent century. *Oronoz / Album Archivo Superstock*

Drawing of the Roman relief o Diogenes and Alexander (1726 made by the Italian artist Pie Leone Ghezzi shortly after it wa excavated. He claimed to have pur chased the relief for one *scudo*. Th drawing is part of the Codex Otto bonianus Latinus 3109, owned b the Vatican Libraries. *Ott.lat.310 113.r © 2022 Biblioteca Apostolic Vaticana, all rights reserved*

Roman statue of Diogenes (ca. second century BCE) owned at some point by Pope Pius VI and heavily restored in the eighteenth century. The right hand may originally have held an oil lamp. *The Metropolitan Museum of Art, Rogers Fund, 1922*

Diogenes (2006) by the Turkish sculptor Turan Baş, Sinop. *Michael F. Schönitzer via Wikimedia Commons*

Silver drachma from Sinope (fourth century BCE). At top is the obverse of the coin, with the head of a nymph; at bottom is the reverse showing an eagle on top of a dolphin and the Greek letters ΙΚΕΣΙΟ[Υ](the name Hicesias in the genitive case) and ΣΙΝΩ (short for Sinope). *Roma Numismatics*

Diogenes (1882) by the English painter John William Waterhouse. *Art Gallery New South Wales, Sydney. Wikimedia Commons*

Fragment of a Roman mold-made pottery lamp (first century CE) with a depiction of Diogenes emerging from his pot. On the right side, reading from top to bottom, the letters DIOGENE are visible faintly. *British Museum, London. The Trustees of the British Museum*

he old *agora* (marketplace) in Athens. In the foreground are visible the remains of the Metroön, a temple omplex for the Mother goddess; Diogenes' pot was located nearby. In the background the Acropolis is isible. *William Neuheisel via Wikimedia Commons*

emains of the so-called Kraneion, a woodsy suburb right outside Corinth where Diogenes also lived in a ır. *Ephorate of Antiquities of Corinthia / Hellenic Ministry of Culture and Sports / Hellenic Organization of ultural Resources Development (HOCRED)*

The School of Athens (ca. 1508–1510) by Raphael in the Papal Palace in the Vatican. Diogenes is lying on th stairs by himself, right of center. *Vatican Museums, Rome. Wikimedia Commons*

Study of Diogenes for *The School of Athens* (ca. 1508–1510) by Raphael. *Städel Museum, Frankfurt am Mai*

Diogenes Drinks (seventeenth century) by the Italian painter Girolamo Forabosco. *Palais Fesch, Musée des Beaux Arts, Ajaccio, Corsica. Wikimedia Commons*

Arrival of Jean Jacques Rousseau to the Elysian Fields (1782), an engraving by Jean Michel Moreau. He is greeted by Socrates, Plato, Montaigne, and Plutarch. Diogenes, sitting on the ground, blows out his lantern, "pleased" because he has found "the human being he was looking for." *Wellcome Collection*

Marat, Conqueror of the Aristocracy (1861), engraving printed by the publisher Villeneuve. Diogenes frees Jean Paul Marat and says: "Fellow *sansculotte*, I have been looking for you a long time." And Marat answers: "The truth was being persecuted, I had nowhere else to go." *Bibliothèque nationale de France*

Picture of Marina Abramović with a visitor (2010) by Andrew H. Walker, during her performance *The Artist Is Present* in the Museum of Modern Art in New York. *Andrew H. Walker / Getty Images*

5

A LONE VOICE AGAINST SLAVERY

There continues to be public debate about how the transatlantic slave trade and slavery in Asia and the Americas during the sixteenth, seventeenth, eighteenth, and nineteenth centuries should be remembered and evaluated. In this context, the universality of slavery across historical periods and geographical regions is sometimes marshaled as an argument against holding enslavers of the past responsible or accountable. Also, the intensity of human suffering under slavery has been compared to the living conditions of the free poor at the time, with some arguing that the working conditions of the enslaved in the colonies were not necessarily worse than those of free workers in the colonizing countries—since, supposedly, the enslaved were "paid" in food and clothing, and living conditions on plantations were generally better than elsewhere in the colonies.[1] These modern conversations about the history of slavery are ultimately rooted in the ways people talked about slavery in Diogenes' lifetime, sometimes directly, sometimes indirectly. When people use the already very old argument that slavery is universal, they often point to the ancient Greeks and Romans. In their eyes the fact that even those much-admired, "high" civilizations relied on slave labor makes the slavery of the early modern and modern periods somehow look less bad. More significantly, the very same arguments that two of Diogenes' contemporaries constructed to defend slavery were later used to justify the institution at several moments in history, including in the antebellum American South.[2]

The contemporaries in question, Plato and Aristotle, viewed slavery as a natural condition. Diogenes, on the contrary, believed that it was a social phenomenon. And, just as he did with other social phenomena based on custom (marriage, political authority), he persistently mocked society's attempts at distinguishing enslavers and enslaved. This does not quite make him an abolitionist, but between his position and the views of his contemporaries lies a big gap that is brought into stark relief by our modern debates about the history of slavery. Simply put: Plato and Aristotle thought that slavery should not be "too" cruel, but they did not at all question the basic premise that some humans enslave other humans. Diogenes, characteristically charting his own course, thought it was completely absurd for one person to own another person.

Diogenes' view was unique for his time and would remain so for centuries to come. To understand how he arrived at it, we must look back even further, starting with the discourse about slavery in ancient Greece long before Diogenes entered the fray.

"BARBARIANS" VERSUS GREEKS: HERODOTUS AND PLATO ON SLAVERY

In ancient Greek thought the term for "slavery," *douleia*, and its cognates were used for a number of different but mutually implicated phenomena. First, of course, there was a literal, legal usage: the fact that humans were bought and sold as commodities, and exploited as means of production, both of their own labor and of their offspring, who automatically became enslaved at birth. Second, the term "slavery" was also used in a geopolitical sense: although the historical reality was more complex, Greeks prided themselves on being "free" because of their somewhat democratic political institutions, while non-Greeks ("barbarians") were assumed to all be living under autocratic despots, "in slavery." The third way the term was used was in a metaphorical sense, in the realm of human psychology. Freedom, according to this way of thinking, is a mental state available to those who are in control of their desires, fears, and impulses, and everyone who has not (yet) achieved this mental state is living "in slavery." Within this framework, those who are legally enslaved can still be "free" mentally if they have achieved self-restraint through philosophical enlightenment, while many who were born legally free are, because of their lack of insight and self-control, "slaves" to their urges nonetheless.

The fact that slavery became a term with political and geographical connotations was due in large part to the historian Herodotus. He lived and worked during the fifth century BCE and is famous for his account of the so-called Persian Wars: the fight of the allied Greek city-states against two successive Persian kings and their invading armies. It was partially because of this conflict that, in terms of how Greeks looked at the world, the dichotomous distinction between themselves and "barbarians" took hold. Ironically, the Greek word *barbaros* itself has a foreign origin, deriving either from an Old Persian word meaning "subservient" or from a Sumerian word meaning "foreign," and it may ultimately have arisen as an onomatopoeia to describe people whose language sounds like incomprehensible babbling.[3] In Herodotus' *Histories* not only the Persians are called "barbarians," but so are people living in ancient Egypt, Scythia, Ethiopia, and India.

In what he styles his "account of his investigation" (the work's title, the Greek word *historiai*, literally means "investigations") Herodotus exhibits a sincere and enthusiastic interest in the way of life of "barbarians." Branding him as a xenophobe would be an unfair simplification. He is, rather, a cultural relativist who finds many reasons to admire the "strange" peoples he describes. But through his overarching juxtaposition of a Greek "us" versus a non-Greek "them," he did solidify the notion that Greeks thrive only in political freedom, while "barbarians" are accustomed and well suited to living in political slavery; he also often depicts non-Greeks as lovers of luxury and as overly emotional, traits readily associated with mental slavery.[4] This juxtaposition, then, laid the groundwork for the theory that there is such a thing as natural slavery (in the legal, literal sense of the word "slavery") and that this state applied to non-Greek peoples. Unlike its (early) modern counterpart, slavery in the ancient Greek world was legally and practically not race-based. During Diogenes' lifetime everyone, Greeks and non-Greeks, was to a certain extent at risk of becoming enslaved through defeat in warfare, kidnapping, or exposure as a child. Still, where in the world you were born was a contributing factor, due to the historical and political situation at any given time. The same was true for socioeconomic circumstances, since parents who already had too many mouths to feed for their means would be more likely to expose a newborn than wealthy ones.[5] Perhaps most importantly, in the ways people thought about slavery, race, or ethnicity was often understood to determine an individual's relative "suitability" for living in freedom or slavery. This ideological connection between race and slavery would prove to be long-lasting, and tragically consequential.[6]

One place where we encounter the notion that "foreigners" were fit to be enslaved is in Plato's treatment of slavery. Given how pervasive the institution of slavery was in everyday life in the ancient Greek cities, discussions of it in ancient Greek texts are surprisingly scarce. This circumstance in itself may be testimony to how self-evident it was to those who had the leisure and education to write to be surrounded by slave labor, perhaps as normal as the oxygen they breathed. This is all to say that Plato by no means wrote a lot about slavery, nor does he seem to have taken a special interest in it. The brief moments where it is discussed in his works are, then, all the more interesting.

Plato's *Laws* is a long philosophical dialogue that, like his *Republic*, centers on the question of how the state should best be governed. It is less utopian and more concrete than that earlier work. The topic of slavery comes up in the context of a discussion of how citizens should run their households. Just prior the interlocutors have considered how one should choose a wife, and it is followed by comments on housing. Slavery is introduced as being a tricky, difficult subject, and the "most complicated" part of it is said to be the treatment of the helots by the Spartans.[7] The helots were the original inhabitants of the area around Sparta, called Messenia, and were enslaved by the city-dwellers. Although it is not made explicit, the reason this is the "most complicated part" in the eyes of Plato's interlocutors is clearly that all of these people—both Spartans and helots—were Greeks. In other words, when the enslaved are Greeks is when slavery becomes difficult. Similarly, in Plato's *Republic*, readers are told that Greek cities should not enslave other Greeks in wartime: the risk that enslaved Greeks would be bought and sold and eventually fall into the hands of "barbarians"—the ultimate disaster—would be too great. Even in peacetime one should, ideally, not buy Greeks, according to Plato's *Republic.*[8]

In the discussion of slavery in *Laws*, Plato's fictional interlocutors also turn to the danger that enslaved laborers will rebel; this is what makes them "a difficult possession." To prevent uprisings, the head of the household must make sure that he purchases enslaved people who are from different regions and who speak different languages. If they have little or no possibility for communication among themselves, organized resistance is less likely to occur, according to *Laws.* When it comes to how the head of household should treat his enslaved workers, the advice is to treat them "correctly," which means "to not abuse them cruelly but, as far as possible, to disadvantage them even less than you would someone who is your equal"—because people show their true character in how they treat "the ones you could easily treat poorly," that is, the enslaved. The interlocutors think it is important to treat the enslaved well, but they also believe it is vital to clearly distinguish between enslaved and free people. They agree that enslavers should, when there is cause, mete out corporal punishment to enslaved workers. Those who only give a stern verbal warning, "like one would with a free man," make the enslaved soft and weak. It is also important to address enslaved workers only with commands. No jokes or niceties are to be used, because those undermine obedience.[9]

In Plato's dialogues slavery as an institution is normalized and legitimized. It is depicted as a yoke borne by foreigners, people from elsewhere, who speak a different language. He consistently approaches slavery from the perspective of the enslaver: (somewhat) humane treatment is required in order to protect one's own moral integrity and to make sure the enslaved will not be driven to extremes such that they would rebel. The passage in *Laws* depicts the enslaved as fundamentally different creatures who need to be approached and spoken to differently than free men. In Plato slavery is not an accidental condition that can happen to anyone; rather, being enslaved is a separate, inferior category of being human. This understanding of the state of being enslaved as something radically other, something to push away, also seeps into Plato's language when he uses the concept of slavery as a metaphor. In his dialogue *Phaedo*, he writes that our nature (*physis*) decides that our body must serve the soul "like a slave." In *Republic* the rebellious, lascivious part of the soul is described as "naturally suited to be enslaved" to the rational part of the soul.[10]

THE "PERFECT" HOUSEHOLD IN ARISTOTLE

The most extensive and influential discussion of slavery from antiquity comes from Aristotle's *Politics*. Plato's star student devoted the two opening sections of his monumental treatise on statecraft largely to this topic. He structures his analysis by dividing the city-state into its smallest possible parts, and he starts with the household, which in its "perfect" form consists of free and enslaved persons. The free enslaver "naturally" leads and uses his mind. People who obey use only their bodies and are "naturally" suited to being enslaved. This state of affairs is mutually advantageous, safe, and just for enslavers and enslaved, according to Aristotle. The connection he makes here between being enslaved and embodiment already shows Plato's influence.

When Aristotle speaks of a slave owner, or "master," to use his own terminology, he is always picturing a man. In ancient Greece many women were involved in the day-to-day overseeing of enslaved workers, and they could also in some cases come to own them, but as a rule they could not manage property, so they could not buy or sell enslaved people.[11] The discussions of slave labor in both Plato and Aristotle are specifically addressed to male heads of household.

Aristotle describes enslaved workers as tools belonging to their owners, and as living property, like livestock. The enslaved belong completely to their owners and not to themselves. Aristotle's answer to the question of what kind of people are slaves by nature is initially frustratingly circular: "one who is able to be owned by someone else and is for this reason owned by someone else." But he adds that the "natural slave" does "not have reason of their own and can only understand another's." Aristotle seems to be saying that enslaved people are able to follow along with the reasoning of free people but are unable to produce rational concepts of their own. The fact that the difference between those who are "natural slaves" and those who are free is on the inside, and therefore invisible, frustrates him. If free people actually had bodies "as distinct as divine statues," then "everyone would agree that the others deserved to be their slaves." In other words, Aristotle wishes free people were divinely beautiful and all the others average-looking or worse, because, he thinks, this would convince everyone that the legal difference between the free and enslaved was justified. Aristotle's complaint strongly suggests that in reality *not* everyone felt that some deserved to be enslaved and that the status quo was just. There were people who criticized slavery.

Aristotle does not say who these people were, but he does evoke one of their arguments—in order to dispute it. Some people, he writes, believe that "the control of slaves by a master is contrary to nature," because "the distinction between master and slave is due to law or conventions," and that "there is no natural difference between them." Aristotle uses this criticism as a prompt to make a distinction between two types of slavery, "by nature" and "by convention." By a sleight of hand, he then goes on to use the argument of the critics to argue against slavery by convention, but he never returns to their fundamental rejection of slavery in all forms.

Slavery by convention, Aristotle explains, occurs when captives in war are sold and enslaved. It is possible, however, that wars are fought for unjust reasons. This means that someone can become enslaved without "deserving" to. It has been argued, Aristotle continues, that Greeks can be enslaved only in this way, through chance circumstances, but not truly, while "barbarians" are enslaved by nature, so everywhere and always. At this point in the text he does not say explicitly whether or not he agrees with that distinction. There are a few comments immediately preceding this passage, however, that suggest Aristotle connected being Greek with being free, just as Herodotus and Plato did. In his introduction to his analysis Aristotle says, in passing, that households in Greece consist of enslaved and free people, while the households of "barbarians" consist only of enslaved people. This is because among the "barbarians" there is no class of rulers—only one autocratic king. He continues with a quote from the tragedian Euripides, saying "that it is proper for Greeks to rule over barbarians."[12] Aristotle explains the verse, saying that it implies that "the barbarian and the slave are the same by nature." Here he combines slavery as a political concept with his ideas about legal slavery and, specifically, his own notion of natural slavery. Politically "barbarians" are already enslaved to their king, but in Aristotle's thinking they are also by nature suited to being enslaved by an owner.

Aristotle concludes his discussion by restating the distinction between slavery by convention or law and slavery by nature. In the case of the latter there is a natural difference between free and enslaved, and it is "just and necessary" for the free to rule and for the enslaved to be ruled. If the free rule badly, this is harmful for enslaver and enslaved; if they rule well, this is beneficial for enslaver and enslaved, according to Aristotle, because, he explains, "the same thing is advantageous for a part and for the whole body or the whole soul, and the slave is a part of the master." When each is in their "natural" role, Aristotle writes, there is a "mutual shared interest and friendship" for "slave and master." By now it is clear that for Aristotle only non-Greeks belong to the category of "slave."[13]

DIOGENES ENSLAVED

Precisely because Aristotle does not name any of the individuals who believe that "the control of slaves by a master is contrary to nature," scholars have long speculated about whom he was thinking of when he wrote this passage. Some candidates have been suggested—orators about whom little is known—but Diogenes has been largely ignored in the context of this debate, likely due to the fact that for a long time now he has not really been taken seriously as a thinker. In my view this is a mistake.

Before turning to Diogenes' criticism of slavery it is worthwhile to assess the other possible candidates Aristotle might have been targeting. So how exactly does Aristotle describe the anonymous opponents of slavery, and how does he present their views? This is what he writes:

> There are others, however, who regard the control of slaves by a master as contrary to nature. In their view the distinction of master and slave is due to law or conventions; there is no natural difference between them: so that this form of rule is based on force and is therefore not just.[14]

To summarize, according to Aristotle the opponents believe slavery is contrary to nature, exists only by virtue of the law, and is enforced through violence, which makes it unjust. Also, they believe that by nature there is no difference between enslaver and enslaved.

Since at least the nineteenth century, scholars looking for the opponents mentioned by Aristotle have pointed to a fragment by an early fourth-century BCE orator, Alcidamas, in which he says: "The divinity made all men free, nature created no one a slave." At first glance this sentiment seems to align well with how Aristotle depicts the critics' views, but it is troubling that the fragment is so brief. Because the sentence is quoted as belonging to a speech titled *Messeniaca*, it is likely that Alcidamas is talking not about enslaved people in general but specifically about the Messenian helots who were enslaved by Sparta. In his lifetime the Messenian territory was freed by Thebes, allowing Messenian refugees from all over the Mediterranean to return home. This may have been the occasion for his speech. If Alcidamas was talking only about the helots, as seems to be the case, he is not a good contender for being an opponent of slavery as described in Aristotle's *Politics*. More recently, scholars have also pointed to the sophist Antiphon, a contemporary of Alcidamas, as one of the critics. The reason is that a fragment has been preserved under his name that reads: "By nature we are all born alike, barbarians and Greeks." Although it would be possible to marshal this statement against Aristotle's account of "barbarians" as "natural slaves," Antiphon himself nowhere mentions slavery at all. Judging by the available fragments, then, he does not seem like a good answer to our quest for the "opponents" in Aristotle either.[15]

On the basis of the texts transmitted from antiquity Diogenes is the most likely candidate for belonging to this group of opponents of slavery mentioned by Aristotle. We call him the "only" critic of slavery, insofar as he alone has left discernible traces of his ideas in the historical record that unequivocally amount to an attack on the institution as such. If we believe Aristotle, there were others too. It seems plausible enough that a few other critical voices were out there, perhaps already before Diogenes' lifetime, that are now lost to us. But it is also possible that Aristotle knew only of Diogenes' criticism and referred to him vaguely as "some people" in order to downplay the significance and value of his voice.

By now we know how much Diogenes liked jokey, often enigmatic punch lines. This also means that a straight-up, concrete rejection of Aristotle's account of natural slavery is not among Diogenes' sayings, whether in Diogenes Laertius' biography or in other sources. Nowhere do we ever see him literally saying that control of the enslaved by the enslaver is "contrary to nature." But if we put Diogenes' views about nature and convention—he taught that we should place nature above convention and the law—together with his comments specifically about slavery, it becomes clear that he held precisely this view and, in his own idiosyncratic way, tried to show his contemporaries that the distinction between free and enslaved is an arbitrary, ridiculous construct that goes against nature.

As we have seen, at some point after moving from Sinope to Athens, likely in the 340s BCE, Diogenes was captured by pirates during a sea voyage to Aegina, an island between Attica and the Peloponnese. We do not know what the reason for Diogenes' trip was. Being captured in a raid by pirates or bandits was probably the most common way people became enslaved in ancient Greece. Armies on campaign also routinely went on plundering excursions for all sorts of booty, including humans, as a side venture from the conflict in which they were engaged.[16] The pirates brought Diogenes to Crete, which would have had a sizable slave market, and put him up for sale. Crete was one of the largest Greek islands and was centrally located. Its inhabitants were known to be involved in piracy, so Diogenes' captors might have actually come from there.

Diogenes Laertius writes that when Diogenes was brought up at the slave market, the auctioneer asked him what he was good at. Diogenes answered: "Ruling over people." And he added: "Make an announcement to ask if anyone wants to buy a master for himself!" With his defiant attitude Diogenes turned on its head the conceptual framework for slavery that Plato and Aristotle carefully constructed. They defined the enslaved as people who are naturally fit to obey others and to be ruled, enslavers as those who are naturally fit to rule. Diogenes imitated their terminology but switched the categories: though enslaved, he was good at ruling others. This means that whoever ended up purchasing Diogenes would be buying a "master" for himself.

Diogenes demonstrates, albeit in a somewhat absurd way, that there are no intrinsic or natural differences between enslaved and enslavers. Whether enslaved or free, humans are first and foremost themselves, with their own peculiarities. If Diogenes happens to be good at telling other people what to do, this characteristic sticks with him, even if by some chance he ends up having to live in slavery.

Still during the auction, Diogenes is told that he is not allowed to sit down. He shoots back: "What does it matter? Fish get sold anyway, regardless of how they are lying around." He goes on to say that he is surprised that when people are buying a pot or a pan they will tap it first to hear how it sounds, but when they buy humans they go by looks alone. Given the situation he is in, these jokes are very daring. But they are more than just jokes: with his remarks Diogenes highlights how slavery dehumanizes the enslaved and treats them like animals or tools. Implicitly, he poses a challenge to everyone present—auctioneer, traders, and buyers: The fact that you are selling me, Diogenes, a human, to another human shows that you do not see me as a human anymore, but as a fish or a pot. Well, in that case, you might as well treat me like I *am* a fish or a pot: allow me to sit down, and maybe even tap my head.

When a buyer presents himself, Diogenes tells the man, named Xeniades, that he will have to obey him, even though Diogenes himself is now enslaved. He also explains why: "When a doctor or a helmsman is a slave he is also obeyed." Enslaved workers were employed in highly skilled professions like medicine and education, and they were sometimes part of the army and navy.[17] So Diogenes' examples are largely realistic. We can read his comment as a response to the argument that the enslaved are suited to their role because they are less intelligent than free people, or even, as Aristotle claims, do not partake of reason at all. If that is so, how can it be that the enslaved perform tasks that clearly require them to have intelligence? If, conversely, they are as smart as their owners, how is their enslavement defensible?

Diogenes' mention of enslaved doctors and helmsmen also brings to mind how philosophers, including Plato and Aristotle, often use these specific professions as metaphors for political leadership. A good leader is like a doctor to the people and does not give them the sweet candies they want, but cures them of their bad habits and desires by prescribing healthy foods and exercise. The leader-as-helmsman is of course the one who makes sure the ship of state stays the course. If those hearing or reading Diogenes' words in antiquity made the same connection, this would make his criticism sting all the more sharply. The enslaved were fully excluded from participation in the civic community of the ancient Greek *polis*. As "live property," they were irrelevant in the prevailing system of power relations among citizens, office holders, and generals. For them only the will of their owner was of significance. How ironic, says Diogenes, that the enslaved perform tasks that only have any value if their owner obeys them, and that precisely these jobs are common models for political leadership.

In a slightly different version of Diogenes' sale, also in the biography, he himself chooses Xeniades as buyer, saying: "Sell me to that man, he needs a master!" After Xeniades purchases him and takes him home to Corinth, what Diogenes predicted happens. The philosopher takes charge of the household and the raising of the children completely. He turns Xeniades' sons into followers, young proto-Cynics. They learn how to live on bread and water, to go around barefoot carrying nothing but their capes, and to scorn appearances and comforts alike. In spite of his harsh regimen, they adore Diogenes. When Xeniades at a certain point protests faintly against this state of affairs, Diogenes responds, again using the doctor analogy: "If you had purchased a doctor because you were sick, you would obey him too, would you not?"

The biography suggests that Diogenes spent the rest of his life in Xeniades' household but also narrates two moments when the possibility of being sold or freed was raised. When his friends wanted to buy Diogenes in order to free him, he forcefully rejected their plan and called them idiots. He turned to another metaphor to explain himself: lions are not enslaved by their keepers, but it is the other way around, because the keepers fear the lions. In other words, Diogenes had so much authority over Xeniades that he did not care whether he gained his freedom or not. The second hint at freedom occurs in his response to Plato calling him a dog: "Yes, I am a dog, because I have returned to those who sold me." Maybe Diogenes' friends did buy and free him at a certain point, and Diogenes stayed with Xeniades as if nothing had changed. An alternative, more philosophical reading of the quip would be that Diogenes wanted to convey that even though fellow humans enslaved and sold him, he was still willing to spend time among people and share his philosophy with them instead of withdrawing from society completely.

As with the episode of his meeting with Alexander, scholars have questioned whether Diogenes was actually enslaved, although Diogenes Laertius cites three early sources for it. This skepticism goes back to the early twentieth century, when the German scholar Kurt von Fritz dismissed Laertius' account as a fiction, because one of the sources he cites is Menippus of Gadara. This early third-century BCE author, from the same town as the philosopher Philodemus, is known to have written some fantastical and satirical works, of which only titles and descriptions survive. But it is of course possible for one author to write different types of works or to write with humor and imagination about real events, not to mention the fact that Laertius did not rely on him alone. His second source, Cleomenes, is thought to have been a student of Crates in the late fourth or early third century BCE and wrote a work, *On Pedagogy*, that mentioned Diogenes' time as an enslaved teacher in Xeniades' household. His third source seems to have been the fourth-century BCE philosopher Eubulides of Miletus (though Laertius mistakenly calls him Eubulus), who was a student of Euclid and wrote a work titled *On Diogenes*.[18]

In a more recent example of skepticism about Diogenes' enslavement, the translator and author Robin Hard has written that the capture may well have happened but that Xeniades did not buy and enslave him, instead paying a ransom to the pirates. The philosopher Luis Navia deals with the episode by claiming that the enslaved in ancient Athens and Corinth were "not really slaves" but rather "servants"—an outdated, overly rosy picture of slavery in the ancient Greek world that has been amply disproven.[19] The living circumstances of the enslaved in ancient Greece varied widely, but they were bought and sold like chattel and were continuously at risk of abuse, torture, and violence, including the possibility of being killed with impunity by their owners. The comments by Hard and Navia illustrate the power and continuing influence of the ideas of Plato and Aristotle. Their theory places the enslaved at such a remove from free people, by othering and dehumanizing them completely, that it becomes hard to imagine that the sharp and witty Diogenes was ever one of *them*.

On the basis of the sources available to us, and the broader historical context of Diogenes' lifetime, Laertius' account of his enslavement appears sound, certainly in its substance if not in all of its details. It should be noted at this point that Laertius also writes that Plato was captured and enslaved once but was immediately bought and freed by an acquaintance. Because Laertius does not cite any sources here, I am inclined to agree with the consensus view that this story is a fiction in this case, and Plato clearly never lived as an enslaved person either way.[20] With Diogenes, on the contrary, we have someone who lived and worked in slavery for an extended period of time but cannot easily be put at a distance or cast aside. Instead, he speaks to us in the first person against the institution of slavery, with courage, defiance, and humor. In this way he presents a powerful counterpoint to his more famous contemporaries who chose to consider it only from the perspective of the enslaver.

DIOGENES, ENSLAVER

According to Diogenes Laertius, at some point in his life Diogenes himself was an enslaver: he owned an enslaved domestic worker named Manes. In light of everything we have just said about Diogenes, the once-enslaved fierce critic of slavery, this may come as a bit of a shock. Laertius does not give any information as to when or where Diogenes owned Manes, which was a name commonly given to an enslaved person. The most likely scenario is that his family might have owned enslaved workers when they were still living in Sinope.[21] It is also possible that Xeniades did free Diogenes at some point. In most slaving societies formerly enslaved people have been known to become enslavers themselves, and ancient Greece was no different in this regard. However, Laertius' report about Diogenes' owning Manes is not as reliable as the account of his enslavement: it lacks detail, he does not cite any sources, and the name is perhaps a bit too stereotypical.

Granting, with some reservations, the possibility that Diogenes did indeed own an enslaved worker, what else does Laertius have to say? He reports that at some point Manes ran away and that certain people told Diogenes to go find him. He answered them: "It would be ridiculous if Manes could live without Diogenes, but Diogenes could not live without Manes." Just as with his own relationship with Xeniades, Diogenes switches everything around. He does not consider Manes' escape a form of disobedience that should be punished harshly—as most slave owners would—but rather views it as a demonstration of admirable independence that should be imitated. For him to need and therefore pursue Manes would go squarely against his fundamental principle of self-reliance.

The biography contains another anecdote about Diogenes that shows him similarly reluctant about being a slave owner. Someone asked him if he had a young enslaved person, boy or girl, living in his house who could carry his body out for the funeral when the time had come. He answered that he did not have anybody, but that whoever wanted his house at that point would simply remove his body from it. The anecdote does not go into detail about the type of dwelling, but on the assumption that he is referring to his pot, the image of someone taking possession of it in this way is pretty humorous, and characteristic of Diogenes' fearless and irreverent attitude toward his own death. It also shows that even if he did bring Manes with him from Sinope, he did not purchase anyone else after Manes escaped.

At times Diogenes spoke in general terms about enslaved people and slavery. On one occasion he encountered a runaway on the road. Instead of stopping him and returning him to his owner, he said: "Go, make sure you do not get caught!" On another occasion, he said he found it surprising that the enslaved watched their owners gorge themselves on food without filching something for themselves. When he saw someone who let an enslaved domestic put on his shoes for him, Diogenes commented: "You will not be satisfied until he also wipes your nose. Once your arms give out, that time will have come." He depicted enslavers as being bound by their endless desires and dependent on their enslaved workers. One time, someone asked Diogenes about the etymology of a particularly derogatory term for enslaved workers: *andrapodon*. This word was formed in analogy with the word for livestock, *tetrapodon*, which literally means "four-footed creature." Both terms are typically used in the plural: *andrapoda* and *tetrapoda*. The (free) person asking Diogenes about *andrapoda* probably expected a jokey answer about the commonality between the enslaved and animals.[22] But Diogenes said the following: "*Andrapoda* have the feet [*podas*] of men [*andron*], and the soul of people like you who are asking me this question." At first glance this reads like an easy insult to the questioner, which then means the enslaved are put down as well, as collateral damage. On a more fundamental level, however, it is a response to Aristotle and like-minded thinkers who, precisely because they had to acknowledge that the enslaved and free looked pretty much the same on the outside, insisted that the difference was on the inside, that the souls of the enslaved lacked reason. Instead of joking about the commonalities between the enslaved and animals, Diogenes insisted on the commonality among all humans, free or enslaved.

Diogenes' criticism of slavery hinges on the arbitrariness of the distinction between free and enslaved. Time and again he showed that those who are enslaved do not stop being humans. Over and against Aristotle's theorization of the enslaved as being animals and tools, as being only fit to be ruled—as being, in sum, foreign and other by nature—Diogenes asserts sameness and what is shared. In his view there are by nature no differences between free and enslaved: the enslaved also have feet and a soul, they also want to be free, they also like food, and they are just as smart as their owners, or more so. Diogenes also points to the dependency that comes with relying on enslaved labor. If you let someone else do everything for you, before too long you will not be able to take care of yourself anymore. This element is connected to Diogenes' critique of possessions in general: the wise person should be able to do without enslaved servants just like they should be able to do without nice clothes and fancy food. In his opposition Diogenes also connects the legal reality of slavery to the metaphorical, psychological use of the concept, but he does so in a very different way than Plato.

For Plato the relations between the rational part of the soul and our desires, and between the mind and the body, respectively, are analogous to the relation between free enslavers and their enslaved workers. In each instance the former is intrinsically higher and better than the latter, which justifies the inferior, restricted status of our desires, of our bodies, and of the enslaved. People who lack mental fortitude, according to Plato, will see the tables turned immediately: they will become enslaved to their passions and desires. Diogenes is similarly worried about this possibility, but unlike Plato he views the body not as inferior to the mind; for someone to live well, both body and mind need to be strong and self-sufficient. As a result, he has a different view of what it means to be an enslaver. Free people do indeed run the risk of becoming "slaves" to their emotions and greed if they are not mentally strong, but, unlike Plato, he believes that owning enslaved labor greatly exacerbates this danger. The enslaver is doubly unfree: he is mentally enchained by his need for luxuries and practically dependent on his enslaved servants.

The other side of this issue is the question of whether those who are legally enslaved can still be free and independent mentally. For Diogenes himself this was certainly the case. This is why he did not think it was necessary for his friends to buy his freedom, and this is how he remained so outspoken and quintessentially Diogenes during the slave auction and in Xeniades' household. But it seems like he did not think this was generally true: he encouraged the runaway to hold on to his freedom, and he loudly rejected the dehumanization in which the buying and selling of enslaved labor is grounded. In other words, the fact that Diogenes himself was able to be mentally free in slavery changed nothing about his view of the institution as utterly absurd. According to Diogenes, the notion that some humans are free and others are not, on the basis of violence and monetary transactions, was an unnecessary and ridiculous social construct.

Why was Diogenes the only one of his own generation and the generations after him—as far as we can tell—to mount such a principled attack on the institution of slavery? We might point to his own experience of being captured, being auctioned, and living in slavery as the obvious reason. We cannot be sure about when exactly he conceived his criticism of slavery, however, and in the remainder of this chapter we will encounter formerly enslaved people with very different views. Another factor might have been his own status of being, at the very least, not entirely Greek. In historical documents dating to around Diogenes' lifetime that list ethnicities of enslaved people, the region of his birth, Paphlagonia, frequently pops up.[23] Diogenes may have found it harder to accept the concept of "natural slavery" because it could be readily applied to himself. But the most important factor probably was Diogenes' ability to think outside of the accepted frameworks and norms. This allowed him also to think outside of slavery and to reject it as entirely unnatural.

APPROPRIATING DIOGENES: THE STOICS ON THE FREEDOM OF THE SOUL

To appreciate fully how exceptional Diogenes' criticism of slavery was, it will be useful to place it side by side with the Stoics' views on the same topic. This movement emerged shortly after his death, and was—via Crates and Zeno—influenced strongly by his ideas. Only the works of the later Stoics, who lived during the Roman Empire, have survived in complete form, and these have actually had somewhat of a resurgence in recent decades, especially the writings of Seneca, Marcus Aurelius, and Epictetus. Their most popular maxim is to concern yourself only with things that are within your control. Although these Stoic thinkers knew of Diogenes' enslavement and were very interested in it, they drew rather different lessons from it than he did.

Epictetus lived from roughly 50 to 130 CE, and we know that he, like Diogenes, also lived in slavery for part of his life. His ideas have been transmitted in lecture notes by his students, most notably the Greek historian Arrian, who also wrote a biography of Alexander.[24] Along with the other Stoics, Epictetus rejects Aristotle's theory of natural slavery: the enslaved and their enslavers are fundamentally the same, because owners are (often) enslaved to their desires and because everyone's lives are controlled by the emperor and the gods to the same degree. Whether or not you have to live in slavery is one of the things that is definitively outside of your control, according to the Stoics. As a consequence, the topic of real, legal slavery is mostly irrelevant within Stoic ethics, while metaphorical, mental slavery is a core concern.

In Arrian's notes on his lectures, generally known as the *Discourses,* Epictetus says nothing about his own experiences living in slavery, but all the more about those of Diogenes. In his view, Diogenes was "truly free," not because his parents were freeborn but because he had rid himself of his bodily desires. In a different passage, Epictetus admiringly tells the story of the slave auction and Diogenes' influence on Xeniades.

He values metaphorical, mental freedom so highly that following this very story he mocks enslaved people who want to gain actual, legal freedom. Such a person thinks, Epictetus says, that once he gains his freedom "everything will be smooth sailing right away." In reality he will have to provide for himself, pay taxes, and maybe even end up having to prostitute himself. In the end, Epictetus says, this freedman will long for his former life in slavery, when someone else gave him "clothing and food," while in return he only had to do "a few things."[25]

The big difference between Diogenes and the Stoics is that the former never loses sight of the reality of living in actual slavery. Epictetus, on the other hand, suggests that the freedman would be less "free" than he was before. Mental freedom and a "carefree" existence are so important in Epictetus' philosophy that he readily sacrifices ownership of one's body to it and is willing to downplay what it means to live in slavery. The way in which he does so is reminiscent of the notion, still defended by some today, that the enslaved working in former European colonies were "paid" in food and clothing.

When it comes to condoning slavery, Seneca goes even further than Epictetus. He was born between 4 and 1 BCE and famously served as tutor and advisor to Emperor Nero, who forced him to commit suicide in 65 CE. His most-read philosophical work is *Letters to Lucilius*, which deals with a large variety of topics that all boil down to the question of how to live a true Stoic life. One of these letters concerns how, as a Stoic, one should treat enslaved workers. Seneca has heard that Lucilius lives alongside his enslaved "on familiar terms." He praises Lucilius for this and considers it a sign of his "prudence" (*prudentia*) and "knowledge" (*eruditio*). Slave owners can be enslaved to their own lusts, greed, fears, or ambitions, and such "voluntary slavery" is "the most shameful," while an enslaved person can, as Epictetus also said, be free "in his soul." Seneca has harsh words for his peers who (sexually) exploit their enslaved workers. Back in the day, he writes with historically unfounded nostalgia, things were different: slave owners engaged their enslaved workers in conversation, and they, in turn, were ready to die for their owners. Seneca concludes, using a metaphor that brings to mind a thorough spring cleaning, that slave owners can erase from the souls of the enslaved all that is depraved by taking good care of them.

In the Stoic approach to slavery all earlier philosophical ideas about it come together. Already in Plato, treating enslaved workers fairly is presented as being important for the development of the owner's character, while it is equally important that he guard against becoming enslaved to his passions and emotions. Aristotle emphasizes that slavery is in the interest of those who are (by nature) enslaved. Diogenes rejects the notion of natural slavery and shows how he remained free mentally and even ruled over others while living in slavery. For Epictetus and Seneca, inner, mental freedom has become so important that actual, bodily freedom ceases to matter. Seneca romanticizes the relationship between enslaver and enslaved so much that he turns it into a path of spiritual growth for both sides, with the owners cleansing the souls of the enslaved.

Historically, in the development of ways of thinking about slavery, the thread of ancient Greek philosophy continues on in the New Testament, as was the case with ideas about sex and desire. In his letter to the Galatians the apostle Paul writes, "There is no longer slave or free . . . for all of you are one in Christ Jesus." In his first letter to the Corinthians he writes, "Slaves or free . . . we were all made to drink of one Spirit."

Just as for the Stoics, there is no difference between free and enslaved people in the eyes of the divine, and, likewise, for Paul bodily freedom is less important than mental freedom through faith in God. "Let each of you remain in the condition in which you were called. Were you a slave when called? Do not be concerned about it," he writes in the first letter to the Corinthians. He adds, however, that when the opportunity arises to gain legal freedom an enslaved person should take advantage of this; this passage, and some other Bible verses, were used by abolitionists later on.[26]

ARISTOTLE AND SENECA IN THE COLONIES

In the European colonies, and subsequently in the newly independent United States, defenders of slavery wielded both the Bible and the texts of ancient philosophers in support of their views. An anonymous author who calls himself "a Southron" writes in the twelfth issue of the *Southern Literary Messenger* of 1838: "To Aristotle, one of the most profound of the philosophers of antiquity, we confidently appeal." This is because, the anonymous author continues, "Aristotle has expressly declared . . . that the distinction which exists between master and servant is a distinction at once natural and indispensable; and that when we find existing among men freemen and slaves, it is not man, but nature herself, who has ordained the distinction."[27] In other words, with thanks to Aristotle, "Southron" argues that slavery is universal and natural, and therefore unassailable as an institution. On May 26, 1850, the Reverend James Henley Thornwell preached a sermon in Charleston, South Carolina, at the dedication of a new church "for the benefit and instruction of the coloured population." In the sermon, titled "The Rights and the Duties of Masters," he enthusiastically quotes Seneca's letter to Lucilius about slavery and several other ancient texts on the importance of not being a slave to one's passions. He concludes, citing Paul, that for the enslaved "to obey their masters in singleness of heart as unto Christ . . . is to be slaves no longer."[28] Just like Aristotle and Seneca, Thornwell preaches that true freedom is on the inside and that for the enslaved it is advantageous to be ruled by their owners.

Jacobus Elisa Johannes Capitein, as he would come to be known later on, was born at the beginning of the eighteenth century in what is now called Ghana. When he was seven or eight years old and (supposedly) an orphan, he was sold to a Dutch captain. Next he was either sold again or gifted to a Dutch trader for the West India Company, who brought him at the age of eleven from Elmina, the center of the Dutch slave trade on the Gold Coast, to the Netherlands. Upon arrival Capitein was automatically free, because slavery was illegal in the Netherlands at the time. He learned Dutch and was baptized. On the condition that he would work as a missionary in West Africa afterward, he was allowed to go to university. Capitein went on to learn Latin, Greek, and Hebrew and earned a doctorate in theology at Leiden University with a thesis on slavery written in Latin. Capitein argues that slavery does not run counter to the Christian faith and that it can be justified if it means that Africans get the opportunity to be baptized. In his thesis Capitein demolishes Aristotle's theory of natural slavery, but he quotes Seneca and Paul approvingly. There are, in his view, no innate differences between enslaved and free people, and everyone who has converted to Christianity is "free" no matter what, even those living in slavery.[29]

According to this way of thinking, conversion to Christianity can accomplish the same thing as Seneca's "cleansing" of the soul: the enlightenment (philosophical or religious) of the soul achieved while in slavery justifies the bondage, and makes gaining legal freedom redundant, because true freedom has already been obtained on the spiritual plane. In the Stoic appropriation of Diogenes' thinking about slavery, two elements were lost, elements that in hindsight were essential. In Diogenes' sayings the fact that an enslaved person can be mentally free or well cared for by their owner in no way detracts from the absurdity of the institution of slavery as such. Also lost was Diogenes' insight that owning enslaved workers is bad for the enslaver, because it removes the possibility of true independence, practical or psychological. For him it did not matter, in contrast to what Plato and Seneca thought, how well or poorly the owner treated the enslaved: he viewed being an owner not as an "opportunity" for building one's own character but as fundamentally harmful.

The consequences of the legal global slave trade and slavery during European colonialism and (in North America) the period immediately following still shape modern societies and are continuously being examined and reexamined. At the same time—even though slavery is now almost universally viewed as morally reprehensible, and all 193 member states of the United Nations officially prohibit it—forced labor persists on a massive scale today: the International Labor Organization estimates that fifty million people are living in modern slavery.[30] Engaging in what-if history is always risky, but it is hard not to wonder whether legal slavery at least might have been banned a bit earlier if Diogenes' own principled stance on slavery had been more influential over time instead of the Stoics' adaptation of it.

Diogenes' attitude toward slavery was indicative as much of his fearlessness as of his ability to think outside of what all his contemporaries took for granted. The same is true of his thinking about what happens when we die. The topic of death will be the last of the five themes central to Diogenes' thought treated in this book before we move our focus to the long afterlife of Cynic ideas from the fourth century BCE up to today. Unlike his stance on slavery, Diogenes' thinking about the very end went on to be greatly influential, as it was taken over by both the Stoics and the Epicureans. He pursued core questions related to death and dying intrepidly and with humor. How should the wise person prepare for death? What is death like? And how should our understanding of what death is affect our life? Diogenes was decidedly out of step with his contemporaries in believing that there is *nothing* after death. This also means that there is nothing to be afraid of.

6

LEARNING HOW TO DIE

"DOING PHILOSOPHY MEANS learning how to die." This is the title of one of the very many essays written by the famous sixteenth-century French humanist thinker Michel de Montaigne. He has taken the phrase from Cicero and offers two alternative interpretations for it. One is that philosophy causes people to live in their heads instead of their bodies to such an extent that it amounts to a sort of internship or dress rehearsal for death. Or the point could be that all philosophical schools ultimately aim at removing people's fear of death. Montaigne himself does not explicitly endorse one or the other reading, but in the remainder of the essay he expounds on why we should not fear death, implicitly choosing the latter option.

Montaigne does not mention that Cicero himself was quoting someone else when he used the phrase—that is, Plato, who in turn presents the words as ultimately deriving from

Socrates. Cicero has taken the sentiment from Plato's dialogue *Phaedo*, where on his deathbed Socrates tells his friends that "those who do philosophy well are practicing for death."[1] The view that Montaigne emphasizes in his essay, that it is absurd to be saddened or frightened by the prospect of dying given that there is nothing after death, is a far cry from the position taken by Plato, who believed in the immortality of the soul.[2] The stronger parallel for Montaigne's attitude toward death is not Plato but Diogenes.

During his lifetime Diogenes was known for making rather morbid jokes—the biography contains quite a few of them—and later literature about Cynicism often depicts Diogenes and his followers laughing up a storm in the underworld. (Such a scenario runs counter, of course, to Diogenes' own insistence that there is nothing after death, but we should understand these texts as playful, imaginary fiction.) Laertius even attributes a book titled *On Death* to Diogenes. This is probably mistaken, because Diogenes did not leave any written works, but the fact that some people thought he did write such a book underscores how important the topic was to him. He agreed with Montaigne, and with Cicero and Plato, that one of the things philosophy should help us do is cope with death.

In modern societies people's feelings and expectations about death are often connected to the religion they belong to, and many find consolation in what their religion has to say about the afterlife. In the ancient Greek world, religion did not have much to offer on how to prepare for death, dying, and loss, or on the likelihood and nature of an afterlife. By comparison, ancient philosophy was much more preoccupied with these questions. We also get some clues from excavated tombs and grave sites about what people thought happens to us when we die, and depictions of the afterlife are a recurring feature in ancient Greek visual art and literature. In some cases the same ideas—for instance, the notion that there is a ferryman who brings souls to the afterlife for a fee—are attested both in literature and in the archeological remnants of funerary culture. Together such sources give us an impression of the most prevalent fears and expectations regarding death and the afterlife at the time, all of which Diogenes ridiculed and rejected.

Diogenes' conviction that death is nothing, and therefore nothing to be afraid of, was a crucial component of his overall outlook. It is the foundation for his fearlessness in the face of power and suffering, and for his insistence that we treat our bodies and souls well in the here and now, since there is nothing that is going to come after. But Diogenes had to develop this way of thinking on his own. For about as far back in time as we can trace any relevant evidence, people living in the ancient Greek world cared a great deal about what happens to our bodies and our souls after we die.

HOMER AND ORPHEUS

Before the spread of the Homeric epics, ancient Greeks seem to have entertained merely a vague, negative notion of some dark underworld. As far as we can tell, they viewed it as a place where the souls of the dead reside and might be punished for their misdeeds. Funerary rites were based on the expectation that the dead continue to exist in one way or another. Burials included so-called funerary gifts: items for the dead to use in the afterlife. Relatives performed annual rituals at the grave to commemorate the deceased, and some funerary monuments had holes to allow poured libations for the dead to pass through.

In the Homeric epic poem *Odyssey*, likely written down sometime around the middle of the eighth century BCE, the afterlife becomes concrete for the first time. We encounter a dark and unpleasant place, named after the god of the underworld, Hades, that is surrounded by dangerous rivers like the Styx and Acheron. It is from there that Odysseus summons the spirits of his deceased fellow warriors and other mythical figures. The *Odyssey* also offers the possibility of a happier version of the afterlife. Menelaus, the husband of the woman (Helen) whose beauty reportedly set off the Trojan War, ended up not in dark Hades but in the Elysian Fields after he died. This place is described as permanently having nice weather.[3]

Closer to the end of the eighth century BCE, an even more detailed picture is provided by the poet Hesiod. In his long poem *Theogony*, he writes that the underworld is guarded by a three-headed dog named Cerberus and that its rulers are Hades and his wife, Persephone. His other poem is titled *Works and Days* and offers a view on life from the perspective of a hardworking farmer. There he writes that heroes go to the "islands of the blessed" when they die, without giving any further information, though the reader is left with the impression that this is a desirable final destination.[4]

So the early poetic tradition paints two possible scenarios for some sort of "life" after death: a gloomy location where the spirits of regular people go and a comfortable hereafter for deceased heroes, although poets sometimes consign heroes to the bad place together with the souls of common dead people. Theater plays and vase paintings from the sixth and fifth centuries BCE add all sorts of additional detail to this picture. Passage to the afterlife is handled by a ferryman, Charon, who conveys the dead across the river for a small fee, and entry is overseen by judges who evaluate how the dead lived their lives. These literary depictions sometimes match developments in funerary culture. For instance, from the sixth century BCE onward, the deceased were often buried with a coin for Charon, either in the mouth or in the hand, though it is impossible to know whether this ritual practice picked up on the new literary theme or whether the influence went in the other direction.

Another example of poetic descriptions of the afterlife cohering with archeological evidence is a fourth-century BCE gravestone from Athens for a young woman named Phanagora. It contains the following poem:

> *Here lies Phanagora having arrived at the end [or "pinnacle"] of every virtue.*
> *She is down here in the chamber of Persephone.*

The fact that the poem refers to the underworld as "the chamber of Persephone," instead of just calling it Hades, is likely connected to the deceased being a young woman, just like Persephone. Incidentally, Phanagora's son was one of Plato's students. They were certainly part of a wealthy family.[5]

Alongside these widespread, more typical ideas about death, there existed also a subset of people who believed in reincarnation. In antiquity the sixth-century BCE philosopher Pythagoras was credited with the concept of metempsychosis, which assumes that human souls can return in the bodies of animals. One century later, the philosopher Empedocles developed this concept further into a cyclical system, in which spirits (what he calls *daimones*) sequentially inhabit all species of living things, ultimately working their way up to divine immortality. The philosophical movement interested in reincarnation was connected with the religious cult known as Orphism, which revolved around honoring the mythical singer Orpheus. He was given special permission to retrieve his deceased wife, Eurydice, from the underworld but immediately lost her again, because he looked over his shoulder to see if she was following him—against the conditions of the deal he struck with the gods. Followers of the cult believed in a cyclical existence for the soul through reincarnation in different bodies. They chose to be buried with Orphic texts inscribed on wafer-thin pieces of gold. Dozens of these have been preserved in (somewhat) readable condition.

There existed other cults, much like Orphism, that also revolved around unconventional ideas about death. These movements are typically called mystery cults, because one could become a member only after an involved process of initiation, and all members were sworn to secrecy about the doctrines and activities of the cult. The most important mystery cult, in terms of both size and longevity, was the cult in Eleusis, near Athens, devoted to the goddess Demeter and her daughter, Persephone, who was also Hades' wife for half of the year. Its secret nature makes it difficult to find out what was promised to those who completed the initiation, but it is clear that they expected an easier, more comfortable afterlife as compared to those who did not complete the initiation. The fiercely independent Diogenes, who expected nothing from the afterlife to begin with, flat out refused to join any of these groups, of course.[6]

FACING DEATH WITH A SMILE

While he was living among them, the people of Athens told Diogenes that he should join the mystery cult at Eleusis. The argument they used in their efforts to convince him, Laertius tells us, is that those who are initiated get "preferential treatment in Hades." Diogenes answered them as follows: "For Agesilaus and Epaminondas to be stuck in the mud for ever after, while some random nobody will go to the islands of the blessed just because he was initiated—what a ridiculous idea." Agesilaus was a Spartan king who ruled for four decades at the beginning of the fourth century BCE. He is praised for his virtuousness at length by the historian Xenophon, who spent some time at his court. Epaminondas was a general and a statesman in Thebes, in Boeotia, who was known for his modest way of life, and who managed to increase the power of his city significantly.[7] He also was a contemporary of Diogenes.

The reason Diogenes used these two men as examples is that neither of them was from Athens. Although in principle initiation was open to non-Athenians, it would be more complicated for them to come to Eleusis and complete the lengthy, multistage process, and they were therefore less likely to do so. In the late first century BCE the Roman emperor Augustus made the trip twice and participated in the rites through the second grade of initiation. The religious authorities at the sanctuary reportedly altered the ritual calendar to accommodate him.[8] Diogenes assumed that Agesilaus and Epaminondas had not been initiated, or he may even have known that this was the case. He used the heroic status the two men had in the eyes of his contemporaries at Athens to ridicule the expectations and aspirations of (would-be) initiates among them. Diogenes did not really think that these heroic men were *more* deserving of preferential treatment after death than a random Athenian who happened to have been initiated. Rather, he wanted to point out the absurdity, in his view, of thinking that regular mortals could by means of secret rituals find a shortcut to a better hereafter that would remain blocked off to the heroes of his generation. The islands of the blessed, Diogenes seems to say, belong to the old epic poems; they were simply beyond the reach of Athenians living in the fourth century BCE. People should just accept this.

Diogenes' mockery of the mystery cult at Eleusis fits well with his overall contrarian nature, but the fact that he mocked it in such an explicit way is still remarkable. The cult was held in the highest possible regard at Athens. Several famous Athenians reportedly were prosecuted for revealing or parodying its rites, including the playwright Aeschylus and the infamous statesman Alcibiades, who had been a student of Socrates. Near the end of the fourth century BCE an eclectic philosopher named Theodorus narrowly escaped the death penalty for this offense. Born in Cyrene, in modern-day Libya, he was inspired by Diogenes' ideas but also followed other philosophical schools. He got in trouble for joking that the priests of the cult at Eleusis themselves were the worst offenders in terms of sacrilege: they revealed the secrets of the cult to non-initiates constantly—namely, each time they shared them with new followers at the precise moment of initiation.[9]

The Cynic tradition of irreverence toward the Eleusinian mystery cult continued in the second century CE with the philosopher Demonax, even if he chose a more diplomatic way to express it. He too, according to Lucian's biography of him, was pressured by the Athenians to undergo the initiation. Demonax's response to the Athenians was so intelligent, Lucian writes, that they admired him for it. He said that it would be impossible for him not to divulge the cult's secret doctrines to others once he had been initiated. If those doctrines turned out to be worthless, he would want to warn non-initiates that this was so. If they turned out to be valuable, he would want to share them with everyone because of his love for humanity. This is why he decided that the safest option for him would be to not be initiated at all.[10] The comments of Demonax and Theodorus on the mystery cult at Eleusis show how influential Diogenes' criticism was: his rejection of the eschatological scenario in which some people are allowed to go to a better version of the hereafter just because of their initiation was adopted by several other (Cynic) philosophers, some living as much as five centuries later.

In addition to the (in his view) pointless expectations of the Eleusinian initiates, Diogenes also targeted conventional ideas about death and dying, as well as the funerary rituals his contemporaries relied on to deal with the death of a loved one. When some people told Diogenes that he should start taking it easy because of his age, he was completely unmoved, saying: "Why would I? If I were running a race, would I want to start slacking off with the finish line in sight? Would I not rather push a little harder?" For Diogenes, there was no point in trying to delay the inevitable. Living with less intensity when you have less time left made no sense to him. He did not view death as something to be afraid of. In the biography Laertius reports that twice people threatened to kill Diogenes. This sort of thing made no impression on him. On both occasions he just shrugged it off. For mortals the risk of dying is never that far away—this was, of course, even more true in the fourth century BCE, in the absence of modern medicine or safe modes of transportation—and in Diogenes' view, we would be wise to keep this in mind at all times.

Diogenes approached the prospect of death for other people just as casually. Some might call him flippant in these moments. When he saw a boy throwing rocks at a wooden cross he said: "Good job, kid, you are sure to hit your target." Just as in English, the Greek verb that I have translated as "to hit" can mean both "to obtain" and "to strike." With his double entendre Diogenes suggested that if the child persisted in his mischief (throwing rocks), he would end up on the cross as a convicted criminal sooner or later. (Although it became more common as a method of execution under the Romans, crucifixion was already used as a form of capital punishment in the Greek world as well.) A joke about a man named Didymon, who had been convicted of adultery, also hinges on a double entendre. "That man deserves to be hanged by his name," said Diogenes. The name Didymon means "double" in ancient Greek, but the same term was also used to refer to testicles. In other words, Diogenes was having fun with the aptness of the man's name to his crime. In addition to this one, the biography contains another handful of jokes about hangings (both as a form of execution and self-inflicted), and again as many about other ways to die.

Diogenes' fondness for morbid humor was clearly connected to his interest in shocking people and breaking down taboos. He showed everyone that he dared speak bluntly and crassly about a topic that society generally feels should be treated with somber respect. At the same time these jokes were a component of his serious critique of the way most people think about death and dying. Fear of death and unease about the topic as a whole are based on the premise that death is something bad. Diogenes rejected this premise. When somebody asked him explicitly whether or not "death is an evil," his answer was: "How can death be an evil, when we are unable to perceive it when it is present?"

Diogenes casts aside the widespread expectation that some part of us remains after we die. Instead, he holds the view that there is actually no point in speaking of "after death" at all. Death is absent while we are alive and are able to use our senses. Once death shows up, we are no longer around to notice. Laughing at Diogenes' morbid jokes is one way of training ourselves to see death as he does: something so trivial and unimportant that laughter is a much more sensible response than fear. He may be flippant, but along the way he is also helping people practice not being afraid of death.

BEASTS AND CORPSES

Many people who believe that death is the end, and that nothing comes after, still remain attached to existing traditions and funerary rites. Even though they know they will not be around to experience any of it, they still care about how their body is treated after they die. Diogenes did not belong to that category: he was fully consistent in this regard and rejected any form of ceremony. According to the biography, while on his deathbed he told his friends to throw his dead body away, outside somewhere, without burying it. That way some animal would be able to eat him.[11] Alternatively—Laertius gives a few different scenarios—he is said to have told them that they should stuff him in a pit and sprinkle a bit of sand on top. The third scenario for what Diogenes said about his own burial is that he wanted his friends to throw him in the river Ilissus in Athens so that he might be "of use to his brothers," by which he probably meant the city's stray dogs. The Dog liked to picture himself as dog food. In this last version, the detail about the Ilissus River is problematic, because we know that Diogenes died in Corinth. But given the similarity of the three scenarios, it does not matter all that much which one was really uttered by Diogenes—he could even have used all of them in different conversations at different times. The salient point is that he did not care about how his body would be disposed of after his death. For Diogenes, being eaten by animals was as good a "burial" as any other.

Diogenes' proposals, as the reader might have guessed, were nothing like the careful funerary rites that in the ancient Greek world anyone who could at all afford to do so performed for loved ones upon their death and, afterward, on the anniversary of their death. Correctly completing the ritual burning of the bodies of the fallen is of utmost importance in the traditional epic hero poems. In the *Iliad* the ceremonies Achilles performs to mourn his beloved comrade Patroclus last several days. King Priam of Troy risks his life to retrieve the body of his slain son Hector from Achilles. In the *Odyssey* the soul of the unburied Elpenor is the first one to come up from the underworld during Odysseus' necromancy ritual. He begs Odysseus to burn his body together with his weapons and to raise a large tomb for him. If Odysseus fails to do so, this will amount to calling down the wrath of the gods upon himself, Elpenor says.

Although there were differences in customs and attitudes in the Greek world depending on location and period—for instance, both cremations and burials were common—the notion that the gods attached importance to the proper treatment of the dead was ubiquitous. The individual's status and dignity in life were celebrated in the funerary rites and confirmed in a lasting grave monument, big or small. Against this background Diogenes' request to have his body left out for the beasts is incredibly provocative. In fact, the prospect that dogs might eat your body on the battlefield if you remain unburied was an oft-repeated, dreaded image in epic poetry. The *Iliad* opens with the gruesome spectacle of the corpses of fighters abandoned to the dogs and vultures, and near its closing Achilles tells Hector, as he is about to kill him, that precisely those animals will soon feed on his body—although when Priam comes to him later, he does relent and give him the corpse instead.[12]

Another instance of Diogenes' disregard for the normative position on the treatment of human corpses is his reported defense of cannibalism: both Philodemus and Laertius attributed the idea to him that there are no good reasons for cannibalism to be taboo. This, in a sense, is the ultimate consequence of his casual attitude toward the deceased human body. It may also have been a way to distinguish himself from others who held unconventional views, like the followers of Pythagoras. They were strict vegetarians because of their belief in reincarnation, and they even refused to eat beans, which they reportedly viewed as representing the heads or genitals of their ancestors. When Diogenes says that there is nothing wrong with eating human flesh, one of the things he does is mock the scruples of the Pythagoreans and their ideas about reincarnation, through the power of sheer contrast.

The stark difference in views between Diogenes and the Pythagoreans was a fruitful topic for philosophically inclined authors working in later centuries. In one of the apocryphal letters written in Diogenes' name by his Roman-era followers,

"Diogenes" writes that if Pythagoras is the new Euphorbus (a legendary Trojan prince in the *Iliad*), he himself is the new Agamemnon. The Argive general, also from the *Iliad*, had a scepter; Diogenes has his staff. Agamemnon had a shield; he has his leather pouch. He explains their difference in hair styles—he is bald, while Agamemnon had thick, luscious hair—with a joke: "If Agamemnon had lived to old age, he would have been bald too." With this silly quip he mocks the notion of reincarnation, and especially the idea that the souls of very famous people who died centuries before would have returned in the bodies of his contemporaries. The mention of Pythagoras' soul makes it abundantly clear which philosopher this fictional "Diogenes" is targeting.[13]

Lucian featured Cynic philosophers in many of his works, and one of these is his series of *Dialogues of the Dead:* brief exchanges set in the underworld, a conceit that allows the author to pair famous individuals who lived in different time periods. He puts Pythagoras together with Menippus, the third-century BCE Cynic philosopher and writer. When he meets Menippus, Pythagoras is famished and begs him for food. But the only thing Menippus has on him is some beans. Pythagoras gladly accepts them nonetheless, explaining that he no longer believes that beans are ancestors' body parts and that he has rejected his own theory of metempsychosis—a victory for the view of the Cynics that our souls die with our bodies. The image of Pythagoras caving to eat the beans is quite striking: according to the philosophy that bears his name, this essentially amounts to cannibalism. In this fictional afterlife scenario Lucian lets Diogenes be right in more ways than one.[14]

DIOGENES IN THE UNDERWORLD

To follow where Lucian takes us—into the underworld with Menippus and other Cynics—not only is a fun trip but also helps us to understand why thinking about death is so important to Diogenes. In one way, the meeting of Pythagoras and Menippus as described by Lucian is actually quite problematic from Diogenes' viewpoint: if it is true that nothing remains of us after we die, how could Menippus' soul have ended up in Hades? But this is resolved when we understand Lucian's work as a piece of philosophical speculative fiction, where the impossibility of this scenario is precisely the point.

A core tenet of Diogenes' criticism of his contemporaries is that they live as if they are immortal. They make plans for the future and allow themselves to become overly attached to their earthly possessions, while death could strike at any moment. Diogenes himself, as we have seen, lived day to day. For him, death was the self-evident endpoint to which he was headed, but it was also the capstone of his outlook on life, confirming the futility of our human obsessions and corroborating his rejection of them.

We should read Diogenes' cheerfulness about death in conjunction with his view that people concern themselves with the wrong things in this life. Obtaining status or wealth typically requires attention and persistence over an extended period of time and entails ignoring or denying one's own mortality at least to some extent. This is not true of the daily tasks of quenching one's thirst and satisfying one's hunger—the only things Diogenes allowed himself to worry about. The connection between Diogenes' own lighthearted attitude toward death and his criticism of people who live their lives as if they will live forever remains implicit in Laertius' account, but Lucian has picked up on it and uses it to create detailed, humorous narratives.

In Lucian's works, again and again Diogenes and his fellow Cynics find themselves in the underworld, where they can finally prove how right they were about the human condition all along. We already encountered a dead Diogenes bullying Alexander so badly it makes the king cry. In the opening dialogue of the same work, *Dialogues of the Dead*, Diogenes sends Menippus an invitation from the underworld. The god Pollux, who was known to split his time between the worlds of the living and the dead, serves as messenger:

> Menippus, Diogenes orders you, if you have laughed enough about the things up above, to come down here and to laugh much more. Up there your laughter is uncertain and many people ask: "Does someone know fully what comes after life?" But here you will not stop laughing, free from doubts just like me, and especially when you see the rich men, the satraps, and the tyrants. They are so lowly and insignificant here, only recognizable from their groans: remembering their lives up above makes them soft and weak.[15]

Menippus seizes upon Diogenes' invitation without delay and joins him in the underworld. Many of the conversations that follow deliver on what Diogenes promised, as they show him, Menippus, and sometimes also Crates and Antisthenes laughing at those who are mourning what death took away from them.

One of the dialogues features Diogenes and Mausolus talking about funerary rituals. Mausolus was a satrap (a local ruler who answered to the king) in the Persian Empire in the fourth century BCE. In Halicarnassus (modern Bodrum, in Turkey) he had a gigantic tomb built for himself that was not destroyed until the Middle Ages, when a severe earthquake laid it low. It is from Mausolus and his massive monument that we get the word "mausoleum" in English. When he encounters Diogenes, he is still convinced that he must be a man of prominence also in the underworld, because of his former position and impressive tomb in the world of the living. But Diogenes tells him that the tomb will not do him any good. As little remains of Mausolus as of himself: bones and a skull. Mausolus asks incredulously if this really means that he is now equal to Diogenes, who answers: "We will not be equal, Your Highness. Mausolus will whine and wail remembering what he had on earth . . . while Diogenes will laugh at him."[16]

In the underworld created by Lucian, Diogenes and his Cynic friends get the better of everyone. Because they already knew that death would take away everything, they did not allow themselves to get attached to anything. Unlike most people, they have not been blindsided by death, they do not miss their scanty possessions, and they are enjoying their *Schadenfreude* at the distress of others who do feel these emotions. The problem is, as already mentioned, that if the Cynics are right, after death nothing remains of them (or anyone else) other than skulls and bones, which means that they would never get to reap the benefits that the underworld would hold for them. Lucian is surely poking fun at the notion that Diogenes would actually get to laugh his joyful laugh in the afterlife. His dialogues do, however, illustrate the important position death and dying hold in Diogenes' thinking, and in Cynicism in general. Philosophically speaking, Diogenes does not need the underworld to confirm the truth of his views: to be satisfied with little in the world of the living and to be without fear or hope for the hereafter is the best path for him no matter what—especially because nothing comes after.

THE DEATH OF SOCRATES

Of the ancient philosophers who were Diogenes' contemporaries, Plato contributed the most to the philosophical discourse on death and dying. Plato was as interested as Diogenes in preparing well for death, and in the question of what comes after. The existing record unfortunately contains no exchanges between the two philosophers on the topic. This might mean either that they never challenged each other on the issue in person or that no report of this conversation survives if they did. They certainly would have had a lot to talk about. Even if, in the end, they disagreed profoundly on what death is like and how one should get ready for it, they were participating in the same debate and may have formulated their views with each other's positions in mind. We also know that their lives—in fact, the lives of their whole generation—were marked by one death in particular.

In 399 BCE Socrates was convicted by a jury of fellow Athenians on a three-part charge: he corrupted the youth, he did not worship the gods of the city, and he worshipped new, different gods. He was sentenced to drink hemlock, and his would become the most famous death in the ancient Greek world (those of the Homeric heroes aside) due almost entirely to his student Plato, who wrote four works about it (*Euthyphro*, *Apology*, *Crito*, and *Phaedo*). Although Socrates would have been dead for about thirty years by the time Diogenes arrived in Athens, the memories of his trial and death were still very much alive. In his works Plato writes about death in ambiguous and often contradictory ways, but Diogenes and Plato's Socrates agree that for them death is not a bad thing. This is why Socrates, like Diogenes, is fearless and even cheerful about his impending death in Plato's dialogues.

In *Apology*, the defense speech that Socrates gave at his trial according to Plato, Socrates responds to the death sentence as follows: "Death is one of the following two things: either it is a kind of being nothing and the dead have no perception of anything, or, as people say, it is a kind of change and a transfer of the soul from here to a different place." Socrates goes on to praise both options. The absence of perception is actually a sleep without dreaming. Who would not sign up for that? A transfer of the soul also appeals to Socrates, because that would mean that he would be able to meet all sorts of dead heroes and poets, like Orpheus, Hesiod, and Homer, and it would allow him to continue his philosophical questioning in the underworld. To emphasize that neither possibility holds any fear for him, Socrates adds that "nothing bad happens to a good man, in life or after," and that such a man is under the care of the gods.[17]

In the dialogue *Phaedo* Plato describes the last moments in Socrates' life. When Crito, one of Socrates' friends, asks how they should bury him, Socrates answers that they should just decide that among themselves. Crito still thinks, Socrates says, that the corpse he will be looking at will be Socrates, while in reality his soul will already have flown away by then. In the same work Socrates speaks in detail about the judgment and punishment or reward of souls in the underworld, but he adds that it is just a little story—a wise man would not claim that it works that way exactly. Still, the soul is immortal no matter what, says Socrates, so it is a good idea to think that this is pretty much what happens to us when we die. At the end of the dialogue Socrates tells his friends that once he has died, they should sacrifice a cock to Asclepius, the god of health and medicine. This seems to be another confirmation that Socrates views his death as a kind of healing or even liberation.[18]

Plato has Socrates talk about the hereafter in other dialogues as well. In *Gorgias* he paints an underworld scenario that basically aligns with the "little story" in *Phaedo*. Again Socrates adds the same caveats and limitations. A striking addition in the version in *Gorgias* is its emphasis on the notion that in the underworld souls are judged naked for their behavior in the world of the living: when we die, we cannot bring anything with us, and the gods have understood that it is fairer to judge souls in the underworld, because there distinguishing features such as good looks, high birth, wealth, or having many friends can no longer cloud the picture.[19]

The end of Plato's monumental work *Republic* consists of the "myth of Er." A man named Er lay dead on the battlefield for twelve days, Socrates tells us. When he came back to life he shared what he had seen in the underworld: after their punishment or reward souls have to choose a new life, they drink from the Lethe (the river of forgetfulness), and then they are reborn. The new life can be as an animal or as a human. The narrative emphasizes that because humans get to choose, they themselves are responsible for suffering in their lives, instead of the gods. In Plato's *Phaedrus*, Socrates talks about the cycle of reincarnation of the immortal soul. In this version the ultimate goal is to be rid of the body forever and be able to gaze upon "the plane of truth" as a winged soul.[20]

Disentangling Socrates' views from those of Plato is, as always, exceedingly difficult. But if, taking Plato's Socrates as accurate enough, we look to *Phaedo*, it seems that Socrates and Diogenes shared a fearlessness about death and an indifference toward funerary rites. Both emphasize, if we take into account *Gorgias*, that when we die we have to leave everything behind in this world. And the first alternative proposed by Socrates in *Apology*, that death could be the absence of sense perception, is practically identical to Diogenes' view. It is, all in all, quite possible that in his approach to death Diogenes was influenced to some extent by the stories he heard in Athens about Socrates, from Plato and others.

On the other hand, however, throughout the dialogues Plato's Socrates keeps insisting on the immortality of the soul, on a divine judgment after death, and even on a cycle of transmigrations of the soul. These are all ideas that run counter to Diogenes' position. In these moments the influence of Pythagoreanism and Orphism on Plato becomes particularly evident: the descriptions Plato attributes to his Socrates show striking similarities to the writings on the wafer-thin gold tablets that followers of the Orphic cult were buried with. Although Plato emphasizes that readers are not to take these "little stories" literally, taken together they do signal loud and clear that our souls will be judged after we die. Later followers of Plato, the so-called Neoplatonists, placed a lot of emphasis on the underworld myths, and their interpretations of these passages, in turn, influenced early Christian thinkers. Apparent similarities between Plato and Christian ideas about resurrection and a divine judgment after death are no coincidence.[21]

The most important difference between Diogenes and Plato's Socrates in how they describe death is to whom that description applies. The latter says he is certain that death cannot be something evil for a good man (like himself). Diogenes says that this is true for everyone. In Plato's thought, the prospect of being judged and punished or rewarded in the underworld means that to prepare for death one should work to be a good person. In Diogenes' thought the ethical imperative to be just and to live in accordance with nature has bearing on this life alone and is evaluated by no other authority than one's own reason. For those who are less confident than Plato's Socrates that they are good people, Diogenes' view of death is a lot more reassuring. Precisely this aspect, the liberation offered by the idea that death is nothing, would become prominent soon after Diogenes' death, thanks to its adoption by Epicurus.

NO MORE FEAR

As mentioned, Epicurus founded a philosophical community in Athens in the late fourth century BCE. His creed would later come to be known as Epicureanism. Epicurus' own works have been lost, but Laertius' biography of him includes three of his letters and a summary of his philosophy known as the *Principal Doctrines*.

Epicurus viewed the fear of death as one of the biggest ills of human existence, and freeing oneself from it as a necessary condition for happiness. The second of his forty *Principal Doctrines* reads: "Death is nothing to us, because that which has fallen apart perceives nothing and that which perceives nothing, is nothing to us." For his followers, the shortened version of this doctrine, "Death is nothing to us," would become a very important phrase, almost like a mantra.[22]

With this statement Epicurus claims, like Diogenes and possibly Socrates in *Apology*, that death is the absence of perception. Epicureanism is based on a materialist, atomistic worldview: the theory that the entire universe consists only of small, indivisible particles and void, nothing else. After we die our bodies separate back into the atoms out of which they were constructed, to be used again elsewhere in the universe in different combinations. Our sense perception disappears from our body the moment we die. Because for Epicureans this is the only way we relate to the world, death is nothing to us.

Compared to Diogenes' jokes and quips, Epicurus' account of death is more theoretical and complex, but the ethical consequences are the same: we should not fear death and there is no point in worrying about what will happen to your body after you die. Aside from the *Principal Doctrines*, our most important source for Epicurus' ideas are three long letters nominally addressed to individuals but intended for a general audience and preserved by Laertius. In his *Letter to Menoeceus* he writes:

> Teach yourself that death is nothing to us. Good and evil exist only in perception, and death is the removal of all perception. . . . He who says he fears death, not because of the pain when it happens, but because of the prospect, is foolish. That which does not hurt when it is present, harms without reason in the expectation of it. . . . When we exist, death is absent, when death is present, we do not exist.

A possible counterargument is that people want to live a long life and fear death because of all the experiences it would take away from them. In the same letter Epicurus responds to this criticism by making a comparison with food: people do (or should) choose not the biggest portion but the tastiest one. In the same way, the wise person prefers a pleasant life over a long life. But, he adds, this does not mean that ending one's life early is choiceworthy in and of itself. Unlike the Stoics, Epicurus and his followers did not advocate for suicide. Only in the most extreme cases, when it is clear that someone's life is unbearable, is it reasonable to end one's own life, and under such circumstances suicide does not carry a moral stigma. Because trained Epicureans can be happy under many different kinds of conditions, the possibility of suicide only rarely becomes relevant.[23]

Lucretius, Epicurus' Roman follower who wrote his lengthy philosophical poem *On the Nature of Things* in the first century BCE, goes after the well-known mythical underworld punishments. He believes that the suffering we inflict on ourselves by our fear that the gods will punish us after we die is far worse than Tantalus' unquenchable hunger and thirst or Sisyphus' interminable labor of rolling the rock—and both are just projections of everyday human suffering, according to the Epicureans. Also, people who have a bad conscience spend so much time thinking about the beatings that await them after death that they preemptively make their lives on earth hellish. Lucretius attacks funerary rites with the same mocking tone:

> If it is bad to be torn to pieces by the jaws and teeth of wild animals after you die, I do not see why it would not also be unpleasant to be placed on a fire and to

> shrivel up in the hot flames. . . . or to be buried and to be squeezed thin by the weight of a pile of dirt.

Either none of these is bad—this is what Lucretius believes, just like Diogenes—or they all are equally bad. The poet wants to show that it makes no sense to be disgusted by the first one but approve of and plan for cremation on a pyre or burial in a tomb.[24]

It is clear that the Epicureans were strongly influenced by Diogenes in their attitude toward death, as was the case with their views on desire and pleasure. But they did not like to admit it. They opposed the Cynics vehemently, both to set themselves apart and to distance themselves from the bad reputation of the troublemaker Diogenes and his followers. This was probably in their best interests; because they mostly withdrew themselves from society, the Epicureans were already getting more than enough flak from their contemporaries.

DIOGENES' SUICIDE?

When it comes to Diogenes' own views on death and dying, one big issue remains: his position on suicide. What did he teach his followers about this, and how did he himself come to his end? A widely held opinion is that Diogenes promoted suicide. The classicist William Desmond, in his standard work about Cynicism, writes that the Cynics "not only condoned suicide but may have even encouraged it," especially in old age, but there is a lot that can be said against this.[25]

Just as would be the case later for the Epicureans, the primary emphasis for the Cynics was on *how* you lived your life. Suicide in itself was not desirable, and your age was of minor importance. Laertius writes that Diogenes "continuously" would say that in our lives we need "reason or the noose" (*logon e brochon*). This is a morbid rhyming pun, but the message is the importance of living in accordance with reason; it is not an exhortation to commit suicide. In other words, using one's reason is *so* essential that if one does not do this, there is no point in going on living. When he met a man who would not give any alms, Diogenes said that if he could, he would convince the man to hang himself. Again, this sounds rather dark and cruel, but the basic principle is the same: living badly is worthless, but living well is very valuable.

Laertius also writes that Diogenes offered his mentor Antisthenes a dagger on his deathbed, saying: "Are you in need of a friend?" The rest of the anecdote shows that this action is a response not to Antisthenes' old age but rather to his behavior. Antisthenes had asked, in a pleading voice, "Who will set me free from these pains?" When Diogenes offered him the dagger, Antisthenes pulled himself together and refused the weapon. Just as in the other examples, suicide is a "solution," according to Diogenes, only for those who cannot stand the pains of living, not for hardened Cynics.

So what about Diogenes' own death? Was it a suicide? In his biography, as mentioned, Laertius offers three different scenarios about the end of Diogenes' life. In one of them he reports that Diogenes died by holding his breath. Laertius emphasizes that this version derives from Diogenes' own friends, who found him dead in the Kraneion in Corinth, wrapped in his cape. He writes: "They assumed [*hypelabon*]"—this is a verb typically used for claims that are questionable in the eyes of the narrator—"that he did this to escape the rest of his life." In terms of his philosophy, holding his breath would have been the perfect death for Diogenes, because it illustrates his utter self-restraint: he was even capable of voluntarily relinquishing the most fundamental of basic human needs, oxygen. But Laertius does not buy it at all, and in the passage that follows he depicts the friends as fools. It does indeed seem most likely that the followers idealized their leader so much that they had a hard time accepting that he might just have died of natural causes.

After Diogenes died, his friends got into a fight about who would get to bury him, to the point of fisticuffs. Only when their fathers and some dignitaries arrived did things calm down. They arranged for Diogenes to be buried next to the gate to the isthmus, and for a pillar with a marble statue of a dog on top to be placed on his grave. In the second century CE the travel writer Pausanias reports seeing the grave in Corinth in that very spot near the gate, though he does not mention the pillar or the dog statue.[26]

This account of the end of Diogenes' life illustrates well how difficult it is to truly accept that death is nothing to us, or that it can come at the most random, banal moment. Diogenes' friends, in spite of everything they had learned from him, were simply unable to separate his body from the person he was. His wish to be thrown to the animals went ignored. But this does not mean that Diogenes' views on death had no effect.

In hindsight, Socrates' two-parter in *Apology* on what death is like was a preview of a historical bifurcation. Plato, the Neoplatonists, and early Christians chose the second option, that the soul moves to a different realm, and they expanded this scenario with a moral judgment in the hereafter, for which the living must painstakingly prepare their souls. Diogenes, and Epicurus after him, chose the first option, that death truly is the end, and strove to live their lives in the here and now, without hope or fear for something else. From late antiquity onward this possibility largely disappeared from view in most of the world, due to the reach and power of monotheistic religions, but it was not completely erased. This allowed for its rediscovery in the Renaissance by humanists such as Montaigne, often specifically through the writings of Lucretius.[27] As a consequence, today, if one wishes, one can choose to use Diogenes' imperturbability in the face of death as a model—or at least one can attempt to do so.

As is already clear from the path of Diogenes' influence on our attitudes toward death, the story of the afterlife of Diogenes' ideas is as rich as it is complex. In this case it was Epicurus' adoption of them that was decisive. Diogenes' conviction that in death human experience ends together with our capacity to perceive, and that therefore there is no reason to be afraid of death, was preserved for us moderns by Lucretius' Epicurean poetry. The liberating power of this conviction, and the accompanying imperative to focus on living in the moment, detaching oneself from the pursuit of wealth, status, and power, was celebrated by Lucian in his underworld fiction. Like Lucretius, Lucian was a favorite of thinkers and writers of the early modern period. At the end of the eighteenth century the philosopher David Hume, the central figure of the Scottish Enlightenment, read Lucian's *Dialogues of the Dead* on his deathbed and took solace in Diogenes' message not to worry about death, but to prepare for it with humor and cheerfulness instead.[28]

In the last two chapters of this book we will trace the story of the afterlife of Diogenes' thought, from the first generation of Diogenes' followers all the way up to the modern day. In what ways did Diogenes' ideas make an impact? Whose lives did he change, and which historical moments might have turned out differently without him? We start by focusing on the revolutionary power of Diogenes' thought. His own ability to think outside of "the way things are," to go beyond the status quo, and to leave no authority unchallenged is what made him loved and hated among his contemporaries. His exhortation to others to be as bold and do the same was heard by people separated by centuries and continents, from the early female Cynic philosopher Hipparchia to those fighting for the French Revolution, and from the earliest Christians living in Palestine to Sufis living in Iran in the Middle Ages.

7

SEEDS OF REVOLUTION

DURING HIS LIFETIME Diogenes embodied rebellion against the status quo. He was uncompromising and he inspired others, but he did not set off any major political or societal revolutions with this rebelliousness, at least not immediately. The most significant upheaval of the period, the takeover of power by the Macedonians, came from the outside. Still, his ideas and his unique understanding of what it meant to do philosophy planted the seeds for a revolution in the minds of his contemporaries that would bloom in the next generation—and, at different times and different places, in many generations after.

The generation that came immediately after Diogenes brought forth a body of thought often called Hellenistic philosophy. Its most salient feature was the turn within and a focus on changing the self. These thinkers grappled with ethics in the primary sense of the word, as the shaping of one's *ethos*. This turn is the legacy of Diogenes, who showed with his own life that philosophy is something that you do, a practice of the mind and the body. He instilled his lessons in the minds of his followers, who passed them on to the next generation and carried his ways and ideas with them to other parts of the world through both oral and written transmission. While many later philosophers appropriated his views, his personality and message remained controversial, and sometimes it seemed most prudent to borrow his ideas without crediting the source, or else to water them down and present that blunted version as the "true" Diogenes.

As a model and symbol of resistance, Diogenes became the inspiration for other revolutionaries. His anti-authoritarian attitude and his willingness to always speak freely stimulated others to think outside of the accepted norms. His meeting with Alexander became a lasting symbol for speaking truth to power. His asceticism, as a method for habituating the body to scarcity and discomfort, is a powerful tool to overcome adverse circumstances that can be used by anyone. For those who are of modest means or low social status, the practice of self-denial introduces the possibility that the poor are superior to the rich in freedom and virtue, and it contains the promise of an overturning of societal hierarchies.

Diogenes' shameless "living in accordance with nature" was in most cases too revolutionary for later generations. Interpretations of him weakened or omitted both his free-spirited sexual morality and the humorous cheekiness he used to mock everyone he met. His relation to power—typically personified as Alexander—is presented as cozier than it was. The trajectory of Diogenes' philosophical legacy was determined in large part by his radicalism. The originality of his ideas and his actions made him a motivating example for other freethinkers, but it has also caused him to be put to the side, or defanged and changed beyond recognition. Yet this is the unavoidable cost of Diogenes' uncompromising intellectual independence. If his ideas had been less radical, they might have been adopted by more people, but they would have lacked their characteristic spark—the very thing that allowed Diogenes to put the human experience in a truly new light.

The revolution Diogenes envisioned consists, ultimately, of conceiving a form of human well-being independent of the community: he turned his back on the *polis* and its trappings (wealth, status, power) to create happiness within, by means of using one's reason and training the body. The new philosophical schools of the third century BCE enthusiastically appropriated his focus on the individual and the gaze inward, but they had a much harder time following through on the rejection of the *polis* and of material possessions. It started, then, with half a revolution.

PICKING AND CHOOSING: STOICS AND EPICUREANS DO (SOME) CYNICISM

After Diogenes' death his followers witnessed the emergence of two large new philosophical movements: Stoicism and Epicureanism. We have just seen how Epicurus adopted Diogenes' view that death "is nothing to us" and made it one of the cornerstones of his school of thought. But this borrowing stands in sharp contrast to how his followers spoke about Diogenes and his philosophy. Among the Stoics we encounter the same paradox.

The Stoics depended on the Cynics in two major ways. In order to claim Socrates as their philosophical ancestor, they had to acknowledge that their founder, Zeno of Citium, had studied with Crates, who had studied with Diogenes, who had been a follower of Antisthenes, who had been a student of Socrates. This was important because Socrates was *the* exemplar of devoting your life to philosophy, even to the point of martyrdom. Also, the Stoics' core tenet of training your mind to care only about the things you can change derived directly from Diogenes' asceticism. Yet in spite of all this, the Stoics continuously put the Cynics down and sought to distance themselves from them. Diogenes' shamelessness was a major point of contention.

In his life of Zeno of Citium, Laertius writes that one day the philosopher heard a bookseller read from Xenophon's *Memorabilia*, his recollections of Socrates. Zeno is so impressed that he asks where in Athens men like Socrates can be found these days. The bookseller points to Crates and says: "Follow him!" Zeno takes the advice and starts spending time with Crates. But soon a problem arises, writes Laertius: the "Cynic shamelessness" makes Zeno uncomfortable. Crates notices this and decides to test him. He tells his student to carry a pot of lentil soup through the streets of Athens. Zeno obeys, but he is so embarrassed that he tries to hide the pot. When Crates sees this, he hits the pot with his staff and breaks it. Zeno runs away. Soup is dripping down his legs, and Crates is calling after him: "Why are you running away . . . ? Nothing bad has happened to you!"[1]

It is a little tricky to assess whether this anecdote was actually grounded in fact—Laertius does not name any sources—but it encapsulates well the problem Stoics had with Cynicism.

Zeno longed for a new Socrates to teach him how to live his life. In his time Crates and the other followers of Diogenes fit this description better than anyone else. But Zeno could not handle the challenge Diogenes set for us, here transmitted by Crates, to show our disdain for social norms through shameless behavior. In the works of Cicero, who was not a Stoic but often shows himself sympathetic to their ideas, we read that the Stoics were still struggling with this two centuries later.

In *On Duties* Cicero writes that Stoics should reject the teachings of the Cynics entirely because they "run counter to proper modesty [*verecundia*]." Cicero warns that Socrates' infractions of societal norms are no justification to do the same. In Socrates' case these offenses were acceptable because of his superhuman virtue. Nowadays nobody comes even close in that respect, so there is no license to transgress. In the same work Cicero criticizes Cynics and "Stoics who are practically Cynics" for their offenses against *verecundia*, yet in the same paragraph he also preaches "living in accordance with nature"—Diogenes' very own line.

Cicero attacks followers of Diogenes, Stoics or otherwise, who practice Cynic shamelessness in his own day. His argument shows how important Socrates still was as a model for Cynics and Stoics. Cicero transfers him to an earlier, quasi-mythical time to neutralize his subversiveness. It is fine for Stoics to worship Socrates as their philosophical forebear, but they should not think that they themselves can be Socrateses. Cicero does not even mention Diogenes: he repeats his well-known lesson without crediting him.[2]

A similarly pointed omission occurs in one of Seneca's *Letters to Lucilius*, a short piece that deals entirely with the desirable attitude toward possessions and outward appearance.

Throughout the Stoic and Cynic ways of life are juxtaposed, yet neither Diogenes' name nor even the label "Cynic" receives any mention. Seneca argues that, unlike Cynics, Stoics should adhere to societal norms, so as not to push people away: "The word 'philosophy' is already unpopular enough. . . . What would happen if we began to exempt ourselves from the general custom? Let us be entirely different on the inside, but let our appearance be like everyone else's." Later on in the letter he turns, like Cicero, to the precept of "living in accordance with nature," a precept that he calls "ours," while "torturing your body" is "against nature." Seneca admits that philosophy requires frugality, but this frugality does not have to be "unkempt." Ancient readers would have understood loud and clear that Seneca is here talking about Diogenes and his followers. He is mocking their strategy of exposing the body to the elements to train it for adverse circumstances, and even branding it as being "against nature." Throughout Seneca is presenting Stoicism as the more palatable philosophical alternative and, what is more, as a truer way of "living in accordance with nature."

The letter closes with some comments on how to deal with wealth. Over and against getting rid of one's possessions, like Diogenes and Crates did, Seneca puts the ideal of "using silver dishes as if they were earthenware." The Stoics preach that there is nothing wrong with being rich, as long as one does not become overly attached to the silver plates. But, he adds in a final stab at the Cynics, "not being able to cope with wealth is an indication of weakness."[3]

Seneca's fellow Stoic Epictetus takes a different approach to dealing with Diogenes' legacy: rather than disavowing him by omission, he remakes him in his own image. In his piece

On Cynicism Epictetus explains to an unnamed interlocutor (probably a real or imagined student) what it means to follow in the footsteps of Diogenes. He accuses him of thinking that a Cynic philosopher simply grabs a cape, a pouch, and a staff and starts begging and letting himself go in public. This is understandable, because in their day, says Epictetus, the "greatness" of Diogenes is no longer around: the new Cynics are "fart machines" who do not really follow the example of their master. According to him Diogenes was really a messenger from the gods, a pioneer who set out to investigate what was good for mankind and what was not. The Cynic philosopher has to be like Socrates and tell people that they are on the wrong path. But he has to protect himself, says Epictetus, through an appropriate sense of shame (*aidos* in Greek, comparable to Cicero's Latin *verecundia*): precisely because the Cynic philosopher does not have a house and does everything out in the open, his *aidos* must ensure that he has nothing to hide. The role of the Cynic philosopher, just like all other destinies in life, is assigned by the gods only to those who are suited for it. If you have been assigned this role, you will have to put everything else aside—being a husband, father, or local politician—to avoid getting distracted.

Epictetus' version of Diogenes, armed with *aidos* instead of shamelessness, allows the Stoic to reconcile himself completely with his Cynic roots. He ingeniously merges Diogenes and Socrates into a single philosopher, a model citizen who rejects the typical societal tasks not in order to turn his back on the community but rather to be able to serve it optimally. It is up to the individual to find out whether the gods have destined him or her to live life as a Cynic—in poverty, without friends, but in maximum freedom and with a clear goal—or as a Stoic. In case of the latter, a much more comfortable and sociable life awaits, even if Stoics cannot allow themselves to become dependent on externals, since true happiness lies within. Epictetus allows that there is some value in the way of Diogenes and that it is related to Stoicism, but he ensures that the way of Zeno comes across as the more attractive option by far.[4]

Emperor Marcus Aurelius is another Stoic who manages to fit Diogenes into his own ideological outlook in a surprising way. In his *Meditations*, written in the second half of the second century CE, he praises Diogenes' anti-authoritarian attitude by asking a rhetorical question: "What even does Alexander mean to Diogenes?" He continues to explain that philosophers like Diogenes, Socrates, and Heraclitus are governed only by their own reason and know about causes and matter in the cosmos. Those in power like Alexander, Julius Caesar, and Pompey (a Roman general who fought and lost a bloody civil war with Caesar) have to concern themselves with so many things that they live in "slavery." In another passage he celebrates Diogenes for his honest critique of other people's arrogance.[5]

What is going on here? It seems rather backward for an emperor to say that rulers are unimportant compared to philosophers. But this is exactly the upshot of the Stoic idea that everyone and everything has its own task in the cosmos. Marcus Aurelius happens to be the emperor, and this means that he cannot and need not be a Diogenes or another philosopher, but he can speak with admiration about how Diogenes performed his task of being Diogenes. His comment here is reminiscent of Plutarch's thought experiment about what it would mean for Alexander to become Diogenes. But this way of thinking runs completely counter to the real Diogenes' call to revolution:

Aurelius' admiration for him does not change a thing about his own involvement with power and wealth.

As we have seen already, the Epicureans were heavily influenced by Diogenes in their thinking. They were just as ambivalent about this as the Stoics. Epicurus does not mention Diogenes' name anywhere in his transmitted letters or sayings, though according to Laertius he did write in one of his works that the wise man should not live like a Cynic philosopher and should not be a beggar.[6] We encounter a similar dismissiveness among later Epicureans. In the first century BCE the Epicurean philosopher Philodemus criticized the Cynics' embrace of poverty and distinguished it from the kind of poverty Epicureans choose. Cynic philosophers have nothing and are beggars, he writes. Epicureans just have few possessions. According to Philodemus, the latter comes with less worry and is more suited to a good life than "the opposite path," the way of Diogenes.

The hostility of the Epicureans toward the Cynics during Philodemus' lifetime, and also in the first two centuries of the imperial period, was rooted in their competition with the Stoics. Philodemus counters Stoic attacks on Epicurean ideas by connecting Zeno to the "scandalous" Diogenes and claiming that both of them advocated cannibalism, sexual licentiousness, and so forth. The Epicureans were always under attack because of their belief that the universe is not being governed by gods but is instead subject to an interplay of laws of nature and chance. They must have been well aware that they ran the risk of being mistaken for followers of Diogenes on account of the many similarities between their own ideas and his—rejection of a teleological worldview with gods at the helm, retreat from political life, harsh critique of marriage, belief in mortality of the soul, and a strong emphasis on mental and bodily well-being—although the Epicureans disagree with Diogenes on the usefulness of suffering (*ponos*) as training of the body. But the largest difference between the Epicureans and Diogenes is that they avoided the kinds of confrontation he most relished. Epicurus, for instance, thought that religious rituals were useless, but he still advised his followers to participate in them, to avoid getting in trouble. Openly embracing Diogenes as a model was, for the same reason, not an option for the Epicureans. They preferred a quiet revolution, secluded in the famous garden of their master, Epicurus.

Both Stoics and Epicureans shared much with Diogenes in terms of their views, and for this very reason they sought to distance themselves from him, since they lacked his shamelessness and fearlessness. As compared to the Stoics, the philosophical borrowings of Epicurus from Diogenes were even more extensive, but the former also stood in a direct line of intellectual genealogy to him, alongside a new generation of Cynics.

HIPPARCHIA: A WOMAN IN PHILOSOPHY

After Diogenes' death, the followers the philosopher had accepted—somewhat in spite of himself—continued to pursue openly and proudly the path he had laid out. Crates became a prominent figure in his own right, and, aside from Zeno, he had other students who *were* able to adopt Diogenes' shamelessness. The rather well-to-do Crates sold all of his family property and divided the proceeds among his fellow Thebans. When the ruler of Athens, at the time appointed by the Macedonians, sent Crates luxury foods, he refused the gifts, just like Diogenes turned down Alexander's overtures. In another example of his imperviousness to authority, Crates said that people should practice philosophy at least until they realize that their generals are nothing more than donkey drivers. He rebuked bystanders who ridiculed him when he did exercises in the middle of the city, saying that they would shrivel up from disease, or simply die long before he would, because they failed to understand what the good life is.

There is one important area in which Crates diverged from Diogenes' path. The sister of his student Metrocles, Hipparchia, was so taken with Crates' teachings that she begged her parents to be allowed to marry him. Crates did everything he could to disabuse her of this idea and to stick to his anti-marriage principles. In a final attempt he took off all his clothes and said: "This is your bridegroom, these are his possessions. You can only be my partner if you also share my way of life." To no avail. Hipparchia married Crates and from then on went through life as a Cynic philosopher herself. They lived in the open air, engaged others in philosophical conversation, and, just like Diogenes, had sex in public, except in their case with each other.[7] The marriage of Crates and Hipparchia served as a model for other Cynics. Not getting married was still the route of choice, but marrying another follower of Diogenes was the next best option. This does not hamper the Cynic way of life too much: you can still get rid of your possessions and live in accordance with nature.

Hipparchia went on to become a heroine within Cynic philosophy and may have inspired other women. Laertius reports a conversation she had with the philosopher Theodorus. Hipparchia outwitted him with a syllogism:

> If what Theodorus does is not wrong, when
> Hipparchia does the same, it is not wrong either.
> When Theodorus hits himself, he does nothing wrong.
> So, when Hipparchia hits Theodorus, she does not
> do anything wrong either.

Theodorus does not know how to counter her smart but (perhaps intentionally) flawed reasoning; frustrated, he tries to pull up her clothes. This does not bother Hipparchia at all, so next he upbraids her for "abandoning, as a woman, her loom." Her response: "I did, it is true, but do you really think that studying philosophy is a bad use of the time I would otherwise spend on weaving?" Laertius concludes his brief biography of Hipparchia by saying that there are "countless" other stories like this one that people tell about her. Unfortunately, these have not been transmitted.[8]

In total Laertius wrote biographies of eighty-two philosophers. Hipparchia is the only woman among them. By actively breaking down the dogma that philosophy is a men-only pursuit, Diogenes' followers were even more radical than he was. Before Hipparchia the only female thinkers in ancient Greece about whom we know anything at all are the Pythagorean philosopher Theano (also Pythagoras' wife), and the influential Aspasia, who was the lover of the general Pericles and an interlocutor of Socrates, though she did not belong to a specific philosophical school.[9] Whether or not Theano really existed is subject to debate; some scholars think that she was merely a legendary figure.[10] That women joined the Cynic movement so early ultimately is a logical outcome of the emancipating premise of Diogenes' own thought: when wealth, social status, or political office are not required for the good (philosophical) life, nothing remains to keep women from pursuing this ideal too.

The importance of Hipparchia for later followers of Diogenes is further corroborated by the large role she plays in the collection of apocryphal Cynic letters. This is a fictive correspondence between Diogenes and Crates, and between them and many other individuals, generally famous ones. Socrates, Antisthenes, and a few other philosophers are also represented as letter writers. All fictive correspondents in the collection espouse Cynic ideas. It is clear from the letters that they were composed by a number of different authors and over the course of a long period of time, though most of them have been dated to around the first century BCE. None of the authors has been successfully tracked down. Out of a total of 131 letters, eight are addressed to Hipparchia, one is about her, and three more are addressed to other famous women. The tone and style of the letters suggest that the collection as a whole aimed to spread Cynic ideas among a wide audience. The letters addressed to Hipparchia and other women may have been intended for female would-be followers, or perhaps for men who were looking for advice about how to talk to their wives about philosophy. It is disappointing that none of the letters is written in Hipparchia's name, but this fits with her role as a student.

A recurring motif in this subset of the letters is that women are just as well suited for philosophy as men—just as female dogs are as strong as male dogs. In a playful reference to Hipparchia's conversation with Theodorus, "Crates" asks her in several letters to stop weaving clothes for him. He does not need them, and Hipparchia should not allow herself to get distracted. Also, he married her not for her love and care but for her like-mindedness in philosophy. In his last letter to her in the collection, Crates praises Hipparchia for giving birth to their child without any wailing, thanks to, he suggests, her physical exercise as a Cynic, which meant that she was already trained in suffering. He advises her to wash the baby with cold water, to give it milk (but not too much), and to use the shell of a turtle for a cradle. As soon as the child can walk and speak she must send it to Athens with a cape, pouch, and staff.

The advice offered in this letter in Crates' name seems to respond to Epictetus' treatise on Cynicism, in which he writes that Cynic philosophers should not have children, because then they will have to obtain a cradle and heat up water all the time to wash the baby. Epictetus wants to emphasize that it was possible to be both a Stoic and a parent, but that this was not true of the "way of the Dog." In the apocryphal Cynic letters, conversely, authors want to make space for this possibility, and they playfully offer some starting points as to how Cynic philosophers should care for their children. Nonetheless, whether or not one should have children at all remained controversial among the followers of Diogenes. A letter from the same collection in the name of Diogenes and addressed to the Stoic Zeno returns to the radical negative position on the issue. "Diogenes" writes that people who get married and have children, hoping to be supported in old age, will regret everything once they realize that in fact both spouses and offspring are heavy burdens.

The collection of letters is not very systematic and is sometimes inconsistent, but almost every letter contains an exhortation to follow in the footsteps of Diogenes' uncompromising way of life. The letters also offer some sympathy about how difficult this is. Would-be Cynics are given comfort and encouragement: they *can* withstand the mean things other people will say to them, as well as their own doubts. In a letter addressed to Plato, "Diogenes" writes: "You are ridiculing my cape and my pouch as if it bothers me to live like this, but I have practiced myself in it with virtue." He blames Plato for living at the court of Dionysius of Syracuse and allowing himself to be won over by power and luxury. He continues to say that no enemy can conquer the man who lives a self-sufficient and simple life and, conversely, that people who live like him will start a war against no king or country. If this fails to convince Plato, he should by all means go on living a life of pleasure and insulting him. It will not hurt Diogenes anyway.[11]

Since we do not know who wrote these letters or who exactly were the people reading them, it is hard to assess what effect they had. But we do know that during the whole period when these letters were being written and circulated, Cynic philosophers remained active in spite of there not being a formal school anywhere. The importance of women in the letters, Hipparchia first and foremost among them, suggests the possibility that there were also female Cynics among the followers of Diogenes around the turn of the millennium. Some of these followers of the Dog got into trouble. As one might expect, their anti-authoritarian outlook, their pacifism, and their outspokenness often rubbed the autocratic and warlike Roman emperors the wrong way—Marcus Aurelius' sympathy for Diogenes and his way of life was the exception in this regard.

STANDING UP TO EMPERORS

The most famous follower of Diogenes in the first century CE—aside from, possibly, Jesus of Nazareth—was called Demetrius. He managed to clash with three different emperors in his lifetime. Most of what we know about him comes from the works of the Stoic Seneca, who was his contemporary and admired him for his simple lifestyle, his complete disdain for luxury, and his devotion to philosophy. Demetrius prided himself on not needing any profound knowledge, only a few rules to live by. Just like Diogenes, he stayed far away from theoretical speculation about the cosmos. Seneca discusses Demetrius in his philosophical treatise *On Benefits*. Just before describing his conflict with Emperor Caligula, he gives Demetrius a long quote in which to lay out his views. Demetrius says that those men are pathetic who think that it will make them happy to have "so much land" that they need "slaves in chains" to work it, and "such a big house that a family of slaves bigger than the most warlike nations" is needed to maintain it. If such men compare what they have with what they still want, they will find out how poor they are, while Demetrius' "kingdom" of wisdom is "large and secure."

When Caligula learns about this philosopher, he is intrigued, just as Alexander was when he heard about Diogenes. He offers Demetrius 200,000 sesterces to join his court—a massive sum of money, more than two hundred times the annual pay of a Roman legionnaire. But Demetrius laughs in Caligula's face and refuses the money, as before him Crates and Diogenes did when rulers tried to "buy" them. His meeting with Caligula illustrates both his rejection of wealth and his willingness to stand up to those in power. On this first occasion there were no serious consequences for Demetrius, but this would change soon.

During the reign of Emperor Nero, Demetrius befriended someone who repeatedly resisted the emperor's rule and would ultimately be forced—just like Seneca himself—to commit suicide. In 66 CE, shortly after attending his friend's death (a scene movingly described by the Roman historian Tacitus), Demetrius was exiled from Rome by Nero. What the precise reason was for his banishment is unclear, but in addition to his having befriended the "wrong" person, the sources report two possible direct confrontations between Demetrius and the emperor. In both cases Nero's decadence is the focal point. Reportedly, Demetrius barged into the emperor's new bathing complex near the Pantheon and yelled at the guests, with Nero also present, that they were "dirtying" themselves there. This was, of course, not a criticism of the facilities but an indictment of the moral weakness of those bathing: they had allowed themselves to become dependent on the luxurious baths *and* the emperor's favor.

Even if this dramatic performance was not the direct cause of his banishment, it does help explain why Nero did not appreciate Demetrius' disruptive presence in the city. Epictetus describes the second confrontation, writing that Demetrius said to Nero, "You may threaten me with death, but nature threatens you." We unfortunately do not know the timing or context of this exchange, but its message is crystal clear: Nero, in spite of his regime of terror, is ultimately more vulnerable than Demetrius, because unlike him he does *not* comprehend that death is the end, even for Roman emperors.[12]

Demetrius' third run-in with an emperor, Vespasian this time, has been recorded by the historian Cassius Dio in his account of Rome in the imperial period. In addition to Demetrius, who must have been allowed to return to Rome after Nero's death, several other Cynic philosophers were also involved. Cassius writes that Helvidius Priscus, the son-in-law of Demetrius' friend who committed suicide under Nero, followed in his relative's footsteps by standing up against Vespasian. Priscus was arrested, and this turned the spotlight on the other philosophers in his circle, including Demetrius, who was reproached for discussing "inappropriate things" in public. Vespasian banned all the philosophers from Rome in 71 CE except for the Stoic Musonius Rufus (although a few years later he was exiled anyway). Demetrius was sent to a remote island, but he remained as loudly critical of the emperor as before. This, writes Cassius, prompted Vespasian to say: "You are doing everything you can to force me to kill you, but I do not kill barking dogs." This insult was intended to place Vespasian miles above the bothersome philosopher, but it also evokes Demetrius' connection to the original Dog and *his* resistance to power.[13]

Cassius offers his own analysis of why Vespasian disliked Helvidius, Demetrius, and their peers so much. Helvidius sowed unrest, chose the side of the common man, and criticized the monarchy. He also gathered people around him, as if "it was the task of philosophy to insult those in power, to stir up the masses, to disrupt the order of things, and to lead in a revolution." Though Helvidius was more closely aligned with Stoicism, Cassius emphasizes the Cynic aspects of his ideas here. In Cassius' narrative the episode of the philosophers under Vespasian ends with the action of two other Cynic philosophers, named Diogenes and Heras. They snuck into the theater, one after the other, to ridicule Vespasian's son Titus because of his intention to marry Princess Berenice from Judea. Diogenes got off with lashes, but when Heras did the same thing, he was sentenced to death and beheaded. The wedding was called off.[14]

The events of Vespasian's reign illustrate once again how ambivalent the Stoics were in their handling of Diogenes' legacy. And, the closer they were to it, the more trouble they faced with the emperor. Cynic philosophers played a big role in this unrest, and together with Priscus they had eyes on bringing about a revolution, according to Cassius. In hindsight the threat to the new Flavian dynasty seems not to have been that serious: Vespasian remained securely on the throne, and after his death, power passed into the hands of his son Titus. But these events could still have seemed truly dangerous as they were unfolding. Either way, the followers of Diogenes were still in the first century CE loudly living up to his radical rejection of those in power.

JESUS AND DIOGENES

The most revolutionary event of the first century CE was arguably the emergence of the Jesus movement in Galilee. In the earliest sources available to us about the life of Jesus of Nazareth, there are many moments in which he sounds almost exactly like a fully fledged Cynic philosopher. A case in point is a passage from what is often referred to as the Sermon on the Mount, an address by Jesus to his followers included in the gospels of Matthew and Luke:

> Do not store up for yourselves treasures on earth, where moth and rust consume and where thieves break in and steal. . . . Therefore I tell you, do not worry about your life, what you will eat or what you will drink, or about your body, what you will wear. Is not life more than food, and the body more than clothing? Look at the birds of the air; they neither sow nor reap nor gather into barns, and yet your heavenly Father feeds them.[15]

If we were to replace the words "heavenly Father" with "nature" in this passage, it sounds rather like something Diogenes of Sinope might have said. In the gospel of Mark, Jesus tells a rich man that he, just like Crates, should sell his possessions and give the proceeds to the poor, because "it is easier for a camel to go through the eye of a needle than for someone who is rich to enter the kingdom of God."[16] Also in the gospel of Mark is the famous scene in the temple in Jerusalem where Jesus chases away the money-changers and other traders.[17]

The Jesus movement would grow slowly over the following centuries, become the official religion of the Roman Empire, and eventually result in the marginalization of anything other than church doctrine in Europe for centuries. But in their time and context the teachings of Jesus were as radically new as Diogenes' philosophy was in the fourth century BCE. The similarities between Jesus' sayings and actions in the gospels and those of Diogenes in Laertius' biography and other sources have spurred a lively scholarly debate about how these similarities are best explained and whether or not Jesus himself had any knowledge of Diogenes' ideas.

Some people find the overlap between Cynicism and the early Jesus movement unconvincing and believe it is canceled out by their ideological differences. Others think that the followers of Jesus who wrote the early texts about him made him look like a Cynic but that this is something they superimposed onto the historical Jesus. A third group of scholars believe that Jesus himself was influenced (directly or indirectly) by the Cynic ideas Diogenes' followers were still living and teaching in the first century CE.

In addition to rejecting wealth and comfort, living the life of a wanderer, and wanting to interact with and include people from all walks of life, the Jesus of the gospels also shares Diogenes' disdain for existing social norms and institutions. In the gospel of Luke he says: "Whoever comes to me and does not hate father and mother, wife and children, brothers and sisters, yes, even life itself, cannot be my disciple." (The gospel of Matthew contains the same idea in slightly different words.)[18] In the gospel of Mark, Jesus rejects his own mother and siblings and says that his followers are his family.[19] This is reminiscent of Diogenes' view that having a family life is irreconcilable with the Cynic life, and of the high demands he and Crates put on their would-be followers. Someone who says that he wants to join Jesus, but only after he has buried his father, receives a response in line with Diogenes' disregard for funerary rites: "Let the dead bury their dead."[20] It also affirms, again, the unconditional devotion demanded of someone choosing the life of the Cynic, *or* a life with Jesus.

Jesus' anti-authoritarian attitude comes out most clearly in his resistance against Jewish leaders, especially the Pharisees, and their rules and customs. When they invite him to dinner, he skips the ritual washing before the meal and is criticized for it. He responds as follows:

> Now you Pharisees clean the outside of the cup and of the dish, but inside you are full of greed and wickedness. . . . Woe to you Pharisees! For you love to have the seat of honor in the synagogues and to be greeted with respect in the marketplaces.[21]

This does not go quite as far as Diogenes relieving himself in the marketplace, but the basic attitude is the same: social norms are arbitrary, and the pursuit of status is superficial and pointless. What is really important is our inner state. When the apostles want to talk about which of them will rule alongside Jesus in the kingdom of God, he tells them that among the gentiles rulers suppress their subjects. He adds: "But it is not so among you; but whoever wishes to become great among you must be your servant, and whoever wishes to be the first among you must be slave of all."[22] Jesus harshly rebuffs the apostles' jostling for power—those who seek it will certainly not get it.

Proponents of the Jesus-as-a-Cynic-philosopher hypothesis point, in addition to the similarities in outlook, to the way Jesus speaks and even to his (reported) appearance. Like Diogenes, he often gives pithy answers and uses animals as examples. And, again like Diogenes, early iconography shows him with long hair, a long beard, and a bare shoulder. Opponents, on the other hand, cite a verse from the gospel of Matthew where Jesus seems to tell the apostles *not* to dress like Cynic philosophers. On their wanderings they should not bring a pouch or a staff, he says. In this way, then, the apostles would actually outdo the followers of Diogenes in simplicity.[23]

The fact that the debate about possible affinities between Jesus and first-century Cynics, and by extension Diogenes, continues to be carried on at a feverish pitch will not be surprising. Just as the Stoics and Epicureans were themselves loath to be associated with Diogenes, the question of whether or not either Jesus himself or his earliest followers had something in common with the Dog is a sensitive one. There is no definitive proof that Jesus knew of the existence of Diogenes and his followers. The New Testament makes no mention anywhere of Cynic philosophers in so many words, unlike the Epicureans and Stoics, who are named. It is certain, on the other hand, that Jewish thinkers were already familiar with Cynicism before the emergence of the Jesus movement, and it is also highly likely that during Jesus' lifetime some people living in Galilee knew about Diogenes' ideas. This means that the opposite claim—that Jesus was in no way, shape, or form influenced by Cynicism—is equally unprovable. We can say, in sum, that it is at the very least possible that this religious innovator and rebel was, perhaps unknowingly, at some point inspired by Diogenes' revolutionary ideas and his legacy.[24]

At the time the similarities between the followers of Diogenes and Jesus, respectively, were without question apparent and striking to their contemporaries. In the first centuries of the common era the two groups were repeatedly mistaken for each other. As a consequence, Cynics and early Christians explicitly tried to distinguish themselves from the other group, as Jesus' comments to the apostles on their appearance suggested. In one example of conflation, the public speaker Aelius Aristides launches a fierce attack on the Cynic philosophers of his day, the mid- to late second century CE, because of their shamelessness, begging, and tendency to speak their minds. He considers them both inferior and impolite, just like, he continues, "those people in Palestine," by which he means Christians. Both groups, Cynics and Christians, lack respect for the "higher powers." This phrase seems to indicate both the traditional gods and the political authorities.[25] Around the same time the philosopher Celsus also criticizes Christians because they go around begging and perform their infamous "tricks" in the marketplace—probably miraculous healings and the like. In this way they attract both the enslaved and free young men, to Celsus' dismay. Origen, a Christian author who quotes Celsus' criticism in the early third century

CE, offers an interesting rebuttal: there is nothing wrong with attracting and engaging the common man in public places, because Cynic philosophers do the same thing.[26] His point, probably, is that Celsus censures Christians for something that his own "kind" (philosophers who are not Christians) do as well. Other Christians of this period accuse contemporary Cynics of hostility toward Christians, and sometimes they use the label "Cynic" as a kind of slur to cast aspersions on Christians whose views are, allegedly, insufficiently orthodox.[27]

In sharp contrast to those Cynics and Christians who sought to emphasize mutual differences, some individuals presented themselves as followers of Diogenes *and* Jesus. The best-documented instance of this phenomenon by far is the case of Peregrinus of Parion, who lived in the second century CE. His contemporary Lucian of Samosata describes in his satirical biography of him how he joined a Christian community in Palestine and quickly worked his way up to being their leader. Peregrinus ended up in prison, where he was dutifully attended by the members of his community. After his release—Lucian writes wryly that the governor suspected Peregrinus would probably welcome being martyred as a source of fame and did not want to give him that pleasure—he returned to his native city, Parion (on the southern shore of the Sea of Marmara in modern-day Turkey), and presented himself as a follower of Diogenes there, wearing his hair long, dressing in a cape, and carrying a staff and pouch. Just like Crates, he donated his possessions to his fellow citizens. Peregrinus returned to his Christian community next, but he was thrown out soon after for violating their dietary restrictions. (Christians were not allowed to eat meat prepared as part of ritual sacrifices for the traditional Greco-Roman gods; it is also possible that the group Peregrinus was a part of was still observing Jewish kosher rules.) From there on out he lived his life as a Cynic philosopher, doing everything that this entailed: he practiced asceticism, masturbated in public, and inveighed against Emperor Antoninus Pius, for which he was exiled. In the end, Peregrinus leapt onto a pyre to be burned alive, in an attempt to showcase the Cynic scorn for death, and to imitate Indian "gymnosophists" like Calanus.

Because both Cynics and Christians vowed themselves to a life of poverty, it was possible for some people to belong to both groups at the same time. Jesus and Diogenes were role models for an uncompromising way of life that does not shy away from clashing with the authorities, and Peregrinus' story shows that they both appealed powerfully to second-century-CE individuals with a rebellious streak.

Diogenes remained an influential thinker in the centuries that followed—Emperor Julian held him up as a model sage in the fourth century CE, and it was during this time that the collections of sayings of Diogenes were being compiled—but the revolutionary power of his thinking next manifested itself clearly in the early Middle Ages, starting in the Islamic world.

DIOGENES IN BAGHDAD

Soon after the city was founded in the late eighth century CE, Baghdad became a center for the translation of ancient Greek philosophical texts into Arabic. Collections of Diogenes' sayings were among the works that were considered important enough to be made accessible for readers who did not know Greek. In the context of medieval Islamic philosophy, Plato and Aristotle are the most influential thinkers from Greco-Roman antiquity, but the large number of sayings of Diogenes that have been transmitted in Arabic show that he too was popular among intellectuals at the time.

Spread out across several collections, a total of about two hundred different Diogenes quotes are extant in medieval Arabic texts. Most of these have been handed down in surviving collections in ancient Greek as well, but there are some that have otherwise been lost. One example is "Do not be surprised about what an enemy says about you, but about what he omits"—a simple, prickly witticism entirely in keeping with Diogenes' ideas. Others seem less fitting. He is, for instance, also quoted as saying that believing in the almighty Allah and respecting one's parents are good qualities. Much like in Epictetus' writings, some of these sayings present a sanitized Diogenes who does not engage in any shameful behavior and has so many friendly interactions with Alexander that he would have had to have spent some time at his court—which we know he most emphatically did not.[28]

Still, Diogenes' sayings, both true and made up, were being translated, shared, and interpreted by intellectuals all over the Islamic world. We find the clearest traces of their impact in texts belonging to the Sufi tradition. With its asceticism and rejection of worldly rulers, the Sufi movement bears a clear resemblance to Diogenes' thought. In his *Letter About Sufism* the eleventh-century scholar Al-Qushayri from Nishapur (in modern-day Iran) writes, in the chapter on contentment, about an unnamed "philosopher." This man has just washed some vegetables in a fountain and is enjoying them when someone comes up to him and says: "If you were in the service of the king, you would not need to eat this." The philosopher answers: "And you, if you were content with this, you would not have to be in the service of the king." This very same saying is attributed to Diogenes in both the Arabic and ancient Greek collections. In Laertius' version the critical interlocutor is Plato, and the king is Dionysius of Sicily.[29] Although stripped of some of his rougher edges, Diogenes still passed on the rebellious kernel of his thought to Sufi Muslims: choosing a simple life over luxuries and refusing to bow to rulers.

For some Christian thinkers of the Middle Ages, Diogenes played a role similar to the one he had in the broader Islamic world: a source of philosophical insight and a model for people undergoing their own inner revolution by learning to embrace an ascetic lifestyle. In a work on the lives of famous philosophers, the thirteenth-century Franciscan theologian John of Wales devotes fourteen chapters to Diogenes, praising him for his steadfastness, self-control, and frankness. These virtues were also attributed to Saint Francis, so it makes sense that the ancient Cynic appealed to the theologian. To illustrate Diogenes' mastery of virtue, John of Wales describes at length how he rejected the gifts Alexander wanted to offer him. In his work John addresses especially the young and points out to them that Diogenes was able to attain virtue using his own reason alone, while they are supported in this by God. He is trying to appeal, it seems, to their competitiveness: when it comes to inner purity, they ought not to let themselves be outdone by a "pagan" philosopher.

The rebelliousness Diogenes inspired in John of Wales and in some like-minded contemporaries targeted, first and foremost, society at large: they felt that most people were living their lives with little regard for virtue or self-restraint. But their Cynic-style criticism became even more venomous when it took aim at the moral shortcomings they saw in corrupt and too-worldly churchmen around them.[30] In the next age Diogenes' biting independence would be used again by a gadfly of the church, though this time a more famous one.

AN ALLY AGAINST THE THEOLOGIANS

As the Renaissance was about to sweep across Europe, the circulation of ancient Greek texts increased drastically on the continent, as did efforts to translate them, this time into Latin. This had already happened in the fourteenth century for Plutarch's *Moral Essays*, in which Diogenes features prominently. Laertius' biographies of philosophers and the apocryphal Cynic letters were translated and distributed widely in the fifteenth century. The Dutch philosopher, writer, and church reformer Desiderius Erasmus, who lived from around 1466 to 1536, participated in this humanist project of gathering, translating, and passing on ancient texts and came away completely enamored with Diogenes.

In Diogenes Erasmus found an ally in his battle against the theologians who split hairs and his contemporaries who thirsted for titles, status, and wealth. Erasmus thought of him as being on a par with Socrates in terms of importance as a philosopher, but in his famous collection *Sayings and Wise Words* (*Apophthegmatum, sive scite dictorum*) Diogenes gets to speak more than twice as often. In the letter accompanying the collection, Erasmus writes that Diogenes is more likely to appeal to students than Zeno is, for instance, and is much more suitable for putting young people on the path of wisdom. Later in his life he would collaborate with the English philosopher Thomas More (author of *Utopia*) on Latin translations of Lucian's works about Diogenes.

Just like John of Wales before him, Erasmus turns Diogenes into a proto-Christian, and even a forerunner of Jesus. His work *Adages* (*Adagia*), a massive collection of proverbs accompanied by essays varying widely in length, contains a piece about the ancient mythical character Silenus. This is where he makes his argument about Diogenes. In Greek mythology Silenus was a companion of the god Dionysus, and he was depicted in art as an ugly old man. In Plato's *Symposium* Socrates is called a Silenus because he seems revolting at first glance but in fact has a pure, divine soul.[31] Erasmus writes that, just like Socrates, Diogenes is a Silenus: people called him a dog, but on the inside he was wise and honorable. This was something that Alexander had already noticed, insofar as the king had said he would have wanted to be Diogenes if he were not Alexander—Erasmus has adopted this bit from Plutarch. He continues with an exclamation: "Is not Jesus the most remarkable Silenus of all?" Jesus too had insignificant, poor people as parents and a modest home and was himself poor, just like the apostles. His life was free from comforts, and he completed the road to the cross hungry, tired, and mocked. But he who has a pure soul, Erasmus writes, sees how rich Jesus was in his poverty, how great in his humility, how strong in his weakness, how glorious in his shame, and how calm in his suffering.

In Erasmus' Silenus figure the Cynic philosopher and the Christian ascetic become one. He wants Jesus and Diogenes to jointly inspire his contemporaries to become Silenuses themselves: uninterested in appearances and always in search of spiritual enlightenment. But Erasmus also takes on some of Diogenes' biting (verbal) aggression. He coins the label "inside-out Silenuses" for bishops who dress lavishly and for stiff philosophers with serious faces. They may look like good and important people, but they are completely rotten on the inside. Diogenes and Crates already understood that wealth is useless ballast, so, Erasmus asks, how can it be that in his own time clergymen still take pride in their riches?[32]

Erasmus wielded Diogenes' spirit to attack the lack of moral fiber in other Christians. As a rhetorical strategy, the anachronism of presenting an ancient philosopher who lived centuries before Jesus as being better at Christian virtue than bishops and theologians is quite powerful. But it also seems like an odd fit. If Diogenes had lived to see the rise of Christianity as an organized religion, with its insistence on doctrine and dogma, he probably would not have been a fan. It is testimony to the indestructible core of what Diogenes stood for that even within the completely foreign context of early modern Christian Europe, he himself, as a symbol, and his ideas were still effective tools for fighting hypocrisy, vanity, and oppressive power structures.

Erasmus' lifetime was a pivotal period in church history. In 1517 the German priest Martin Luther penned his incendiary Ninety-Five Theses (whether or not he actually nailed them to the door of the Schlosskirche in Wittenberg is disputed), which would set off the Protestant Reformation and split the Catholic Church. Erasmus and Luther were engaged in a public debate through their writings, and Luther approved of Erasmus' revised bilingual edition of the New Testament (containing the original ancient Greek and a Latin translation), which had come out just a year earlier. Although they disagreed on certain theological issues—Erasmus would stay within the Catholic Church until the end of his life—they also had much in common. Both rebelled against the hierarchy of the church, and both felt that Christians should be empowered to investigate religious questions for themselves, instead of being told what to believe by the clergy. According to many scholars, Erasmus' criticism of the church, inspired by Diogenes, was a vital precursor to the Reformation.[33]

DIOGENES' MONKEY AND THE FRENCH REVOLUTION

The primacy of reason, practiced in complete freedom. The overthrowing of old hierarchies. Natural law in place of unjust political institutions. Revolutionary ideas like these were brewing in eighteenth-century Western Europe, under the sway of the Enlightenment. Just like Erasmus had two centuries earlier, thinkers turned to Diogenes yet again because of his biting recalcitrance, which could be used against the traditional elites and ruling classes of any age. His praise of poverty and embrace of low social status prefigured the notion that in terms of inner freedom and virtue "the little guy" is equal to the elite or even superior. Erasmus gave the poor the status of Silenus and the prospect of satisfaction through the grace of God. Enlightenment thinkers promised something even more radical: societal change in the here and now.[34]

In 1753 the philosopher Jean-Baptiste le Rond d'Alembert wrote: "Every age, and especially ours, would need a Diogenes. The difficulty is in finding men who have the courage to be him, and men who have the courage to endure him." This appeal comes from an essay about how intellectuals should relate to their benefactors. Together with Denis Diderot, its author compiled the *Encyclopédie*, the major achievement of the French Enlightenment, gathering the then available knowledge on seventy thousand different subjects. The reason he brings up Diogenes, d'Alembert writes, is that in his poverty Diogenes "withstood" Alexander, and he was "the most abused philosopher of antiquity" because "his intrepid truthfulness caused him to be the bane of the philosophers." Diogenes did lack the "propriety" to be truly a model philosopher, but d'Alembert still considers him to be among those who "have shown the greatest understanding of mankind, and of the true value of things."[35] With his shamelessness removed, the ancient symbol of independence and free speaking could function as a blueprint for the kind of progressive but refined intellectual d'Alembert was looking for. But as the French Revolution loomed, the figure of Diogenes would regain his sharp edge and be used for decidedly less refined purposes.

In 1770 the German writer Christoph Martin Wieland published a philosophical novel that playfully purports to be a translation of works written by Diogenes himself, espousing cosmopolitanism and republicanism. Supposedly, the author stumbled upon a Latin translation of an Arabic version of the Greek original. Wieland's novel was quickly translated into French and admired by Diderot and the other *philosophes*. Its popularity inspired more writing about and "thinking with" Diogenes and was emblematic of his importance for Enlightenment intellectuals. The big players of the French Enlightenment—Diderot, Voltaire, and Rousseau—were forced time and again during this period to position themselves vis-à-vis d'Alembert's Diogenes. Would they be able to "endure" their age's Diogenes, or even to be him? And, if so, what kind of Diogenes would that be?

Initially, among the *philosophes* "Diogenes" is a proud moniker for anyone who strives for freedom, is able to remain independent through their own virtue, and enters the intellectual arena with courage. But his name also becomes a slur for those who overstep the boundaries of civilized intellectual discourse, show too much aggression or hunger for change, and, in this way, come under suspicion of being shameless. Diderot went on to write a novel of his own, titled *Rameau's Nephew*, in which the two sides, the two ways of being a Diogenes, are personified and put into conversation—or rather, a raucous debate—with each other. Through his ingenuous characterization of both the shameless and free-speaking younger man, a sponger referred to as "Lui" in the dialogue, and the austere and idealistic older narrator, a well-to-do philosopher referred to as "Moi," Diderot shows that ultimately the one cannot do without the other. Both speakers lay claim to being the "real" Diogenes, but Moi needs Lui to prevent him from becoming complacent, while Lui needs Moi for the dialogue to have any philosophical integrity and for self-control to reenter the picture.[36]

Outside of the world of philosophical fiction, no one was plagued more by the tensions and ambiguity of what it meant to be Diogenes than Jean-Jacques Rousseau, famous for his treatises *The Social Contract* and *Émile, or On Education*. His theory that by nature man is good but has been corrupted by society and civilization and has become unfree shows much kinship with Diogenes' ideas about living in accordance with nature. He viewed himself as a Diogenes, looking for a true human with his lantern, and others also saw him as a Cynic hero. An engraving from 1778 by Moreau on the occasion of Rousseau's death depicts a scene where Diogenes blows out his lantern because Rousseau has arrived in the Elysian Fields: in him Diogenes has found his true man.

Moreau's positive posthumous appraisal of Rousseau as a Cynic stands in sharp contrast to the intense disapproval

Rousseau experienced toward the end of his life. The Prussian king Frederick offered Rousseau political asylum, which he, like a true Diogenes, refused. The king retorted that he was an "egocentric philosopher" who tried to bring Diogenes back to life after two millennia and thought he could survive by "eating grass." Voltaire, Wieland, and Diderot ultimately also felt that Rousseau went too far in his primitivism, his polemics against others, and his embrace of poverty. He was, in the words of Voltaire, *le singe de Diogène*, "Diogenes' monkey." They rejected Rousseau not only for the radicalism of his ideas but also for the shamelessness of his way of life, which he broadcast by public readings from his autobiographical work in progress, *Confessions*.

In 1789 the hunger for change in the here and now, the desire for more social equality, and the resolve to overthrow old hierarchies and institutions—all of which Enlightenment thinkers inspired by Diogenes had helped formulate—culminated in the start of the French Revolution. During the atrocities of the following years Diogenes' name continued to reverberate. Proponents of the revolution used his name as a pseudonym to write anonymous pamphlets in which they justified the executions. A satirical cartoon shows Diogenes, again with his lantern, as he pulls up Jean-Paul Marat through the window of a cavernous half-basement. Marat had been imprisoned for a short while because of conflicts among the revolutionary parties—the same Girondins who wanted a more moderate course and would plot his murder a year later had indicted him—and in this cartoon he steps on a snake symbolizing the aristocracy. Diogenes, himself donning the characteristic red cap worn by the revolutionary workers and small business owners who called themselves *sansculottes*, says: “Fellow *sansculotte*, I have been looking for you a long time.” And Marat answers: “The truth was being persecuted; I had nowhere else to go.”

During the Enlightenment Diogenes was crowned as the hero of critical reason, but he also came to symbolize the dangers of radical critique. Rousseau’s detractors viewed him as the embodiment of the shameless Lui of *Rameau’s Nephew*: fearlessly independent reason gone wild. The atrocities committed in the name of the revolution formed a dark illustration of what overturning all existing norms and institutions could entail once violence is accepted as a tool for bringing this about. Even though nothing in Diogenes’ thought would support such terror, his Cynic radicalism was now tied to the derailment of reason into the violence of the revolution. Thinkers of the nineteenth and twentieth centuries were left to pick up the pieces: How could things get so out of hand? Is true societal critique possible at all? And what purpose, if any, could Diogenes’ Cynicism still serve after the Enlightenment? The most famous revolution Diogenes’ life and ideas helped spark became a heavy burden that required reckoning with, and in the process would usher in an entirely new interpretation of Cynicism.

8

HOW TO BE A DIOGENES IN THE MODERN WORLD

It may be surprising that, in a book about the founder of Cynicism, it has taken until nearly the end for cynicism with a small "c" to make an appearance. There is a boring, practical reason for this: Cynicism and cynicism simply do not mean the same thing. The Germans, who capitalize all nouns, have actually adopted different spellings for the two phenomena in order to avoid confusion: the ancient philosophy of Diogenes is written *Kynismus*, while modern cynicism is *Zynismus*. What English speakers call cynicism with a small "c" did not even emerge as a concept until the very end of the eighteenth century, roughly at the same time as the period historians refer to as modernity, and exactly where we have just left off tracing the influence of Diogenes through history. On the timeline of the afterlife of Diogenes' Cynicism, small-"c" cynicism arrives very late and appropriately enters the picture only in this final chapter.

So, what do we actually mean when we call someone cynical in colloquial American English today? According to Merriam-Webster's online dictionary, "cynical" describes persons and attitudes that are "contemptuously distrustful of human nature and motives," or "based on or reflecting a belief that human conduct is motivated primarily by self-interest." As synonyms for "cynical," it offers "misanthropic" and "pessimistic." With his belief that the human mind and body are capable of anything, and that nature has given humans all they need to live a good life, Diogenes the Cynic seems like a poor fit for the twenty-first-century label "cynical." Admirers of Diogenes and his philosophy emphasize this and take pains to separate modern cynicism from ancient Cynicism. At the end of the twentieth century the German philosopher Peter Sloterdijk even argued that we should fight *Zynismus* with *Kynismus*: modern cynicism, in his view, is a perversion of ancient Cynicism that can be remedied only by a return to Diogenes' true, original philosophy.

But how did we get from the Dog's vivacious Cynicism—recall the etymology from the ancient Greek word for dog (*kyon*) via the cognate adjective "doggish" (*kynikos*) and its Latin spelling, *cynicus*—to the modern pessimistic cynic? The beginning of this story lies in the eighteenth-century polemic between Enlightenment thinkers about the true meaning of Diogenes' ideas and about their value: Were they dangerously radical and shameless, or much-needed catalysts for liberation and reform? The protagonist of that polemic, Jean-Jacques Rousseau, has the questionable honor of being one of very few historical figures to have been called both a Cynic and a cynic. Among the most important reasons for his acquiring the latter label is the autobiographical work *Confessions*, in which he gave a far from flattering account of his tumultuous personal life. His critics, observing a sharp contrast between his life and his lofty philosophical ideals, concluded that those ideals must have been false. Here the word first acquired a new set of meanings, that of being a misanthrope, a hypocrite, and a dissimulator.[1]

An early victim of the new uses to which the word "cynic(al)" could now be put was the English political philosopher Thomas Hobbes, famous for his work *Leviathan* (1651) and his description of the life of man in his natural state as "nasty, brutish, and short."[2] A critic, writing in 1814, posthumously accused him of being motivated not by a search for philosophical truth but by fear and a desire to save his skin: Hobbes' argument in *Leviathan* that sole rule by a sovereign is the only way out of the natural state had been nothing but a surrender to the king from "our cynical Hobbes."[3] The contrast between Diogenes' honest outspokenness, especially in the face of power, and the cynic as an insincere opportunist who bows to the king could not be greater.

The large gap between the Cynic and the cynic, and between Cynicism and cynicism, might raise the question of whether the modern variant is even relevant to the history of the development of Diogenes' ideas. But in fact the two phenomena would continue to be intensely mutually implicated well into the twentieth century.

While the thinkers of the Enlightenment played a vital role in carrying the legacy of Diogenes' ancient Cynicism into the modern era, later critiques of those same Enlightenment thinkers paved the way for the prevalence of modern cynicism. One possible definition of the Enlightenment is that it asks us to leave behind all our preconceptions and assumptions to face the world with a critical and inquiring mind, relying on the power of human reason alone: a liberating project that was going to bring about ever-advancing progress for mankind. Diogenes was a productive model because he propagated independent use of human reason and pushed back against preconceptions and received opinion. That the fully "enlightened" individual, freed from all norms and assumptions, could also become a disillusioned, hardened, selfish, and raging small-"c" cynic—instead of the hoped-for progressive and self-reliant yet philanthropic individual—was the nightmare Diderot had already explored artistically in his novel through the character Lui and which Rousseau's critics felt he embodied in real life. But for this part Diogenes could also serve as a model, except now as a "raving Socrates" (one of Plato's labels for him): a man who, unmoored from norms, traditions, and society, is at risk of succumbing to the visions of his own derailed and deranged mind.

As we move from the late eighteenth century into the nineteenth, the most important thinker to grapple with the two faces of Diogenes' legacy was Friedrich Nietzsche. He was steeped in ancient Cynicism but equally well aware of its modern small-"c" counterpart, and he has often been accused of the latter by others. Nietzsche cultivated a connection between the two phenomena by intentionally letting the two versions overlap and spill over into each other, showing Diogenes both as the independent and rational ideal sage and as a nightmarish, unhinged madman—sometimes at the same time.

NIETZSCHE'S *CYNISMUS*

A madman is walking around the town square in broad daylight carrying a lantern and yelling: "I am looking for God! I am looking for God!" Bystanders laugh and hecklers shout mocking questions back at him: Did God get lost? Or did he emigrate? He looks back at them with piercing eyes. "Where is God?" he screams. "I will tell you. We have killed him—you and I! We are all his murderers." He continues his rant, describing the murder as "washing away the horizon" and "loosening the earth from the sun." As a consequence, humanity is in free fall, he yells, while no one smells that God is decomposing. They have committed the greatest deed ever, and humans will have to become gods to become worthy of the murder they have committed.

No longer amused, the bystanders fall silent. The fool smashes his lantern: he realizes that he has come too early and that people, even though they are the ones responsible for this murder, do not yet understand what has happened. He starts barging into the local churches the same day, so the story goes, to pray loudly for eternal peace for God. Whenever he is removed violently, he just says: "What are these churches anymore, if not the burial chambers and tombs of God?"[4]

The author of this story, Friedrich Nietzsche, undoubtedly borrowed the image of the fool with a lantern from the anecdote about Diogenes' search for a human being. He had learned ancient Greek and Latin in school by the time he was fourteen, and as a high school senior wrote an essay on the sixth-century BCE poet Theognis of Megara, not exactly a household name. Nietzsche may well have become acquainted with Diogenes during his high school days in Prussia too, or at least very soon after. Less than a month after his twentieth birthday he wrote that he had been studying Laertius' biographies of the philosophers, and just a few years later he published an article on which sources Laertius had used for them. He started work on a dissertation on the same topic but never submitted it, nor did he ever complete the formal examination. When he was twenty-four, the University of Basel, in Switzerland, offered him a professorship on the basis of the research he had already done. He was able to accept the offer after receiving an honorary doctorate from the University of Leipzig and renouncing his Prussian citizenship. Nietzsche held the position of professor of classics in Basel for ten years, until 1879. He continued working on Laertius' biographies, completing two further publications on them, but also took up other Cynic topics, like the third-century BCE Cynic philosopher Menippus of Gadara.[5] After he left his professorship, he traveled all over Europe and wrote profusely for the next decade.

Nietzsche's long aphorism "The Madman" was published in *The Gay Science* in 1882, and it is as difficult to interpret as Diogenes' own sayings in Laertius' biography—but we can attempt to decipher its meaning. The madman's reference to a washing away of the horizon and the loosening of the earth's chain to the sun point almost certainly to the Enlightenment ideal that humans might be able to free themselves from religion and existing societal structures through their use of reason. This suggests that the death of God proclaimed in the story is equated with the Enlightenment's commitment to the notion of human progress. At the same time Nietzsche forces us, by giving the madman a lantern, to think of Diogenes, who was looking not for God but for a human being—the same human being put on a pedestal by the Enlightenment. As discussed,

Diogenes either was mocking Plato's philosophical ambitions with his performance or wanted to show that it was impossible to find good humans—or possibly both. For Diogenes too the gods are already dead, at least in the sense that they do not play any role in running the universe.

With the madman's loud quest Nietzsche dramatized Diogenes' complex role in the disillusionment of the post-Enlightenment age perfectly. The model of his rationalism was one ingredient in bringing about the Enlightenment—that is to say, he did indeed help to "kill God"—while his shameless, lonely raving in the marketplace is a symbol for the possibility that freedom from all norms and assumptions might lead to immorality, atheism, and even madness, exactly as Rousseau's detractors had feared. But many ambiguities remain: If God has really been killed, why do we hear the news from a screaming madman? And if it is true, was this the greatest deed ever or a tragic crime? Are humans capable of filling the void that is left behind? Nietzsche confronts his readers with a towering dilemma—whether the Enlightenment was a glorious liberation or an out-of-control mass delusion—but he does not resolve it for them. They have to do this on their own.

The ambiguity of the Diogenes figure in "The Madman," who is made to be a wise Cynic and a raging, misanthropic cynic at the same time, is emblematic of Nietzsche's approach. In all of his writings—both those derived from his research in classics and the philosophical works he published after leaving his professorship—Nietzsche uses one and the same word for Cynicism and cynicism, spelled *Cynismus*, instead of relying on *Kynismus* for the former and *Zynismus* for the latter. This decision illustrates that he still strongly connected modern cynicism to Diogenes, and it allows him to create puzzles for the reader as to which one he means. In *Ecce Homo* (1888) he writes that his own books "here and there" achieve "the highest thing that can be achieved on earth, *Cynismus*."[6] If we read *Cynismus* here as modern cynicism, Nietzsche's remark would seem to be satirical, a provocation meant to shock the reader. But what if Nietzsche was actually referring to Diogenes' Cynicism? Would he have described that, sincerely, as "the highest" achievable thing on earth? We can ask the same question about an aphorism from *Human, All Too Human* (1878): "To look for people you must first find the lantern. Will it have to be the lantern of the *Cyniker*?" The title of the aphorism is "The Modern Diogenes."[7] So does Nietzsche view grabbing "the lantern of the *Cyniker*" as an embittered choice, doomed to fail from the outset, or as a courageous endeavor?

For Nietzsche, as for Diogenes, living and doing philosophy were one and the same thing. Nietzsche adopted an asceticism and discipline for himself that, unlike the guilt-driven Christian practices of mental and bodily self-flagellation he despised, was not punishing but aimed at virtue. He embraced his life as an exile—both from his home country and from academic and other elite social circles—and viewed himself as an outsider. The phrase *Umwertung aller Werte* (typically translated as "revaluation of all values"), which he uses in *Ecce Homo* and *The Antichrist* to describe his philosophical project, is strongly reminiscent of Diogenes' disruption of the *nomisma* (the existing norms and customs). In *Beyond Good and Evil* (1886) Nietzsche writes that moral outrage is as mendacious as the *Cynismus* of a laughing madman is honest.[8] In order to be truthful, he was willing, it seems, to take on the role of the laughing madman himself. Tragically, Nietzsche would end up suffering from mental illness toward the end of his life and had several strokes.

With his provocations, his rejection of Christian morality, and his satirical, sometimes obscure writing style, Nietzsche brought upon himself the suspicion of being a cynic in the modern sense of the word, and he was often branded (and sometimes still is) as such. It is quite conceivable that, in his playful recalcitrance, he refused to clearly distinguish between Diogenes' philosophy and modern cynicism in his writings for this very reason. And, ultimately, cynicism and Cynicism are always connected in Nietzsche's life and thought. Striving for the revaluation or reversal of all values—just like killing God—always comes with the risk of falling into burned-out, empty cynicism instead. If madness and wisdom are barely distinguishable from each other, what is the point of it all?

But Nietzsche was too much like Diogenes to be *just* a cynic. His contemporaries would sometimes ask Diogenes whether he thought life as such was something bad. He answered with a play on words: "Not life itself, but living badly." In his works Nietzsche likewise chose humor and spiritedness, which is to say that as a philosopher, in spite of everything, he too chooses life.

In 1894 Nietzsche's sister, Elisabeth Förster-Nietzsche, founded the Nietzsche-Archiv to preserve and promote his writings and ideas. Although he would go on to live for another six years in her care in Weimar, the philosopher himself had by this time already lost his mind. Förster-Nietzsche was a German nationalist, and under her stewardship Nietzsche's unpublished papers were edited by intellectuals who shared her worldview and adapted these texts to prop up their own developing ideology: Nazism. The philosophical debate as to whether or not Nietzsche's own thought had any affinity with later Nazi ideology has been highly contentious, but the current majority view is that its appropriation of some of his concepts rested on misinterpretation.[9]

The complex and ambivalent *Cynismus* of Nietzsche had been a critique of the Enlightenment's unchecked progressivism and a response to how eighteenth-century thinkers had grappled with Diogenes. Nietzsche resisted a simple, heroizing understanding of the philosopher and presented the Cynic as both sage and madman. The next important stage of reflection on the Enlightenment and on Diogenes' legacy took place in the second half of the twentieth century, in the aftermath of the massive atrocities wrought by Hitler's totalitarian Nazi state.

SLOTERDIJK AND CYNICISM'S FALSE CONSCIOUSNESS

The title of the only twentieth-century work of philosophy dedicated entirely to cynicism is a joke. By calling his book *Critique of Cynical Reason* the German philosopher Peter Sloterdijk was not so subtly alluding to the magnum opus of nearly one thousand pages by another German philosopher, Immanuel Kant: *Critique of Pure Reason*. With his choice of title Sloterdijk is cheekily underlining his unbridled ambition as a philosopher. On the other hand, the notion that in 1983 another Kant would stand up in West Germany would have been so absurd that those in the know would have understood the title as a big fat wink. And this very absurdity is an integral part of the problem that Sloterdijk raises in his book. His work is still part of the processing of, and recovery from, the

Enlightenment, of which in Germany Kant's *Critique* was one of the main texts.

Shortly after the end of World War II the members of the so-called Frankfurt School had pointed out the complicity in the horrors of fascism and totalitarianism of both the Enlightenment's uncritical devotion to the notion of human progress and Kant's ideal of universal reason. The fiction that the truth always wins because of the superiority of reason, as if in a power vacuum, was responsible, they argued, for the fact that it had been possible to put human reason to such cruel ends. For Sloterdijk in the 1980s, political totalitarianism was no longer the biggest threat; rather, the threat came from the internalized disillusionment and apathy that followed the realization that both the old certainties of church and tradition as well as the critiques of them had failed—that is, modern cynicism.

Sloterdijk defines modern cynicism as "enlightened, false consciousness." Modern cynics know both the lessons of the Enlightenment and the critiques that followed them inside out, and they withdraw into pragmatic, realistic opportunism. They comfort themselves with the knowledge that at least they are not naïve. Sloterdijk writes:

> For cynics are not dumb, and every now and then they certainly see the nothingness to which everything leads. The apparatus of their soul has become elastic enough to incorporate in themselves as a survival factor the permanent doubt about their own activities. They know what they are doing, but they do it because, in the short run, the force of circumstances and the instinct for self-preservation are speaking the same

> language, and are telling them that it has to happen. Others would do it anyway, perhaps worse people.[10]

In the opening sections of his book Sloterdijk immediately juxtaposes this opportunistic *Zynismus* with the *Kynismus* of Diogenes, who does not need anyone and places himself at a remove from society by means of his biting criticisms. Alexander, on the other hand, anachronistically embodies the definition of modern *Zynismus*, according to Sloterdijk: he said he wanted to be Diogenes, which means that he had glimpsed the truth, but still he continued on as king.

Diogenes can point the way for us to get out of the apathy of modern cynicism, Sloterdijk thinks, because he offers an alternative to the Enlightenment that is actually viable: cheekiness (*Frechheit*). Philosophers are almost never able to live entirely in accordance with their own ideals, which means that hypocrisy is always right around the corner. Diogenes' cheekiness is needed to unmask this hypocrisy and to honestly account for life as it is being lived. According to Sloterdijk, Diogenes created a "rude enlightenment" by starting a "non-Platonic dialogue." With his satirical and humorous way of speaking, he cracked open Plato's methodology right as it emerged. The impasse of modern cynicism is, as Sloterdijk sees it, the endpoint of the dialectical tradition that started with Plato. To break out of this impasse and to resuscitate the critique undertaken by the Enlightenment, people should return to the satirical strategy Diogenes employed in his confrontation with Plato.[11]

Aside from his satirical humor, the way Diogenes used his body is also essential for Sloterdijk. The criticism of the Enlightenment formulated by the Frankfurt School had already raised the issue of the suppression and denial of the body by reason.

Sloterdijk continues this thread. "In the dialogue of heads only head theories [*Kopftheorien*] will ever emerge," he writes. This means that the physical is always inevitably sidelined from the get-go. Diogenes battles the cerebral ideas of the Athenians with his shameless actions. Instead of mounting an attack on theoretical grounds, he uses his body. German idealism—the philosophical school of Kant and Hegel—justifies the existing world order by placing "pure" ideas at the top and "impure" matter at the bottom. Sloterdijk asks how matter can defend itself against this humiliation, since it is excluded from academic discourse:

> What can be done? The material, the alert body, actively presents the proof of its sovereignty. The excluded lower element goes to the marketplace and demonstratively challenges the higher element. Feces, urine, sperm![12]

Not without cheekiness, Sloterdijk once again points to Diogenes' resistance to Plato as a blueprint for a strategy against the *Zynismus* to which the Enlightenment gave rise. Plato was so deflated by Diogenes that he saw no alternative other than to call him a "raving Socrates"—in his eyes the greatest insult, but according to Sloterdijk, the highest form of recognition.

FOUCAULT AND THE COURAGE OF TRUTH

A year after the publication of Sloterdijk's *Critique of Cynical Reason*, the French philosopher Michel Foucault taught his last course at the Collège de France in Paris. A few months later, in the summer of 1984, he would succumb to the consequences of AIDS. Of the nine lectures he gave during this course, five were about Diogenes. Foucault had not had the opportunity to read Sloterdijk's book, but he too points to Diogenes' Cynicism as a remedy for the apathy of his own time. He thought that returning to Diogenes would allow philosophy to make good on the promise that the critique attempted in the Enlightenment had made but failed to keep.

In his earlier works Foucault, like the members of the Frankfurt School, had studied the entanglements of the Enlightenment's commitment to the ideal of ever-advancing human progress with power and oppression, especially the ways in which knowledge and technology are used to control individuals and force them into the mold of "normality." In the prison system, for instance, changes that may seem like progress—no more corporal punishment, private cells, and psychological care—in fact amount, Foucault argued, to a more dangerous and more invasive form of using power: to transform human beings into docile and disciplined subjects.

In his later works Foucault adopted a more positive outlook toward the Enlightenment. He returned to Kant's essay "What Is Enlightenment?" to reinterpret the title as a historically specific question instead of a universal one. Every generation must answer this philosophical question for themselves and use it to investigate their own relation to the present. This makes Enlightenment into something like what "the Greeks called an *ethos*," Foucault writes—that is, a habit for life.[13] In the last years of his life Foucault wrote two books, *The Use of Pleasure* and *The Care of the Self*. He turned to ancient Greek philosophers, especially Plato, Aristotle, and the Stoics, to find starting points for shaping the self by means of daily, practical exercises that should ultimately produce greater positive freedom for the subject. These two elements—reactivating the critical outlook of the Enlightenment and the search for practical everyday ethics—come together in his lectures about Diogenes' Cynicism.

The course Foucault taught in the spring of 1984 was recorded on tape. The lectures were transcribed but did not get published until 2009, under the title *The Courage of Truth*. In the opening lectures Foucault turns to Socrates to investigate the ancient Greek virtue of *parrhesia*, "speaking freely," but along the way he realizes that Diogenes is a better model for what he is trying to achieve. In ancient Cynicism Foucault finds a way to redefine the relationship between the self and the truth, which also offers the possibility of reshaping the relationship between truth and power: "Life as the immediate, resounding, and savage presence of the truth—this is what is manifested in Cynicism."[14] Diogenes' way of life, to Foucault, is the embodiment of his interpretation of the task given to us by the Enlightenment: an always ongoing critique and questioning of the present. In Foucault's analysis the Cynics' choice of a simple and sober existence is entirely in the service of speaking freely: Diogenes had to liberate himself from desires and dependence in order to speak the truth ruthlessly, with nothing to lose.

Foucault starts his discussion of Diogenes with a close reading of a passage from Laertius' biography:

> One day he was asked what the most beautiful thing among humans is. The answer: *parrhesia*. You see how the theme of the beauty of existence, of the most beautiful form one can give to one's existence, and the

> theme of the exercise of *parrhesia*, of free-spokenness, are directly linked here.[15]

What Foucault is getting at is that *parrhesia*, which he equates with speaking truth, is not simply an activity for Diogenes but actually a way of life. The literal meaning of *parrhesia* is "saying everything," and already in antiquity it was understood as an attitude of ruthless honesty. Foucault adds to this the notion that as a practical exercise *parrhesia* is an exchange between two people: "For there to be *parrhesia* . . . the subject must, in speaking this truth which he signs as his opinion, his thought, his belief, be taking some kind of risk, a risk which concerns his very relationship with the person to whom he is speaking." And this risk, Foucault emphasizes, is considerable: "In speaking the truth one must open up, establish, and confront the risk of offending the other person, of irritating him, of making him angry and provoking him to behaviors which may even be extremely violent. So that is the truth, in the risk of violence."[16] The speaker's courage to speak the truth in spite of everything must be reciprocated by the addressee with magnanimity to accept that they are being told the truth, even if it is painful to hear. Initially Foucault also ascribes this form of *parrhesia* to Socrates, but he goes on to argue that Diogenes applied this practice in his own unique way.

In contrast to Socrates, Foucault writes, Diogenes uses not only his words but also his body to tell the truth. His asceticism is a condition for being able to exercise *parrhesia* without any fears or commitments, but it is also in itself a form of speaking truth. With his way of life he demonstrates that conventions and norms are superfluous, and by concerning himself only with basic necessities he shows what really matters.

Where Sloterdijk emphasized Diogenes' shamelessness, in Foucault this aspect is overshadowed almost entirely by Cynic self-discipline.

Foucault points to a second difference between Socrates and Diogenes, which lies in what they understand the task of the philosopher to be. Socrates, initially, is out on his own quest for the truth, which he hopes may benefit others as well, while Diogenes displays a burning passion for overturning the *nomisma* to change the world. Foucault writes: "So you see that the Cynic is of service in a very different way than through leading an exemplary life or the advice he can give. He is useful because he battles, he is useful because he bites, he is useful because he attacks."[17] The Cynic sees himself as a fighter in the vanguard of a special mission. His task is so demanding, according to Foucault, that few people will be able to take it up.

That second distinction between Socrates and Diogenes is less convincing than the first one. If we take seriously what Socrates says in the defense speech Plato wrote for him, known as *Apology*, he did want to put his life in the service of the city of Athens and his fellow citizens. Also, Foucault himself acknowledges that his understanding of Diogenes has been strongly influenced by Epictetus' version of him, and Epictetus had very specific motives for depicting Diogenes as a heroic, unflappable, and pioneering do-gooder. He wanted both to clear the reputation of the forefather of his own philosophical school, Stoicism, and to show that, unlike Stoicism, Cynicism was a feasible option only for a select few. But other sources about Diogenes show time and again that, according to Diogenes himself, the path of the Cynic—living in accordance with nature and using one's reason—is open to everyone who is willing to try.

The most obvious and powerful illustration of how speaking freely can redefine "the relationship between power and truth" would of course be Diogenes' famous meeting with Alexander. Foucault uses the lengthy fictionalized version written by Dio Chrysostom in which Diogenes lectures Alexander about leadership, and unpacks it in great detail. For Foucault the fact that the meeting took place at all, with Alexander seeking out Diogenes, is in itself a negation of the power differential between the two men. Alexander would want "to be Diogenes" if he were not himself because he views Diogenes as the only person in the world who can compete with him. Sure enough, in their confrontation Diogenes confirms that he, not Alexander, is the true king. Alexander needs an army, guards, allies, and armor to defend himself and his power. Diogenes needs nothing more than self-control. His kingship relies on no one outside of himself, and he cannot lose it through misfortune or setbacks. Foucault writes: "The king Diogenes will roll in the burning sand in summer, and in the snow in winter, solely in order to be able to practice on himself an ever more complete, harsh, and accomplished endurance."[18] Diogenes' control over his mind and body renders him sovereign over himself. This sovereignty is superior to Alexander's precarious political sovereignty, which is a sham. The Cynic's power to shape the self can render worldly structures of power null and void.

Foucault ends with a brief historical sketch of the different ways in which, in his view, Cynicism has been practiced outside of philosophy after antiquity. Starting with the early Christians, religious believers have practiced Cynic asceticism, and some Cynics became Christians—here Foucault mentions the infamous Peregrinus specifically. In the Middle Ages, Foucault sees Cynicism primarily among the begging, traveling

Franciscans, and afterward in those who rose up against the institutions of the Catholic Church during the Reformation. Even though Foucault does not mention him here, we can think back to Erasmus' criticism of the church at that time, which was directly inspired by Diogenes' Cynicism.

Foucault sees another historical thread of Cynicism in art, starting around the end of the eighteenth century. The modern idea that the life of the artist imbues the work of art with authenticity and even is a work of art in its own right is a continuation of the Cynic idea that the life of the philosopher manifests itself as a "scandalous rupture" through which the truth becomes concrete. Examples he gives, all compatriots, include the painter Eduard Manet, the poet Charles Baudelaire, and the writer Gustave Flaubert, who wrote *Madame Bovary.* Foucault locates in modern art a "polemic relationship" with cultural and social norms, "a permanent Cynicism toward all established art."[19] For Foucault Cynicism can take many different forms. It can be practiced just as well through a painting or a novel as through a philosophy lecture, as long as it is truthful and critical.

Foucault and Sloterdijk both viewed the Cynicism of Diogenes as a potential solution for the challenges of their own time. Their intense engagement with him happened against the backdrop of the severe global economic crisis of the early 1980s, which led to mass unemployment worldwide, including in France and West Germany. At the time Cold War tensions were still high. That the Berlin Wall would come down by the end of the decade seemed far from likely. In this mood of understandable pessimism and apathy Diogenes called out to Foucault and Sloterdijk as a life-affirming voice, even if they emphasize different aspects of him.

While Sloterdijk opposed modern, "bad" cynicism to ancient, "good" Cynicism, for Foucault there was only one Cynicism. This carries the promise in itself, if it is practiced sincerely and without presuppositions, of being able to change the world. In other words, what Sloterdijk calls "modern cynicism" would in Foucault's eyes probably not even deserve the label. It is neither courageous nor sincere, and—the most important thing—the "truth" of the modern cynic is discordant with their own way of life. Sloterdijk's "good" Cynic is more humorous and embodied than Foucault's, but the core of lived courage and real honesty is just the same.

These thinkers' efforts notwithstanding, in our everyday usage today modern cynicism is far more prevalent than Diogenes' Cynicism. As the ambivalence of Nietzsche's *Cynismus* already illustrated, the disruption of the *nomisma* is psychologically so risky and overwhelming that one might easily fall into emptiness. Overturning all prevalent norms and institutions can produce an outlook devoid of any values in which everything, including opportunism, can be justified. Moreover, the high demands of the shameless and ascetic Cynic way of life coupled with the immutable imperative that the Cynic must live in accordance with their Cynic ideas render it all but impossible to achieve this ideal. We know that Diogenes himself was acutely aware of this risk. One way he tried to circumvent it was with his description of himself as a choir conductor. With his life he is setting the tone just a little too high, and whoever tries to follow him will necessarily fall short, but that means they will actually be hitting the right note. People who think they should be perfect Cynics are missing the point and are doomed to fail. The self-described Cynic Rousseau was accused of hypocrisy because he was unable to live out his ideals. Sloterdijk's pragmatic modern cynics choose apathy instead: they do not even try to live up to their own enlightened insights because they have decided beforehand that they cannot do it.

This is not to say that modern cynicism was able to arise only as an aberration of ancient Cynicism. We can imagine that even without Diogenes the attitude we now call cynicism might have emerged. But it has become clear, to answer our question from the opening of the chapter, what ancient Cynicism and modern cynicism share, in spite of the vast differences between them, and how the transition happened over time. Someone who attempts to follow in Diogenes' footsteps by overturning all values but loses sight of the fact that nature offers us the possibility of a joyful, good life can descend into nihilism or even insanity. Likewise, whoever takes too seriously their own efforts to live out their Cynic ideals and prides themselves on perfection will sooner or later inevitably be shown up as a hypocrite. There are several ways to start out from Diogenes and end up with modern cynicism.

But what about the other path? Foucault and Sloterdijk insisted that a modern Cynicism is also possible and even necessary. Does that still hold true? The very fact that small-"c" cynicism seems to be all around us would mean, in their view, that Cynicism is more necessary than ever. Whether it is also possible is a question that is more difficult to answer.

A DIOGENES FOR OUR TIME?

The Enlightenment thinker d'Alembert claimed that every age could use its own Diogenes. Nietzsche, Foucault, and Sloterdijk agreed with d'Alembert on this for the nineteenth and twentieth centuries, respectively. They also seem to have fulfilled the task of being a Diogenes themselves, arguably more so than any of their contemporaries. This raises the question of whether or not we, at the beginning of the twenty-first century, need someone to be a Diogenes for our time. If so, who could it be?

A common denominator in (quasi-)democratic countries around the world over the past few decades has been the rise of populism. In nearly all of them leaders have emerged who present themselves as champions of the people. In many cases such claims are accompanied by a provocative style and challenges to the political establishment, which is painted as deceitful and unreliable. Such challenges are then frequently dressed up with a certain shamelessness. The new leaders prove their status as outsiders vis-à-vis the traditional political elites by ostentatiously breaking the accepted rules of engagement. Much of their charisma is derived from playing the part of the rogue. They do and say everything that most of their followers would want to do and say but do not dare to.

So are these populists the Diogeneses of our time? There are clear points of contact. Diogenes too was an outsider, and by flagrantly ignoring accepted norms and values he tried to show that they were both useless and hypocritical. But at the same time Diogenes' resistance was much more radical. Populist politicians are attacking the representatives of the establishment in order to topple them and then take their place. Diogenes' aim is to show that the establishment does not have real power. In other words, Diogenes does not want to be Alexander, and he does not actually need to overthrow him, because he is already free. Diogenes undermines those in power by showing others that there is no need whatsoever to obey the king or to get into his good graces, because the Cynic way of life offers true wealth and protection.

This particular contrast in their respective attitudes toward power produces a host of other differences between Diogenes' Cynicism and contemporary political populism. The self-restraint and simple life on which Diogenes' sovereignty rests are typically absent in the populists' narratives. Also, Diogenes' shamelessness was all-encompassing, while the cult of personality that populists rely on renders them vulnerable: they carefully have to pick and choose which brand of shamelessness will appeal. And Diogenes' message to his followers is that in order to achieve happiness they have to change their lives themselves. Populists, conversely, promise that they will solve everything *for* their followers. Finally, Diogenes' vision for changing the *nomisma* is to allow people to shape their lives in accordance with nature and reason. Populist politicians often pride themselves on not having any ideals at all. As a result, one of the most difficult tasks of Cynicism—namely, to put one's philosophical ideals into practice—is completely irrelevant to them. Contemporary populism is akin to modern cynicism as analyzed by Sloterdijk in its pragmatic opportunism and its "false consciousness" of the failure of both the old certainties and their critiques. But while the cynicism of the 1980s translated into apathy and a seamless participation in the machinery of the much-maligned establishment, for current populist movements the lack of new ideals is no impediment to going on the attack. In sum, while the shameless roguishness of contemporary populists partakes of some of the same tools as Diogenes did—mainly performativity and shock value—it is starkly different in its motives, application, and ultimate objective.

When Foucault was thinking through the possibility of being a Diogenes in his own time, which for him meant to exercise the courage of speaking truthfully through one's way of life, he looked to art and found Cynic elements there. Would that still be true for the twenty-first century?

In 2010 the Serbian artist Marina Abramović sat at a table for eight hours a day every day for three weeks in one of the big exhibition spaces of the Museum of Modern Art in New York City. Visitors were allowed to sit down across from her at the table. Abramović looked straight at every visitor who did so and did not break eye contact. In total 1,545 people sat down with her, some just for a few minutes, some for an entire day. Many of these visitors found it to be an emotional experience. Abramović, who has been engaged in performance art since the 1970s, has said about her work: "The first time I put my body in front of [an] audience, I understood: this is my media." She has described her work as a form of asceticism: "I am interested in how far you can push the energy of the human body and then see how energy is almost limitless. It is not about the body, it is about the mind, pushing to the extremes that you never could imagine." And about the 2010 work, titled *The Artist Is Present:* "Nobody could imagine . . . that anybody would take time to sit and just engage in mutual gaze with me."[20] Like Diogenes, Abramović trains her body to understand, and then show, what it is capable of. Also like him, she makes herself available to people, not as a teacher, but for a meeting and a form of shared inquiry.

Foucault's observations that in art life itself has become an artwork and that artists stand in a permanent relationship of Cynicism to culture and society were based in the developments he saw in art in the eighteenth and nineteenth centuries, but they seem to apply almost as well to developments in the art world since then. In the provocative work of Abramović and other performance artists, the body, the art, and the message overlap entirely. Her ascetic exploration of the limits of the body—in other works she has wounded herself, or allowed others to wound her—is not necessarily representative of all performance art, but it is a recurring theme. For these artists the central objective is to challenge and question existing social norms and power structures without aspiring to political power, just as for Diogenes but in sharp contrast to contemporary populists.

The American art critic, poet, and classics PhD Thomas McEvilley (1939–2013) saw a direct link between performance art and Diogenes, whose philosophy he called "performance philosophy" in the magazine *Art Forum*. According to McEvilley, the kind of work that Abramović and similar artists make has both an artistic goal ("the discovery of new art forms beyond the old boundaries") and an ethical one ("by refocusing life as art, it is hoped to purge it of conventional motives and restore it to a fresh and disinterested appreciation"). In 1994 McEvilley undertook a project to encourage people to make their own performance art inspired by Diogenes. On eleven lead tablets he had as many anecdotes about Diogenes' life engraved, which he called "philosophical performance pieces." They were intended, it seems, as short scripts for the recipients to perform themselves, in any given order. The collection was titled *Diogenes: Defictions*. This was probably wordplay referring both to the de-fictionalized, "real" aspect of performance art and to the fact that ancient lead curse tablets were called *defixiones* in Latin. McEvilley presented the tablets in a ceramic box, and they were playfully billed as fake copies of an object found during an archeological excavation in Corinth. How often people have actually used *Diogenes: Defictions* for their own performances is hard to know. Today most of the fifty copies that were made are owned by galleries and library special collections and preserved as art objects.[21]

Our final example of a potential twenty-first-century Diogenes is the artist and writer Jenny Odell, who, like McEvilley, is explicit in her admiration of the Dog. As artist in residence at a waste-disposal site in San Francisco, she photographed and catalogued objects from other people's trash.[22] In her book *How to Do Nothing: Resisting the Attention Economy* she has collected scraps of texts from other writers (artists, critics, and philosophers), and Diogenes is a recurring character. Odell writes, referring to d'Alembert: "We need a Diogenes not just for entertainment, nor just to show that there are alternatives, but because stories like his contribute to our vocabulary of refusal even centuries later." Odell includes, of course, Diogenes' refusal of Alexander's offer of wealth, the story of him rolling his jar up and down the Kraneion in Corinth in wartime, and his interest in emulating the simple life of a mouse. She describes her work as an artist as "searching for frameworks that allow us to perceive something new about everyday reality."[23] The *nomisma* she tries to break with her book is our contemporary devotion to productivity and to the online world: like Diogenes, she urges us to refuse, to withdraw from working, and to get closer to our own embodiment and to the natural world.[24] In short: to engage in the radical act of doing nothing.

The attempts to carry on societal critique in the spirit of Diogenes through the art of Odell, McEvilley, and Abramović differ quite a bit from one another in scope, medium, and reach, but all three artists used their work to try to spur their recipients into some kind of action. The recipients have to be participants, not passive consumers, and they have to realize that it (the art) is all about *them*, just as much as Diogenes' lived philosophy was about the people he engaged with in the marketplace in ancient Athens and Corinth, and continues to be about whoever is willing to engage with it today. Whether Diogenes' Cynicism is still possible ultimately depends on how we live our own lives.

CODA

You gotta be your own,
You gotta be your own dog.
Don't let nobody put a leash on you.

—dEUS, "Fell off the Floor, Man"[1]

What does it really mean to speak freely? According to Foucault, true *parrhesia* requires two parties: a speaker and a listener. What this means is that even the fully independent and courageous free speaker has to rely on someone outside of themselves to put their *parrhesia* into practice. An unpracticed intention of *parrhesia* counts for nothing at all. The same predicament affects the Cynic project in general.

Laertius tells us that one time Diogenes suddenly started humming because the people were passing him by while he was talking about something serious. Immediately after he started making a funny noise, people stopped and a large crowd gathered around him. He then proceeded to harangue his audience because they were not interested in the serious, important stuff but were drawn right away to his silliness. The anecdote shows that Diogenes was well aware that in order to be able to pass on his message about the Cynic way of life, he had to be able to get people's attention. With his rejection of the *polis* he ran into the irresolvable problem that the same *polis* was the stage that allowed him to live out his philosophy for everyone to see.

To write a book about Diogenes is to share in this irony. There is an insoluble contradiction between living out for oneself the message of radical independence and connecting with an audience in order to share this message with others. Whoever wants to stay away from the apathy of Sloterdijk's modern cynic but also wants to keep the energy of Diogenes' ideas alive has no other choice but to embrace this philosophical impurity. And the willingness to do so yields something of value: a critical guide both for discerning and exposing the injustices of the status quo and for pushing back whenever collective devotion to progress in the abstract loses sight of human, embodied realities.

As I was wrapping up this book a snippet of an almost forgotten nineties song lyric kept popping into my head: "You gotta be your own dog." And I realized that this is what it all boils down to in the end. Rather than finding a modern Diogenes to put on a pedestal, we must act in our own lives. Diogenes was once observed trying to enter a theater just as everyone was leaving. When asked why, he answered: "This is what I have been doing my whole life." The truth Diogenes teaches us is to cut against the crowd, to swim upstream—things that only we ourselves can do—and to never accept a leash.

ACKNOWLEDGMENTS

Before I wrote this book, I wrote a philosophical biography of Diogenes of Sinope in Dutch, which was published by Athenaeum–Polak & Van Gennep in Amsterdam in 2022. *Diogenes: The Rebellious Life and Revolutionary Philosophy of the Original Cynic* is the result of a process not only of translation but also of adaptation. The substance and overall thrust of this "English *Diogenes*" is the same as that of my "Dutch *Diogenes*," but I have eagerly taken advantage of the opportunity to add material, to expand on certain issues, and to further accentuate some persistent themes throughout the book as I was translating it. I wish to thank Sander van Vlerken, Gaia Cerpac, and Jolijn Spooren at Athenaeum–Polak & Van Gennep for their support in helping my *Diogenes* cross the Atlantic. This crossing never would have come about in the first place without the generous encouragement and expert guidance of my agent, Rob McQuilkin, of Massie & McQuilkin Literary Agents. I extend my deep gratitude to him and members of his team, Sophie Weiler and Max Moorhead. It has been a great pleasure to work on this project with Basic Books, and I wish to thank Brian Distelberg for placing his trust in me and the book. My editor, Brandon Proia, has been a brilliant sounding board and astute reader throughout the process. His feedback has improved this book in countless ways. I also wish to thank Alex Cullina, Melissa Veronesi, and Sue Warga at Basic Books for their help during the production process. I want to thank all of my colleagues and students at the Department of Classics at the University of Virginia for creating the most supportive and inspiring environment to teach, think, and write in. I owe special thanks to my colleagues Ted Lendon, for believing in this project and introducing me to my agent, and Giulio Celotto, for taking the time to read and provide helpful feedback on the full manuscript. I wish to thank my dear friends and family for sustaining me with love and inspiration. Last but foremost, I want to say thank you to my partner, Steve, for sharing his love of ideas, of language, and of life with me.

NOTE ON SOURCES

In writing this book I have relied on the works of countless predecessors and colleagues in the fields of philosophy, classics, ancient history, and beyond. The notes that follow serve to acknowledge this debt, but they are also intended to provide starting points for readers who want to know more about Diogenes, ancient Cynicism, or any of the related topics that have come up in this book. I also make mention of the ancient sources cited or consulted. With just a few exceptions these are always available in English translation in the Loeb Classical Library series by Harvard University Press, or in the Oxford World's Classics series by Oxford University Press. Please note that in the case of ancient sources references are not to page numbers but to the generally accepted section or line numbering system for that author.

Our most importance source text for Diogenes' life is Diogenes Laertius' *Lives of the Philosophers* 6.20–81. In order to avoid repetition, I have omitted references to this work in the endnotes. So, whenever I discuss an anecdote or saying without explicitly attributing it to another ancient author or work, I have derived it from Laertius. As discussed in Chapter 1, *Lives of the Philosophers* is far from an unproblematic source, primarily because of the several centuries that elapsed between Diogenes' lifetime and its composition. It is, nevertheless, more reliable than many other works because of Laertius' intent—he does not engage in philosophical polemic but wants to preserve and hand down the information he has gathered—and his use of many earlier sources now lost to us, including authors who were Diogenes' contemporaries. That being said, there is, of course, a real possibility that sometimes anecdotes and sayings were transmitted inaccurately. In all instances where I use Laertius' *Lives of the Philosophers* to reconstruct Diogenes' life and ideas, I do so because in my view his version brings us closest to what Diogenes actually said and did. Just exactly *how* close this is we can, sadly, not ascertain without time travel.

NOTES

INTRODUCTION: SEEING THE WORLD DIFFERENTLY

1. On the murder of Philip and the first weeks and months of Alexander's reign, see Diodorus, *Library of History* 16.91–95, 17.1–4; Arrian, *Education of Alexander* 1.1.1–3; Plutarch, *Life of Alexander* 10–14. Most scholars now date Philip's murder to the end of October 336 BCE; on the issues, see Nicholas Hammond, "The Regnal Years of Philip and Alexander," *Greek, Roman, and Byzantine Studies* 33.2 (1992), pp. 356–361.

2. Plutarch, *Life of Alexander* 14. Translations of texts originally written in a language other than English are my own, unless mentioned otherwise.

3. For the debate about this, see Duane Roller, *Cleopatra: A Biography* (Oxford, 2011), pp. 165–166.

4. Georg Friedrich Hegel, *Vorlesungen über die Geschichte der Philosophie* (Frankfurt am Main, 1979 [1817]), pp. 56–57 and pp. 19–20. For Hegel's influence on perceptions of Diogenes as a philosopher, see Heinrich Niehues-Pröbsting, *Der Kynismus des Diogenes und der Begriff des Zynismus* (Berlin, 1988 [1979]), esp. pp. 293–296.

CHAPTER 1: IN SEARCH OF A HUMAN BEING

1. Remarkably, in the two most recent biographies of Diogenes the earliest sources about him get short shrift. Jean-Manuel Roubineau's *The Dangerous Life and Ideas of Diogenes the Cynic* (Oxford, 2023) omits all three of the earliest sources (Aristotle, Metrocles' papyrus text, and Teles);

Luis Navia's *Diogenes the Cynic: The War Against the World* (Amherst, MA, 2005) only includes the earliest one of these three.

2. Aristotle, *Rhetoric* 1411a.

3. Diogenes Laertius, *Lives of the Philosophers* 5.43.

4. *Papyrus Vindobonensis Graecus* 29946, in Katarzyna Jazdzewska, *Greek Dialogue in Antiquity* (Oxford, 2022), pp. 79–82.

5. Teles, *On Self-Sufficiency* 12–13.

6. Philodemus, *On the Stoics* 15–22 = *Papyri Herculanenses* 155 and 339.

7. Cicero, *Tusculan Disputations* 5.92.

8. Robin Hard, *Diogenes the Cynic: Sayings and Anecdotes* (Oxford, 2012), p. xxii.

9. Pierre Bayle, *Dictionnaire historique et critique. Tome cinquième* (Paris, 1820 [1697]), pp. 522–523.

10. Seneca, *On Benefits* 5.4–6.

11. *Paulys Realencyclopädie der Classischen Altertumswissenschaft V.1* (Stuttgart, 1903), p. 767.

12. William Tarn, "Alexander, Cynics, and Stoics," *American Journal of Philology* 60 (1939), p. 48.

13. Mentions of Onesicritus as a source: Plutarch, *Life of Alexander* 8; Arrian, *Anabasis of Alexander* 7.2–3.

14. Philip Bosman, "King Meets Dog: The Origins of the Meeting of Alexander and Diogenes," *Acta Classica* 50 (2007), p. 52.

15. The lemma for Diogenes in the *Suda* is δ1142.

16. Up until the Hellenistic period, tombstones typically did not list the ages of the deceased at all, and when people start to include this information in the Roman period they use round numbers so often as to suggest that they are rounding off the ages.

17. Herodotus, *Histories* 4.12; Thucydides, *History of the Peloponnesian War* 1.111–2.55; Plutarch, *Life of Pericles* 20.

18. Xenophon, *Anabasis* 5.5.13–25. On the theme of ethnicity in this section of *Anabasis*, see Emily Baragwanath, "A Universalist Moral Compass: Depicting Greeks and Foreigners in *Anabasis* 5 and 6," in *Xenophon's Anabasis and Its Reception*, ed. Tim Rood and Melina Tamiolaki (Berlin, 2022), pp. 131–155. For a detailed timeline of the march, see Iordanis Paradeisopoulos, "A Chronology Model for Xenophon's Anabasis," *Greek, Roman, and Byzantine Studies* 53 (2013), pp. 645–686.

19. Polyaenus, *Stratagems of War* 7.21; Arrian, *Anabasis of Alexander* 3.24.4. On the ancient history of Sinope, see the chapter on the Black Sea region by Alexandru Avram, John Hind, and Gocha Tsetskhladze in *An Inventory of Archaic and Classical Poleis*, ed. Mogens Herman Hansen and Thomas Heine Nielsen (Oxford, 2004), pp. 960–963.

20. Navia, *Diogenes the Cynic*, p. 23.

21. The remark about his mother is *Florilegium Monacense* 157; he is called a "heavenly dog" in *Cynic Epistles* 7.

22. C. T. Seltman first connected the coin finds to Diogenes' biography in a lecture at the Cambridge Philological Society on February 21, 1929 (*Proceedings of the Cambridge Philological Society* 142/144 [1929]), p. 7. See Herbert Bannert's "Numismatisches zu Biographie und Lehre des Hundes Diogenes," in *Litterae Numismaticae Vindobonenses*, ed. Wolfgang Szaivert (Vienna, 1979), pp. 49–63, for a critical assessment. The question hinges on the precise dating of the coins: in order to treat them as evidence for the notion that Diogenes got exiled because his father tampered with the coinage, one needs to accept an early date of ca. 370–365 BCE. In the standard study of the coins they are tentatively dated to the broad period of 360–320 BCE but not assigned a precise date (*Recueil General des Monnaies Grecques* [Paris, 1925], pp. 193–200.) In my view it is possible that the relevant coins are in fact a few years older.

23. Plato, *Apology* 21a–23c.

24. Aristophanes, *Knights* 792.

25. Sigmund Freud, *Civilization and Its Discontents* (London, 1930 [1929]), pp. 66–67n1.

26. Pausanias, *Description of Greece* 2.2.4.

27. The attempt was spearheaded by the conservative Islamist Erbakan Foundation, named for the late Turkish prime minister Necmettin Erbakan, who, like Diogenes, was born in Sinop. "Erbakan Foundation Members Demand Removal of Philosopher Diogenes Statue in Sinop," Turkish Minute, August 23, 2017, turkishminute.com/2017/08/23/erbakan-foundation-members-demand-removal-of-philosopher-diogenes-statue-in-sinop.

CHAPTER 2: WHAT IT MEANS TO KNOW SOMETHING

1. Plato, *Parmenides* 126a–127d; Plutarch, *Life of Pericles* 4.3. For an overview of Zeno's life, see Diogenes Laertius, *Lives of the Philosophers* 9.25–29.

2. The paradox is given by Aristotle in *Physics* 239b15–20. On modern solutions to the paradox, see Joseph Mazur, *The Motion Paradox: The 2,500-Year-Old Puzzle Behind All the Mysteries of Time and Space* (New York, 2007). On the drinking cup, see Herbert Hoffmann, "Zeno's Tortoise," *Antike Kunst* 47 (2004), pp. 5–9.

3. On Thales, see Diogenes Laertius, *Lives of the Philosophers* 1.22–44. For his tumble, see, for example, Plato, *Theaetetus* 174a; Aesop, *Fables* 40; Aristophanes, *Clouds* 168–180. (This is actually a parody of the story.)

4. Plato, *Phaedo* 95e–102a. The extent of Socrates' involvement with natural philosophy remains a point of controversy, just like the reliability of accounts of his life in general. On these issues, see, e.g., Jörn Müller, "Socrates and Natural Philosophy: The Testimony of Plato's *Phaedo*," in *Socrates and the Socratic Dialogue*, ed. Alessandro Stavru and Christopher Moore (Leiden, 2018), pp. 348–368; David Johnson, *Xenophon's Socratic Works* (Abingdon, 2021).

5. Diogenes Laertius, *Lives of the Philosophers* 2.108–109.

6. Homer, *Odyssey* 1.157, 4.70.

7. On washing away moral stains, see Robert Parker, *Miasma: Pollution and Purification in Early Greek Religion* (Oxford, 1983). On ancient Greek religion in general, see *On Greek Religion* (Ithaca, NY, 2011) by the same author.

8. Aristophanes, *Knights* 32–35.

9. Xenophon, *Symposium* 34–44.

10. Diogenes Laertius, *Lives of the Philosophers* 6.1–19.

11. Herodotus, *Histories* 4.46, 4.76–77. Ten letters in the collection of *Cynic Epistles* were written in character as being by Anacharsis.

12. See, for instance, Martin West's classic *Early Greek Philosophy and the Orient* (Oxford, 1971), and, more recently, the essays in Richard Seaford, ed., *Universe and Inner Self in Early Indian and Early Greek Thought* (Edinburgh, 2016). Already in antiquity people thought Pythagoras' wisdom originated from India; Philostratus, *Life of Apollonius of Tyana* 6.11.9–13.

13. On Indian asceticism, see Patrick Olivelle, *Samnyāsa Upanisads: Hindu Scriptures on Asceticism and Renunciation* (Oxford, 1992), and on Greece and India, see Richard Stoneman, *The Greek Experience of India: From Alexander to the Indo-Greeks* (Princeton, NJ, 2019). Onesicritus' report is quoted by Strabo in his *Geography* 15.1.63–65.

14. Diogenes Laertius, *Lives of the Philosophers* 3.1. It used to be thought that Plato's date of birth was 428 or 427 BCE, but many scholars

are now persuaded by Debra Nails's argument for a later date in *The People of Plato* (Indianapolis, IN, 2002), as am I.

15. Plato, *Republic* 596a–b.

16. Plato, *Statesman* 266e.

17. On Plato's life, see Robin Waterfield, *Plato of Athens: A Life in Philosophy* (Oxford, 2023). Diogenes Laertius (*Lives of the Philosophers* 3.9) says Plato did take money from Dionysius II; Plutarch says he did not (*Life of Dion* 19).

18. In his book *The Dangerous Life and Ideas of Diogenes the Cynic* (Oxford, 2023 [2020]), p. 7) Jean-Manuel Roubineau takes a different view. He accepts the quotes in Philodemus as actually being from a treatise by Diogenes titled *Republic* (see my Chapter 1), positing "many works" by him besides, but does not address Diogenes Laertius' comment that Diogenes wrote nothing.

CHAPTER 3: ON HAVING A BODY

1. The title of this chapter is inspired by Simon Critchley's account of the deeply human and often humorous experience of both "having" and "being" a body in his book *On Humour* (London, 2002), pp. 41–52.

2. Dio Chrysostom, *Oration* 13.1, 19.1–2. On the exile, see John Moles, "The Thirteenth Oration of Dio Chrysostom: Complexity and Simplicity, Rhetoric and Moralism, Literature and Life," *Journal of Hellenic Studies* 125 (2005), pp. 112–138, and on his life in general, see Christopher Jones, *The Roman World of Dio Chrysostom* (Cambridge, MA, 1978).

3. Dio Chrysostom, *Oration* 8.

4. Julian, *Oration* 6, esp. 202b–c. On Julian the Apostate's life and reign, see Hans Teitler, *The Last Pagan Emperor: Julian the Apostate and the War Against Christianity* (Oxford, 2017).

5. Galen, *On Affected Parts* 419–420. For an introduction to Galen's life and works, see Susan Mattern, *The Prince of Medicine: Galen in the Roman Empire* (Oxford, 2013).

6. It becomes even more doubtful when compared to no. 42 among the *Cynic Epistles*, which are all fictional; basically the same thing happens, although it is unclear here whether or not the woman in question is a prostitute.

7. Plato, *Protagoras* 320d–322a.

8. Aristotle, *Politics* 1253a.

9. Euripides, *Phoenician Women* 40.

10. Plato, *Phaedo* 82e. The other relevant passages are *Cratylus* 400c, *Phaedrus* 250b–c, and *Gorgias* 493a. For some context on Plato's approach to the body, see Douglas Campbell, "The Soul's Tool: Plato on the Usefulness of the Body," *Elenchos* 43.1 (2022), pp. 7–27.

11. Diogenes Laertius has devoted all of book 10 of his *Lives of the Philosophers* to Epicurus, which includes his letters and the *Principal Doctrines*. For Lucretius on love and sex, see *On the Nature of Things* 4.1037–1287.

12. On the founders of Stoicism, see book 7 of Diogenes Laertius' *Lives of the Philosophers.* A good starting point on Stoicism is Brad Inwood, *A Very Short Introduction to Stoicism* (Oxford, 2018). For a more in-depth consideration of Stoic and Epicurean ethics, see Martha Nussbaum's classic work *Therapy of Desire: Theory and Practice in Hellenistic Ethics* (Princeton, NJ, 2009 [1994]). On the influence of both schools in Republican Rome, see Katharina Volk, *The Roman Republic of Letters: Scholarship, Philosophy, and Politics in the Age of Cicero and Caesar* (Princeton, NJ, 2021).

13. Corinthians 1:6–7. On Paul and sexuality, see Peter Brown's classic *The Body and Society: Men, Women, and Sexual Renunciation in Early Christianity* (New York, 1988), pp. 44–57, and David Wheeler Reed's more recent *Regulating Sex in the Roman Empire: Ideology, the Bible, and the Early Christians* (Oxford, 2018), pp. 65–73. On Paul and Hellenistic philosophy, see the first part of Ward Blanton and Hent de Vries, eds., *Paul and the Philosophers* (New York, 2014), pp. 1–85.

CHAPTER 4: SPEAKING TRUTH TO POWER

1. On Demosthenes and his adversaries, see Raphael Sealey, *Demosthenes and His Time: A Study in Defeat* (Oxford, 1993); on the reign and conquests of Philip II, see Nicholas Hammond, *Philip of Macedon* (Baltimore, 1994).

2. Lucian, *How to Write History* 3. For my interpretation of this work I have drawn on Alexander Free, *Geschichtsschreibung als Paideia. Lukians Schrift „Wie man Geschichte schreiben soll" in der Bildungskultur des 2. Jhs. n. Chr.* (Munich, 2015).

3. Lucian cites no source for the anecdote. The only other instance of it is the erroneous inclusion in one manuscript of Diogenes Laertius' *Lives of the Philosophers* (at 6.69). It probably made its way into that manuscript from a collection of sayings now lost to us, and this is also where Lucian would have found it. See Tiziano Dorandi, *Capitoli sulla tradizione*

manoscritta e sulla storia del testo delle Vite dei filosofi di Diogene Laerzio (Berlin, 2009), pp. 97–99.

4. Plutarch, *On Exile* 606c. Diogenes Laertius has included Dionysius the Stoic in *Lives of the Philosophers* 7.166–167.

5. In Laertius' biography in *Lives of the Philosophers* there are five moments where he places Alexander and Diogenes together. I consider the following genuine: at 6.32 Alexander says he would have wanted to be Diogenes if he were not Alexander; at 6.38 Diogenes asks Alexander to get out of his sun; at 6.68 Alexander asks Diogenes if he fears him. These are in line with the accounts of Plutarch and Arrian and must go back to Onesicritus. The following cannot be genuine: at 6.60 Alexander says to Diogenes he is the great king, but he did not get this title until after his campaigns, and they must have met beforehand; at 6.44 Diogenes makes a snarky comment about a letter Alexander sends to Antipater, which would assume he spent time at Alexander's court, which he did not. On these issues, see also Chapter 1.

6. On Harmodius and Aristogiton, see Thucydides, *History of the Peloponnesian War* 1.20, 6.53–59; Herodotus, *Histories* 5.55–57, 6.109, 6.123.

7. On Onesicritus, see Diogenes Laertius, *Lives of the Philosophers* 6.75–76, 6.84; Truesdell Brown, *Onesicritus: A Study in Hellenistic Historiography* (Berkeley, CA, 1949); Lionel Pearson, *The Lost Histories of Alexander the Great* (Oxford, 1960), pp. 83–111; Michael Whitby, "Onesikritos (134)," *Jacoby Online: Brill's New Jacoby Part II* (2011).

8. Lucian, *How to Write History* 40.

9. Onesicritus' report is quoted by Strabo in his *Geography* 15.1.63–65.

10. Plutarch, *On the Fortune or Virtue of Alexander* 331e–332c.

11. Plutarch, *To an Uneducated Ruler* 728b.

12. Plato, *Republic* 449a–466d. Whether Plato intended for the "ideal city" in *Republic* to be understood by his audience as a deterrent dystopia or as a true model worthy of emulation continues to be a source of major disagreement among scholars. For a recent argument for the former that pays particular attention to the status of the family, see Jacob Howland, *Glaucon's Fate: History, Myth, and Character in Plato's Republic* (Philadelphia, 2018).

13. Philodemus, *On the Stoics* 15–22 = *Papyri Herculanenses* 155 and 339. On Philodemus' own life and philosophy, see Voula Tsouna, *The Ethics of Philodemus* (Oxford, 2007).

14. Martha Nussbaum, *The Cosmopolitan Tradition: A Noble but Flawed Ideal* (Cambridge, MA, 2019), pp. 1–2.

15. Nussbaum, *The Cosmopolitan Tradition*, pp. 71–72.

16. On this strand in scholarship, see Luis Navia, *Diogenes the Cynic: The War Against the World* (Amherst, MA, 2005), pp. 153–155.

17. Nussbaum, *The Cosmopolitan Tradition*, p. 69; *Cynic Epistles* 47.

18. Although the fact of their concurrent deaths on this special date has never been disputed, it has been argued that it was not truly a coincidence, but rather planned in some way or another; see Margaret Battin, "July 4, 1826: Explaining the Same-Day Deaths of John Adams and Thomas Jefferson," *Historically Speaking: The Bulletin of the Historical Society* 6.6 (2005).

19. Dio Chrysostom, *Oration* 4.

20. Lucian, *Dialogues of the Dead* 13. On the deification of Alexander, see Ernst Badian, *Collected Papers on Alexander the Great* (London, 2012), pp. 244–281, and Ernst Fredricksmeyer, "Alexander, Zeus Ammon, and the Conquest of Asia," *Transactions of the American Philological Association* 121 (1991), pp. 199–214. On his death and burial, see Peter Green, *Alexander of Macedon, 356–323 B.C.: A Historical Biography* (Berkeley, CA, 2013), pp. 385–387, and James Romm, *Ghost on the Throne: The Death of Alexander the Great and the Bloody Fight for Crown and Empire* (New York, 2011).

CHAPTER 5: A LONE VOICE AGAINST SLAVERY

1. These arguments are derived from the Dutch historian Piet Emmer's work on slavery in the European colonies. For a contrasting account, with a focus on the Dutch colonies, see *Slavery: An Exhibition of Many Voices* (Amsterdam, 2021). On the transatlantic slave trade broadly, see Marcus Rediker, *The Slave Ship: A Human History* (London, 2008). On North America, see, for instance, John Swanson Jacobs, *The United States Governed by Six Hundred Thousand Despots: A True Story of Slavery; A Rediscovered Narrative, with a Full Biography*, ed. Jonathan Schroeder (Chicago, 2024), and Nikole Hannah-Jones, *The 1619 Project* (New York, 2021). I choose to use the term "enslaved" rather than "slave," because doing so underscores that slavery is an economic and social fact, not a natural condition: no one is born enslaved, and anyone who has gone (or is going) through life as a "slave" has been enslaved by others. In (translated) quotations I maintain the terminology used in the original.

2. For an account that places ancient Greek and Roman slavery side by side with contemporary, modern, and early modern slavery, see Page

Dubois, *Slavery: Antiquity and Its Legacy* (London, 2010). On uses of classical antiquity in North American debates about slavery, see Margaret Malamud, *African Americans and the Classics: Antiquity, Abolition and Activism* (London, 2019), pp. 105–146, and Carl Richard, *The Golden Age of the Classics in America: Greece, Rome, and the Antebellum United States* (Cambridge, MA, 2009), pp. 181–203.

3. See Edith Hall, *Inventing the Barbarian: Greek Self-Definition Through Tragedy* (Oxford, 1989), p. 4, and Hyun Jin Kim, "The Invention of the Barbarian in Late Sixth-Century BC Ionia," in *Ancient Ethnography: New Approaches*, ed. Eran Almagor and Joseph Skinner (London, 2008), pp. 34–36.

4. For an introductory overview on Herodotus, see Jennifer Roberts, *A Very Short Introduction to Herodotus* (Oxford, 2011). For his descriptions of non-Greeks, see James Redfield, "Herodotus the Tourist," *Classical Philology* 80 (1985), pp. 97–118, and Chris Pelling, "East Is East and West Is West—or Are They? National Stereotyping in Herodotus," *Histos* 1 (1997), pp. 51–66. See also the contributions in Thomas Harrison, ed., *Greeks and Barbarians* (Edinburgh, 2002).

5. On slavery in the ancient Greek world, see Sara Forsdyke, *Slaves and Slavery in Ancient Greece* (Cambridge, 2021). On the rare ancient philosophical discussions of slavery, see Peter Garnsey, *Ideas of Slavery from Aristotle to Augustine* (Oxford, 1996); Christopher Tuplin, "Fear of Slavery and the Failure of the Polis," in *Fear of Slaves, Fear of Enslavement in the Ancient Mediterranean*, ed. Anastasia Serghidou (Besançon, 2007), pp. 57–74; and Ilaria Ramelli, *Social Justice and the Legitimacy of Slavery: The Role of Philosophical Asceticism from Ancient Judaism to Late Antiquity* (Oxford, 2017).

6. There is a long-standing debate on whether or not "race" is a concept that can be applied to describing ancient societies. I follow recent scholarship by Denise McCoskey and Sarah Derbew in positing that, although they did so using categories, demarcations, and terms different from our modern ones, the inhabitants of the ancient Greco-Roman Mediterranean did have a concept of race that played a role in how they understood the world around them. See Denise McCoskey, *Race: Antiquity and Its Legacy* (London, 2012); Sarah Derbew, *Untangling Blackness in Greek Antiquity* (Cambridge, 2022); and the contributions in Denise McCoskey, ed., *A Cultural History of Race in Antiquity* (London, 2022).

7. Plato, *Laws* 776b–778a.

8. Plato, *Republic* 469b–c.

9. Plato, *Laws* 776b–778a.

10. Plato, *Phaedo* 80a and *Republic* 444b.

11. Eva Cantarella, "Gender, Sexuality, and Law," in *The Cambridge Companion to Ancient Greek Law*, ed. Michael Gagarin and David Cohen (Cambridge, 2006), pp. 247–250.

12. Euripides, *Iphigeneia at Aulis* 1400.

13. Aristotle, *Politics* 1251b1–1255b40.

14. Aristotle, *Politics* 1253b20–25.

15. The Alcidamas fragment has been preserved in the scholia to Aristotle's *Rhetoric* 1373b18. The Antiphon fragment comes from the Oxyrhynchus papyri no. 1364 fr. 2 and no. 3647. On both fragments, see Giuseppe Cambiano, "Aristotle and the Anonymous Opponents of Slavery," in *Classical Slavery*, ed. M. I. Finley (London, 1987), pp. 21–41.

16. Forsdyke, *Slaves and Slavery in Ancient Greece*, pp. 53–59.

17. On the professions and tasks of enslaved workers, see Forsdyke, *Slaves and Slavery in Ancient Greece*, pp. 102–160. For the Roman period there is ample evidence for enslaved doctors, for earlier times less so, but see, for instance, Plato, *Laws* 720a–e. For this topic, see Mária Bujalková, "Sklaven in der antiken Medizin," *Graeco-Latina Brunensia* 18.2 (2013), pp. 67–76.

18. Kurt Von Fritz, *Quellenuntersuchungen zu Leben und Philosophie des Diogenes von Sinope* (Leipzig, 1926), pp. 22–27. On Cleomenes, see Diogenes Laertius, *Lives of the Philosophers* 6.95; on Eubulides, see 6.108–112.

19. Robin Hard, *Diogenes the Cynic: Sayings and Anecdotes* (Oxford, 2012), p. 209; Luis Navia, *Diogenes the Cynic: The War Against the World* (Amherst, MA, 2005), p. 58.

20. Diogenes Laertius, *Lives of the Philosophers* 3.19–20.

21. As in the version of Aelian, *Historical Miscellany* 13.28.

22. More common terms were *doulos* ("servile one") or *oiketes* ("household servant"), which generally but not exclusively referred to the enslaved, or *pais*, which literally means "child" but was used for the enslaved regardless of their age. On this topic, see Rachel Zelnick-Abramovitz, "Greek and Roman Terminologies of Slavery," in *The Oxford Handbook of Greek and Roman Slaveries*, ed. Stephen Hodkinson, Marc Kleijwegt, and Kostas Vlassopoulos (Oxford, 2018).

23. Forsdyke, *Slaves and Slavery in Ancient Greece*, pp. 95, 173–175.

24. On Epictetus and Arrian, see Raffaella Cribiore, *Listening to the the Philosophers: Notes on Notes* (Ithaca, NY, 2024), pp. 79–86.

25. Epictetus, *Discourses* 1.9.29 (implicit mention of his own enslavement), 4.1.1–14, 1.13.4–5 (everyone is enslaved), 4.1.152 (true freedom of Diogenes), 4.1.115–117 (Diogenes enslaved), 4.1.34–47 (life of the freedman).

26. Galatians 3:28, Corinthians 1 12:13, 7:20–21. Translations from *The New Oxford Annotated Bible* (Oxford, 2018).

27. Southron, "Thoughts on Slavery," *Southern Literary Messenger* 4.12 (1838), p. 738.

28. James Henley Thornwell, *The Rights and the Duties of Masters* (Charleston, SC, 1850), pp. 78–80. The reference is to Ephesians 6:5. On Thornwell and Seneca, see also Stephanie McCarter, "Seneca's Lost Cause: The Myth of the Noble Stoic/Southern Slave Owner," *Eidolon*, February 1, 2019.

29. For Capitein's thesis, see the annotated translation by Grant Parker, *The Agony of Asar: A Thesis on Slavery by the Former Slave, Jacobus Elisa Johannes Capitein, 1717–1747* (Princeton, NJ, 1999).

30. *Global Estimates of Modern Slavery: Forced Labour and Forced Marriage* (Geneva, 2022). This estimate consists of around twenty-eight million people working as forced laborers and twenty-two million women living in forced marriages. The International Labor Organization is part of the United Nations.

CHAPTER 6: LEARNING HOW TO DIE

1. Cicero, *Tusculan Disputations* 1.30.74; Plato, *Phaedo* 67e.

2. Montaigne, *Essays* 1.20.

3. The underworld is described in *Odyssey* 11, the Elysian Fields at *Odyssey* 4.561–569. In these early mentions the Elysian Fields seem to be an entirely separate place, but later on they will be described as a subsection of Hades.

4. Hesiod, *Theogony* 310–312, 767–774; *Works and Days* 166–174.

5. *Corpus Epigraphicum Graecum* 510.

6. On popular Greek ideas about death and dying, see Christiane Sourvinou-Inwood, *Reading Greek Death* (Oxford, 1995); Sarah Iles Johnston, *Restless Dead: Encounters Between the Living and the Dead in Ancient Greece* (Berkeley, 1999); and Suzanne Lye, *Life/Afterlife: Revolution and Reflection in the Ancient Greek Underworld from Homer to Lucian* (Oxford, 2024). On the ideas about the soul of Pythagoras and Empedocles, see

Maria Michaela Sassi, *The Beginnings of Philosophy in Greece* (Princeton, NJ, 2018), pp. 110–138. On Orphism, see Radcliffe Edmonds III, *Redefining Ancient Orphism: A Study in Greek Religion* (Cambridge, 2013). Jan Bremmer's *Initiation into the Mysteries of the Ancient World* (Berlin, 2014) contains chapters about both Orphism and the mystery cult at Eleusis.

7. In Xenophon's *Hellenica* Agesilaus is a recurring character from the third book onward, and he is the protagonist of Xenophon's (if it is indeed by him) encomium *Agesilaus;* see also Nepos, *Life of Agesilaus*, which makes use of the former. On Epaminondas, see Pausanias 9.13.1–15.6; Diodorus Siculus, *Library of History* 10.11.2, 15.38–16.2; Nepos, *Life of Epaminondas*; and Xenophon, *Hellenica* 7.1.41–42, 7.4.40–7.5.24.

8. Dio Cassius, *Roman History* 51.4.1, 54.9.10.

9. Diogenes Laertius, *Lives of the Philosophers* 2.101.

10. Lucian, *Life of Demonax* 11.

11. Cicero quotes this version at *Tusculan Disputations* 1.104.

12. *Iliad* 1.3–5, 22.335–336, 24.468–676.

13. *Cynic Epistles* 19. Pythagoras himself claimed to have been incarnated as Euphorbus; Diogenes Laertius, *Lives of the Philosophers* 8.4–5.

14. Lucian, *Dialogues of the Dead* 6.

15. Lucian, *Dialogues of the Dead* 1.1.

16. Lucian, *Dialogues of the Dead* 29.3.

17. Plato, *Apology* 40c–41d.

18. Plato, *Phaedo* 115c–d, 114d, 118a.

19. Plato, *Gorgias* 523a–525e.

20. Plato, *Republic* 614b–621d; *Phaedrus* 248a–249d. A helpful introduction to Plato's underworld narratives is available at the online, open-access *Stanford Encyclopedia of Philosophy*, in the entry titled "Plato's Myths" (2009/2022), authored by Catalin Partenie.

21. For an introduction to the relation between Neoplatonism and Christianity, see Andrew Smith, *Philosophy in Late Antiquity* (London, 2004), pp. 105–130.

22. Diogenes Laertius, *Lives of the Philosophers* 10.139.

23. Diogenes Laertius, *Lives of the Philosophers* 10.125–127. On the Stoic view of suicide, see James Ker, *The Deaths of Seneca* (Oxford, 2012).

24. Lucretius, *On the Nature of Things* 8.978–1023, 8.858–893. On the Epicurean view of death, see James Warren, *Facing Death: Epicurus and His Critics* (Oxford, 2004).

25. William Desmond, *Cynicism* (Stocksfield, 2008), p. 130.

26. Pausanias 2.2.4.

27. On Montaigne and Lucretius, see Stephen Greenblatt, *The Swerve: How the World Became Modern* (New York, 2011), pp. 242–249.

28. On Hume and Lucian's underworld fiction, see my article "Laughter in Lucian's Utopias of the Dead," in *Utopias in Ancient Thought*, ed. Pierre Destrée, Jan Opsomer, and Geert Roskam (Berlin, 2021), pp. 255–276.

CHAPTER 7: SEEDS OF REVOLUTION

1. Diogenes Laertius, *Lives of the Philosophers* 7.3.

2. Cicero, *On Duties* 1.148, 128.

3. Seneca, *Letters to Lucilius* 5. He does mention Diogenes by name three times in other letters, of which there are 124 in total: a brief reference to his slavery (47.12), a criticism of his candidness (29.2), and a positive comment on his simple way of life (90.14). For comparison, he uses the phrase "in accordance with nature" (*secundam naturam*) sixteen more times in the letters.

4. Epictetus, *Discourses* 3.22.

5. Marcus Aurelius, *Meditations* 7.2.3, 11.2.

6. Diogenes Laertius, *Lives of the Philosophers* 10.119.

7. On Crates' life, see Diogenes Laertius, *Lives of the Philosophers* 6.85–93.

8. On Hipparchia, see Diogenes Laertius, *Lives of the Philosophers* 6.96–98.

9. On Aspasia, see Plutarch, *Life of Pericles* 24. Useful modern treatments are Madeleine Mary Henry, *Prisoner of History: Aspasia of Miletus and Her Biographical Tradition* (Oxford, 1995), and Rebecca Futo Kennedy, *Immigrant Women in Athens: Gender, Ethnicity, and Citizenship in the Classical City* (London, 2014), pp. 68–96.

10. On Theano, see Diogenes Laertius, *Lives of the Philosophers* 8.42–43, and Dorota Dutsch, *Pythagorean Women Philosophers: Between Belief and Suspicion* (Oxford, 2020), pp. 1–70.

11. The *Cynic Epistles* to and about Hipparchia are nos. 1 and 28–33 among those by "Crates" and nos. 3 and 43 among those by "Diogenes"; the letter by "Diogenes" to Zeno is no. 47, and the one to Plato is no. 46.

12. Seneca, *On Benefits* 7.1–2, 8–11; Tacitus, *Annals* 16.34–35; Philostratus, *Life of Apollonius of Tyana* 4.42, 5.19, 7.16; Epictetus, *Discourses* 1.25.

13. Cassius Dio, *Roman History* 65.13 (epitome); Suetionus, *Life of Vespasian* 13. For modern accounts of Demetrius and his circle, see Miriam Griffin, "Cynicism and the Romans: Attraction and Repulsion," in *The Cynics: The Cynic Movement in Antiquity and Its Legacy*, ed. Robert Bracht Branham and Marie-Odile Goulet-Cazé (Berkeley, CA, 1996), pp. 190–204, and Donald Dudley, *A History of Cynicism* (London, 1937), pp. 125–142.

14. Cassius Dio, *Roman History* 65.12, 15 (epitome).

15. Gospel of Matthew 6:19, 25–26. Translations of passages from the New Testament are from *The New Oxford Annotated Bible: Fifth Edition* (Oxford, 2018).

16. Gospel of Mark 10:25.

17. Gospel of Mark 11:15–16.

18. Gospel of Luke 14:26; Gospel of Matthew 10:37.

19. Gospel of Mark 3:33–35.

20. Gospel of Luke 9:60.

21. Gospel of Luke 11:39, 43.

22. Gospel of Mark 10:42–44.

23. Gospel of Matthew 10:9–10.

24. The strongest proponents of Cynic influence on Jesus and the Jesus movement are Gerald Downing, *Christ and the Cynics and Other Radical Preachers in First-Century Tradition* (Sheffield, 1988), and Bernhard Lang, *Jesus der Hund: Leben und Lehre eines jüdischen Kynikers* (Munich, 2010). For more moderate assessments of the evidence, see Hans-Dieter Betz, "Jesus and the Cynics: Survey and Analysis of a Hypothesis," *Journal of Religion* 74.4 (1994), pp. 453–475; Marie-Odile Goulet-Cazé, *Cynicism and Christianity in Antiquity* (Grand Rapids, MI, 2019); and Philip Bosman, "Cynics in the Crosshairs: The Loci Classici for the Anonymous Cynics of the Early Roman Empire," in *Ancient Philosophy and Early Christianity*, ed. Philip Bosman and Gideon Kotzé (Leiden, 2022), pp. 85–86.

25. Aelius Aristides, *Oration* 46.309.

26. Origen, *Against Celsus* 3.50.

27. Goulet-Cazé, *Cynicism and Christianity in Antiquity*, pp. 203–205.

28. Dimitri Gutas, "Sayings by Diogenes Preserved in Arabic," in *Le Cynisme ancien et ses prolongements*, ed. Marie-Odile Goulet-Cazé and Richard Goulet (Paris, 1993), pp. 475–518.

29. Translation from Dimitri Gutas, *Greek Wisdom Literature in Arabic Translation: A Study of the Graeco-Arabic Gnomologia* (New Haven, CT, 2016), p. 465.

30. John of Wales, *Compendiloquium de Vitis Illustrium Philosophorum* 3.2.1–14. On John of Wales and some of his contemporaries who similarly admired Diogenes, see Sylvain Matton, "Cynicism and Christianity from the Middle Ages to the Renaissance," in *The Cynics: The Cynic Movement in Antiquity and Its Legacy*, ed. Robert Bracht Branham and Marie-Odile Goulet-Cazé (Berkeley, 1996), pp. 246–248.

31. By his onetime student, the controversial statesman and general Alcibiades; see Plato, *Symposium* 215a–222b.

32. This section of the *Adages*, which also circulated on its own, is titled *Sileni Alcibiadis*. On Erasmus' life, see James Tracy, *Erasmus of the Low Countries* (Berkeley, 1996), and, yet to appear in English translation, Sandra Langereis, *Erasmus: Dwarsdenker* (Amsterdam, 2021).

33. On Erasmus and Luther, see Michael Massing, *Fatal Discord: Erasmus, Luther, and the Fight for the Western Mind* (New York, 2018).

34. This section is greatly indebted to Louisa Shea's book *The Cynic Enlightenment: Diogenes in the Salon* (Baltimore, 2010), pp. 45–105. Also relevant are David Mazella, *The Making of Modern Cynicism* (Charlottesville, VA, 2007), pp. 110–142, and Michael Sonenscher, *Sans-Culottes: An Eighteenth-Century Emblem in the French Revolution* (Princeton, NJ, 2008), pp. 134–201.

35. Jean-Baptiste le Rond d'Alembert, "Essai sur la société des gens de lettres et des grands, sur la réputation, sur les mécènes, et sur les récompenses littéraires," *Œuvres de d'Alembert, tome IV, deuxième partie* (Paris, 1822 [1753]), pp. 335–373.

36. Denis Diderot, *Rameau's Nephew*, trans. Margaret Mauldon (Oxford, 2006). Diderot wrote the work between 1761 and 1774, but he did not dare circulate it, and it was published only posthumously.

CHAPTER 8: HOW TO BE A DIOGENES IN THE MODERN WORLD

1. *Monthly Review* 67 (September 1782), pp. 227–233; David Manzella, *The Making of Modern Cynicism* (Berkeley, 2007), pp. 171–175.

2. Thomas Hobbes, *Leviathan* 1.13.62.

3. Isaac D'Israeli, *Calamities and Quarrels of Authors* (London, 1871), p. 440; Manzella, *The Making of Modern Cynicism*, pp. 138–142.

4. Friedrich Nietzsche, *The Gay Science* 3.125. In Nietzsche's work *Thus Spoke Zarathustra*, published one year later, the death of God would again be a major theme.

5. On Nietzsche's scholarship on ancient Greek and Latin literature, see the essays in Anthony K. Jensen, ed., *Nietzsche as a Scholar of Antiquity* (London, 2014), and especially the chapter on his work on Diogenes Laertius by Jonathan Barnes, pp. 115–137. On his classical education see Sue Prideaux, *I Am Dynamite! A Life of Nietzsche* (New York, 2018), pp. 23–38.

6. Friedrich Nietzsche, *Ecce Homo* 3.3. Only the online critical edition of Nietzsche's complete writings retains Nietzsche's idiosyncrasy in this regard (*Digitale Kritische Gesamtausgabe Werke und Briefe*, www.nietzschesource.org); in print editions it tends to be obscured by the editorial practice of printing either *Kynismus* or *Zynismus* as the editor sees fit. On the issue, see Heinrich Niehues-Pröbsting, "The Modern Reception of Cynicism," in *The Cynics: The Cynic Movement in Antiquity and Its Legacy*, ed. Robert Bracht Branham and Marie-Odile Goulet-Cazé (Berkeley, CA, 1996), p. 354, and Cheng Guo, *Cynismus bei Nietzsche* (Berlin, 2022), pp. 12–15.

7. Friedrich Nietzsche, *Human, All Too Human* 2.2.18.

8. Friedrich Nietzsche, *Beyond Good and Evil* 26.

9. The bibliography on the complex afterlife of Nietzsche's philosophy is vast. Some places to start are Prideaux, *I Am Dynamite!*, and Walter Kaufmann's classic *Nietzsche: Philosopher, Psychologist, Antichrist* (Princeton, NJ, 2013 [1950]).

10. Peter Sloterdijk, *Critique of Cynical Reason* (Minneapolis, 1987, p. 5 = Frankfurt am Main, 1983, p. 37). The first page references are to the English translation, the second ones to the German original; the translations are my own directly from the German.

11. Sloterdijk, *Critique of Cynical Reason* (102 = 205).

12. Sloterdijk, *Critique of Cynical Reason* (104 = 210).

13. Michel Foucault, "What Is Enlightenment?" in *The Foucault Reader*, ed. Paul Rabinow (New York, 1984), p. 39.

14. Michel Foucault, *The Courage of Truth* (Basingstoke, 2011, p. 173 = Paris, 2009, p. 160). The first page references are to the English translation, the second ones to the French original; the translations are my own directly from the French.

15. Foucault, *The Courage of Truth* (166 = 154).

16. Foucault, *The Courage of Truth* (11 = 12).

17. Foucault, *The Courage of Truth* (279 = 257).

18. Foucault, *The Courage of Truth* (278 = 255–256).

19. Foucault, *The Courage of Truth* (188 = 173–174). For a critical appraisal of Foucault's engagement with Diogenes, see James Porter, "The Cynics with and Without Foucault," *Arethusa* 56 (2023), pp. 363–389.

20. These quotes are from the educational section on the Museum of Modern Art website: www.moma.org/learn/moma_learning/marina-abramovic-marina-abramovic-the-artist-is-present–2010/.

21. Thomas McEvilley, "Diogenes of Sinope (ca. 410–ca. 320 B.C.): Selected Performance Pieces," *Art Forum* 21.7 (1983). The 1994 work *Diogenes: Defictions* was produced in a paper edition as well. McEvilley collaborated with the printer Peter Koch on both the lead tablets and the paper reproduction. The ceramic box was made by the sculptor Stephen Braun.

22. The project was titled "The Bureau of Suspended Objects" and is still accessible online: www.jennyodell.com/bso.html.

23. Quote from Jenny Odell's own website: www.jennyodell.com/about-news.html.

24. Jenny Odell, *How to Do Nothing: Resisting the Attention Economy* (Brooklyn, NY, 2019), pp. 65–69, 72–73, 92–94. The Greek performance artist Georgia Sagri is of the same generation as Odell, and she also explicitly cites Diogenes as an inspiration, but her work is closer to that of Abramović in the way she uses her body. Her 2012 work *Diana Very Dog*, for instance, featured photos of Sagri roaming the outskirts of Athens naked, "in conversation with Diogenes" (www.centralfine.com/diana-very-dog-by-georgia-sagri).

CODA

1. From the lyrics of "Fell off the Floor, Man" by Tom Barman, Stef Kamil Carlens, Rudy Trouvé, and Craig Ward, for the album *In a Bar Under the Sea* by the band dEUS (1996).

INDEX

INDEX

Credit: Cora Hendriks

Inger N.I. Kuin is an associate professor of classics at the University of Virginia. Born in the Netherlands, she worked as a journalist before receiving an MA in philosophy from the University of Amsterdam and a PhD in classics from New York University. She divides her time between Rotterdam, the Netherlands, and Charlottesville, Virginia.

Thank you for reading this book and for being a reader of books in general. We are so grateful to share being part of a community of readers with you, and we hope you will join us in passing our love of books on to the next generation of readers.

Did you know that reading for enjoyment is the single biggest predictor of a child's future happiness and success?

More than family circumstances, parents' educational background, or income, reading impacts a child's future academic performance, emotional well-being, communication skills, economic security, ambition, and happiness.

Studies show that kids reading for enjoyment in the US is in rapid decline:

- In 2012, 53% of 9-year-olds read almost every day. Just 10 years later, in 2022, the number had fallen to 39%.
- In 2012, 27% of 13-year-olds read for fun daily. By 2023, that number was just 14%.

TOGETHER, WE CAN COMMIT TO RAISING READERS AND CHANGE THIS TREND. HOW?

- Read to children in your life daily.
- Model reading as a fun activity.
- Reduce screen time.
- Start a family, school, or community book club.
- Visit bookstores and libraries regularly.
- Listen to audiobooks.
- Read the book before you see the movie.
- Encourage your child to read aloud to a pet or stuffed animal.
- Give books as gifts.
- Donate books to families and communities in need.

Books build bright futures, and **Raising Readers** is our shared responsibility.

For more information, visit JoinRaisingReaders.com

Sources: National Endowment for the Arts, National Assessment of Educational Progress, WorldBookDay.org, Nielsen BookData's 2023 "Understanding the Children's Book Consumer"